THE COMPLETE ENCYCLOPEDIA OF

CHICKENS

THE COMPLETE ENCYCLOPEDIA OF

CHICKENS

ESTHER VERHOEF
AAD RIJS

© 2003 Rebo International b.v., Lisse, The Netherlands

This 8th edition reprinted in 2007.

Text: Esther Verhoef and Aad Rijs
Photographs: Esther Verhoef
Layout: Studio Imago, Amersfoort, The Netherlands
Typesetting: Artedit, Prague, The Czech Republic
Cover design: Minkowsky Graphics, Enkhuizen, The Netherlands
Proofreading: Jeffrey Rubinoff
Editing: Blanka Rambousková

ISBN: 978-90-366-1592-1

Contents

Introduction

First and foremost, this encyclopedia has been written for those who like chickens, but have little experience in keeping them. Often such people have lots of questions about feeding, housing, behavior, and other matters. The questions that beginners have put to experienced breeders over recent years have served as a starting point for Part One of this book.

In the section on the various standard or purebreds (sometimes also called 'true-breeding' breeds), you will find a vast range of chickens: about 120 different purebreds are reviewed. Still, there are far more breeds world-wide. This encyclopedia, however, does not intend to discuss all the various breeds exhaustively, but aims to give an idea of the different types, backgrounds, and purposes. In this encyclopedia you will find the most common breeds, as well as some of the special ones that are only very rarely raised. With each breed we have done our best to explain what its specific qualities are so that it will become clear whether this breed, or one resembling it, will fit in with your situation. Harmonizing the requirements of a particular breed with the future owner's wishes is a healthy principle in keeping any kind of animal. That is why we have tried to provide as much practical information as possible.

Apart from this, many people are of course interested to know what colors can be found in a particular breed and whether the poultry they have bought more or less meet the standard of perfection for the breed in question. That is why we also look into every breed's range of color patterns and their typical features. Most breeds come in two different sizes, large and bantam. Should the book only include one of these forms, it does not mean the other form does not exist.

Almost all chickens dealt with here are bred or kept in many different countries. This means that, not only for the common breeds, but also for the unusual exotic-looking ones, you will often be able to find a breeder less than a few hours' drive from your home. You can always contact such a person through the various national and local associations, professional journals and breed clubs, or by way of an international show catalogue. People breeding rare birds in which usually not much interest is shown–quite unjustly so–will certainly appreciate that you, as a beginning fancier, are interested in their fowls. They will gladly take the time to answer your questions and help you along, should you decide to raise any. The present standard breeds no longer have any real utility value, as in the past. This task has been taken over by the egg and table hybrids. The many hundreds of chicken breeds which we have world-wide today would have been extinct by now if there had not been any fanciers, who, from generation to generation, had taken trouble over these birds. If you just want a couple of chickens for the hell of it, then it is certainly to be recommended to get a rare standard breed, instead of some crossbred egg-layers from a vendor. What is more, if you then also let them breed once in a while, you will contribute towards preserving this rare heritage, saving it for generations to come.

There are different ways of classifying the many hundreds of breeds that are found in the world. Each classification has its supporters and opponents. In this book, we have decided to classify them according to their original purpose, so either as table birds, layers or game birds. After the rise of the hybrids, all of these standard breeds were more or less converted into show breeds, in which 'good looks' are usually among the main criteria. However, breeds also have many other qualities that are each time handed down together with the selected genes and most certainly leave an important stamp on the breed's present form. Classifying them into groups according to their original utility or breeding objective therefore has its point.

The standard of perfection as regards to its size, accepted colors, marking patterns and other anatomical features may vary from country to country. Standards are certainly not rigid facts; they change in the course of time, depending on whether a new breeding direction is taken, a new color is introduced, or a color or variety disappears due to lack of interest. Thus it also happens that an entire breed is simply cancelled in a certain country due to lack of enthusiasm, only to be recognized again a few decades later. Therefore, in this book, we have chosen not to include any precise standard requirements of the breeds discussed, but instead offer a rather more general description of their appearance. Also in regards to colors and markings, we have given as much attention as possible to what is going on internationally. Some colors you encounter in this book may therefore not be recognized by your club, although they may certainly be bred and exhibited in a neighboring country or state.

We hope this encyclopedia will help improve your insight into chickens, thereby improving their care and well-being. In this way, you can get more pleasure and success out of keeping and perhaps breeding these charming and pleasant domestic birds.

Esther Verhoef
Aad Rijs

Part One:
General Information

For centuries, chickens in Europe ran free around farmsteads.

1   History

Evolution

Our domestic chickens have probably evolved from the Common or Red Jungle Fowl (*Gallus gallus*), a wild gallinaceous bird found in South-East Asia. The influence of other wild members of the order of Galliformes cannot be entirely refuted, but by now it is evident that the Red Jungle Fowl is the most important ancestor. In what way the process of domestication precisely took place is not entirely clear, but we do know that by the year 3200 B.C. domesticated fowl were being kept in Asia, particularly in India. Marco Polo's travel book, for instance, mentions a domesticated Silk Fowl with black skin. Also there are indications that the Egyptians and the Chinese were keeping chickens from 1400 B.C. onwards. The first domestic chickens arrived in Southern Europe around 700 B.C. At first, they were mainly kept and bred at monasteries like so many other domestic animals; the monks and nuns keeping these birds on account of their meat and eggs. Nowadays chickens are found practically all over the world.

Cockfights

In all probability, the earliest domesticated chickens were initially not so much kept for their meat or eggs, but for cockfights. Findings from excavations point in this direction. From time immemorial, cockfights have been very popular in the Middle East and Orient, and later on also in the West. Nowadays this cruel sport has been banned in almost all countries of the Western world, though it is still practiced illegally. In a number of Eastern countries, notably the Philippines, the popularity of this bloody pastime has remained undiminished over the ages, being part of an ancient culture. In today's Western world, game breeds tend to be mainly kept for their

Red Jungle Fowl (Gallus gallus)

special build and are bred for beauty, in order to put them on show. The Aseel, a chicken from India, is a very old game fowl breed, perhaps even the oldest. For that matter, the name Aseel basically refers to a large group of Asiatic game fowl. This group consists of various breeds, including the Madras Aseel and the Rajah Aseel.

Chickens in Europe

For centuries, chickens in Europe ran free around farmsteads. Usually, they just had to forage for themselves and were at the most given a little extra feed on the side, roosting in barns, trees and stables. The eggs were gath-

ered by the farmers for personal consumption, at least when they could be found. If this was not the case, the outcome would often be a new batch of chicks. Superfluous animals were butchered for the pot. Due to the isolated nature of many rural areas, there was hardly any exchange of genetic material. The inevitable inbreeding of these chicken stocks resulted in many country fowl breeds. Not un-

Drenthe Fowl

til the end of the nineteenth century did one start to focus on the economic value of poultry, and then the animals were mainly housed in hencoops that could accommodate between one hundred and several hundreds of chickens. During the daytime they wandered about the meadows freely. All the work, like feeding and gathering the eggs, was done by hand. Due to improved henhouses and nutrition there were more eggs to be gathered, though in actual practice the old breeds did not prove suitable for commercial poultry farming. The Mediterranean breeds were however known to lay far bigger eggs, consequently many imports followed. Notably the Leghorn has vastly contributed towards the development of poultry farming. A market-directed demand for chicken meat, brown eggs or eggs during the winter months also saw to a lot of crossbreeding with imported Asiatic breeds. From all of these imported or indigenous birds new breeds sprung, initially exclusively kept for their utility. These include the New Hampshire, the North Holland Blue, the Barnevelder and the Welsummer. Those breeds held out for decades, but eventually succumbed to the modern hybrid chicken. Fortunately, these often handsome breeds with their many useful qualities have been preserved as hobby fowl. The rise of the hybrid commercial chicken also meant an end to small henhouses. And so began the era when chickens were locked up in battery cages and deep litter systems of 'free-range' commercial poultry farms.

Shows

Standard-breed chickens have been around since the sixteenth century, which is why in paintings from that period we see specimens of breeds still existing today, like the Japanese Bantam. However, in the countries of the Western world, one generally only became interested in breeding purebreds as late as the eighteenth century. Usually, the rich kept them for decorative purposes on their large country estates. Owning beautiful ornamental chickens of rare foreign breeds was a way of

Japanese Bantams, a very old ornamental breed.

demonstrating one's wealth, and there is a similar display of affluence in the exotic plants and trees that adorn these country estates. From owning these breeds in order to let people see them sprung the need to secure certain features in stocks, subsequently comparing the animals with one another. In this manner, the various breeding standards came about in the course of time, prescribing what the ideal specimen of a breed should look like. By way of these standards, judges evaluate the birds that are entered in shows. The first serious shows were probably not held until the nineteenth century, and only during the second half of that period did they become truly popular. Also at that time the first poultry clubs arose. Nowadays, keeping and breeding chickens is a hobby pursued by people all over the world.

2 Considerations Beforehand

Look before you leap!

If you are thinking of keeping chickens, make sure that you have the time to give these birds the care they need, and that the work involved appeals to you. Chickens are far less demanding than most other domestic animals, but they do require feed and fresh water every day, and a henhouse requires regular cleaning. If you are away for a couple of days or more, then you cannot leave these animals to their own devices. In that case, you need a reliable person to take care of them during your absence. Keeping chickens need not be expensive, certainly not when you only have a few birds. Whatever the case may be, you will have to consider buying or making a solid and durable henhouse, which as a rule is not cheap. Also, your chickens might contract a disease for which they must see a veterinarian, and although this could be expensive, your animals should not go without

because of the costs. As chickens can live ten or even fifteen years (and sometimes even more), it is sensible to carefully up all the pros and cons beforehand. You should realize that your chickens cannot choose whether to live with you or not, and that they depend entirely upon you for their well-being. There are a few examples of municipalities prohibiting chickens within a residential area, or of fanciers having to get rid of their chickens because neighbors complain about the noise. So, before acquiring chickens, it is wise to inquire about such matters at your town hall.

Why standard breeds?

Many people have chickens that they have bought at a market or from some local dealer. Such animals are usually crossbreeds between several breeds, or they are white, black or brown 'egg-layers'. It regularly happens that

Whether you start breeding chickens or not, a henhouse is a minimum requirement.

Chickens of non-standard breeds are 'surprise packages'.

Cornish Bantam: extremely tame and nosy by nature

owners are disappointed in their birds, for instance because they keep on getting into neighboring gardens, crow very loudly and often, lay poorly or absolutely refuse to be tamed. This is in fact the disadvantage of animals that are not purebreds–it is hard to predict how their behavior is going to develop and what qualities they may either have or lack. With standard-bred poultry, this problem is virtually nonexistent. For, in standard or true-breeding birds, not only have their physical features been fixed, like build, type of plumage and color, but also qualities like broodiness, whether or not they are good layers, and the color and average size of their eggs. Furthermore, the breed also determines those features that may be best described as 'character'. There are breeds with which an owner can easily form an attachment and which, when well treated and cared for, will follow him or her around like little dogs and sit on his or her lap. But there are also breeds that react rather aggressively or shyly to people. Furthermore, you find breeds that can fly quite well and those that never do so, and there are roosters with a rather soft voice and ones that crow really loud. The fact that such qualities are 'ingrained' in a breed is very handy for people who have certain requirements or wishes as to their new pets. Some folk merely want chickens because they are decorative, just to look at. They have the space to let the birds run free safely and it does not bother them if they do not get very tame. And there are others who have a small backyard where they would like their chickens to go

about freely, expecting them to remain at the right side of a low garden fence and not to scratch about in the flower beds. Or there are those who only have a balcony, where they would nevertheless like to keep a few bantam hens in a space no larger than a mere square meter (10 sq ft). Still, all this is possible. But should one have such wishes, then the chance of success is far greater if one picks a breed that has qualities corresponding with one's requirements and possibilities. Apart from that, it is an old wives' tale that hybrids are stronger than purebreds. There are indeed some breeds that are a bit more susceptible to certain diseases and parasites, but this is usually easily prevented by vaccination or adapted housing. Most breeds are downright tough.

Appearance and care

If you have to make a choice for a certain chicken breed, then please consider, before simply going out and buying 'just' a few chickens, that every standard breed tends to have its particular physical features demanding spe-

On a wet lawn, soon nothing is left of an attractive feather crest or beard.

The Lakenvelder is an attractive and hardy breed.

cific care. If you for instance want to let a few chickens wander about your backyard, then you had better not buy a breed with crests, beards or lots of feathers on their feet. After a few days of scratching around, or even sooner, they will usually look pretty bedraggled. If you don't want your poultry to upset your garden, you can put a check on this by choosing chickens with feathered feet. These are less fanatic diggers, but then again you should see to it that they are able to roost in dry conditions, so that their leg feathers can dry. A short-legged breed like the Japanese Bantams cannot get about very well in a yard, nor can frizzle-feathered breeds that have a problem with rain.

Booted Bantams; the garden remains tidier because of their foot feathers.

If you have got very little space, then needless to say you should pick some bantams or else a bigger placid breed that does not need a lot of room. If you don't know much about chickens and you do not intend to look into the matter very deeply, you will do better to get a hardy breed instead of a rather delicate one needing special care. If you are of a slender build yourself or if your kids also like taking care of the chickens together with you, then don't settle on a large, heavy breed, but pick a more manageable size instead. Also consider the fact that big chickens produce more droppings than small bantams do. As a rule, large chickens take more work in cleaning the garden or henhouse, and of course having many chickens is also a lot more trouble than just keeping a few. Thus all breeds, types and sizes have their own specific features, making the birds either suited or not to your situation and requirements.

Breed-related qualities

There are chickens of all sizes, shapes and colors, with all kinds of feathers, and with a variety of temperaments. Thus one finds noisy chickens, chickens that love to fly and are constantly escaping from their run to visit your next-door neighbors (as well as the ones across the road), chickens that by nature are very calm and docile, and those that are known for their jumpiness or even for being quite aggres-

The Araucana is known for its bluish green eggs.

The Cochin is by nature a tame and very placid chicken.

sive. If you yourself are rather lively and excitable, then you will do better to settle on a calm breed. Your animals will actually reflect your disposition, resulting in your temperamental chickens growing agitated, and when you walk into the coop, literally all hell breaks loose, leaving you in a cloud of feathers. There are also differences in laying capacity: there are breeds specially selected for laying relatively large and many eggs (even in winter) and breeds that lay very few indeed. Besides, hens of some breeds are broody at the drop of a hat, while others almost never are. Frequent broodiness is a nuisance if you chiefly keep chickens for their eggs, because a broody hen is not in lay. So if you want hens for the eggs, see to it that you get a breed of prolific layers that are not prone to broodiness.

Frisian Bantams are quick as lightning and hardly need to be tamed at all.

As both the external and inner qualities are usually fixed in a breed, it is clear that one does not only pick a breed for its attractive appearance. The best thing to do is to carefully consider beforehand what qualities you would appreciate in your new pets, choosing the breed that complies with this best. This way, you will prevent the enterprise from turning out a disappointment. However, do remember that character not only depends on breed, but is also connected with stock. Thus a breeder, by consciously or unwittingly selecting certain traits, will embed them in his or her stock, so that chickens from this breeder might be more placid than is normally the case, or just the opposite.

Annoyance

Most breeds do not need a lot of space, and any garden or even a balcony is able to accommodate a few small chickens. If you keep their coop sufficiently clean and your chickens stay on your own premises, few neighbors will object to your hobby. Only when you do not clean your henhouse well will this attract flies and vermin, for which local residents may quite rightly blame you. But most people like chickens as their scratching around creates a positive atmosphere. This may however take a very different turn if your neighbors are confronted with the crowing of one or more roosters. Although many people actually enjoy the sound, there are unfortunately also those who find that it gets on their nerves. That is why it is sensible to inquire beforehand whether your neighbors object to your keeping a cock. If you expect problems, it is better to just have hens,

Some of the smaller breeds can even be kept in a flat, for instance this Grubbe Bearded Bantam.

The crowing of a cock does not sound sweet to everyone's ear (here a Vorwerk cock).

otherwise you might find yourself involved in a law suit and a neighborhood quarrel. For that matter, hens also tend to cackle when laying an egg, or when startled by some noise or other. A chicken, whether cock or hen, is never entirely silent.

Is a rooster necessary?

If you don't want to breed your birds, then strictly speaking you need not get a cock. Hens do not need a rooster to be happy, and the pecking order within a flock is usually not a problem either. Often one of the hens takes on the cock's role. She becomes a bit more dominant and starts behaving in a 'testy' manner like a rooster. Thus, very dominant hens sometimes even make a modest attempt at crowing. But if you find roosters handsome birds and it is possible for you to keep one, then you will have to take into account that he is going to fertilize your hens. That is of no consequence, as long as the hens don't sit on the fertilized eggs. A fertilized egg is similar to an unfertilized one, so you can simply eat it

and not taste the difference. Still, it is something else if the fertilized egg has been brooded on for a couple of days. The developments in a hardset egg go very quickly: within a couple of days a system of blood vessels is already evident, and on the fourth day one can clearly distinguish an embryo. If you are aware that you occasionally tend to forget to gather the eggs for a day or more, then it is best to select a breed that is rarely, if ever, broody ('non-sitters'). Otherwise you might happen to break a set egg over the frying pan. Many an inexperienced chicken buff can tell you horror stories about this.

Preventing annoyance

If you want your birds to have offspring, then getting one or more roosters is unavoidable. In that case, it is good to know that any potential noise pollution can be largely prevent-

A breeding flock of Brakels

ed. Most people who are irritated by crowing basically have a problem with the early hour at which a rooster starts to herald the new day, for they normally crow at dawn. A blinded and sound-proofed hen-roost may prevent a cock from crowing in the early hours of the morning and causing trouble. This insulation however has the disadvantage that not much fresh air can get into the henhouse, which is in fact indispensable to the animals' vitality and health. So this is only wise if you have a spacious roost with few birds. Apart from that, a cock may occasionally happen to crow in the middle of the night. In that case, the animal has almost certainly been disturbed in its sleep. A door slamming or a car starting is usually more than enough to get him to crow once or several times. The advantage of this is that you have a cheap burglar alarm, but your neighbors will probably appreciate it less. Another possibility is to separate your cock from your hens at night before they go to roost, putting him in a box or some special, well-insulated cage in your barn or elsewhere on your premises. After nine o'clock in the morning, the rooster can be placed with the hens again.

Roosters crow to let their rivals know what their territory is.

The Old English Game Bantam is known for its relatively soft voice.

Real game fowls, like this Malay Bantam, are practically monogamous.

However, there are breeds of roosters which are known to crow less shrilly and also more briefly than the average cock. The Old English Game Bantam is one of them. But whatever measures you may take, you will never be able to stop the crowing entirely, as it is a natural quality of roosters. By doing so, the animal lets its rivals know where it lives and what its territory is. It is perhaps a good idea to now and then treat your neighbors to a box of free-range eggs from your chickens: then they will enjoy the benefits as well as suffer the inconveniences of your hobby.

The number of hens and cocks

How many hens and cocks you are able to keep depends on what you want to do with the birds, the amount of space you have and the breed you choose. Do you merely want a few animals as a pastime, without intending to go to shows with them or to breed them? Then it does not matter whether or not all of the eggs are fertilized. In that case, you can get a rooster with at least two or three, but possibly even

more hens, depending on the breed and the space available. If it is indeed important to you that the entire clutch is fertilized, then you should preferably get no more than six hens to one rooster. In regards to light, temperamental breeds, you can increase the number of hens to ten or twelve, but with large, heavy breeds, like the Brahma or the Cochin, three to five hens are more than enough. There are also breeds that are still very close to nature and are prac-

Frisian Bantams are active– a cock may very well 'serve' ten to twelve hens.

21

tically monogamous. This is notably the case with the Asiatic game breeds.

Keeping several roosters together

If you seriously intend to start breeding, you eventually will have to get more roosters. Keeping several cocks together can sometimes cause problems, even when they each have their own harem. There are placid breeds where the roosters usually accept one another very well, but many cocks get into a scuffle right away. Certainly the temperamental breeds then fight on until the weakest rooster kicks the bucket. This is notably the case in confined runs where the space is limited, so that the animals cannot avoid each other and there is no escape. If you have sufficient room and it is possible to let your birds run free in your yard, then aggression among roosters is often no problem, or far less so. In that case, the animals can avoid one another, and the hens can join the harem they feel happiest in. An exception are the breeds that have been selected to be aggressive among themselves, the real game breeds. It is almost always impossible to keep cocks of these breeds together, not even with lots of space, for they will seek each other out to pick a fight. You can best keep these animals in pairs, as cock and hen will usually remain faithful to each other for life. If you do not have the possibility of letting your chickens roam about freely, or if this is undesirable for some reason, then

The cocks of game breeds, like this Shamo, have to be kept strictly separate from one another.

There are not many cocks that can be kept together – usually they start fighting.

for each breeding flock you could make a separate run with an inner section. But whatever your choice may be, chickens are not made to live alone. Therefore you should at least get two hens, so that they can keep each other company.

Required space

Most chicken breeds do not need very much room to lead a happy life. As a rule, the living space for large, medium heavy and light breeds should at least be 15 square feet per bird. The small or miniature breeds and bantams usually need no more than half of this. However, these are minimum requirements, and it goes without saying that every inch (or centimeter) more you can offer your animals is welcome. It will enhance their zest for life and their vitality, and keeping few chickens in a large area is less work than keeping many in a small space. The likelihood of diseases breaking out is also greatest when many animals are together in cramped conditions. If it is possible for you to have a larger hen-roost

If the chickens are allowed to stretch their legs every day, a henhouse need not be so very large.

and outside run, you should certainly do so. Keeping more animals together often means

Few chickens in a large area afford less work than many chickens in a small area.

that you can give them somewhat less room than the minimum: a large group or 'flock' strictly speaking requires less space per bird, as they are sharing the henhouse's overall area with their own kind. In a run of 4 square meters (40 sq ft), one would in fact only be able to keep five bantams, but, if you take good care of the animals, it is all right to house a few more. There are also many fanciers who keep their animals in relatively small coops, but give them the opportunity to stretch their legs in the garden for a few hours every day. Then a henhouse need not be very big, if only your are sure your animals will still get their daily freedom when the novelty wears off.

Youngsters or yearlings?

If you intend to get chickens for breeding, you will be better off with yearlings than with young birds. Note that in the world of poultry one calls an animal a 'yearling' when it was born the year before. So it is not a term for a chicken born this year, as some people think. Yearlings are usually to be preferred, because at their age one can tell whether they have developed well. In young animals, good qualities may be present in rudimentary form, but it is difficult to predict whether these will actually materialize. However, don't get animals that are too old either. On average, a cockerel is for instance able to start fertilizing hens from the age of six months. How long a rooster remains fertile, depends very much on the breed

Breeding flock of white Rheinlander Bantams

Heavy breeds like the Brahma are often infertile sooner than light ones.

A rooster will have to be at least six months old before he can be used for reproduction.

and on the bird's condition. Heavy, placid breeds that easily grow fat are often soon infertile, while light and active breeds frequently remain fertile longer. On average, a rooster stops being fertile when it is six years old. Pullets may already start laying at a mere six months (pullets that age are often called 'point-of-lay'), though the pullets of most breeds are not broody yet at that time. For that, one must wait another half a year or longer, depending on breed, nutrition and weather conditions among other things. As a rule, when a hen reaches the age of five, she virtually stops laying, although it may still happen once in a while. Such occasional eggs can go on up to a ripe old age, considering the many instances of chickens older than ten still laying the odd egg now and then.

Most chickens die when they are between ten and fifteen years old. How old they grow depends on all sorts of factors, like feed, stress and housing, but age often also has to do with breed or type. Heavy chickens, originally bred for meat production, usually do not grow as old as light country fowl breeds.

Chickens and other domestic animals

Apart from chickens, you probably also have other pets, or there are other animals that you would like to keep alongside of your chickens. Generally, this is no problem, though you should always keep a watchful eye. Some animals are better not placed together.

CATS AND DOGS

Cats and poultry often get on well together. The odd cat tends to chase chickens, but very few cats really harm them. Your own cats will usually accept your chickens as simply part of it all, though their hunting instinct may sometimes lead them to chase the chickens of other people in the neighborhood. If you have chicks or rather small chickens, then you had nevertheless better keep them in a safely enclosed run or an inside coop where a cat cannot get at them.

Dogs react variously to chickens. Some dogs do not show any interest at all, or they might even tend to protect them, while others love going after them, trying to make a hole in the

With a little tact, the contact between chicken and dog can often be excellent.

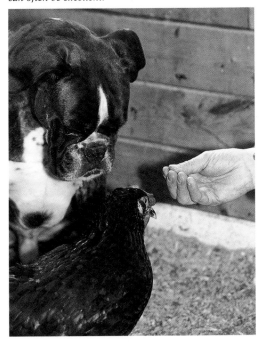

run in order to get at them and even kill the birds when they get hold of them. It goes without saying that you can only keep chickens if your dog is reliable in this respect, and if that is not the case you will have to see to a safe run and an inside coop the dog can not get into.

Many sheepdog breeds appoint themselves chicken guards.

RABBITS, GUINEA PIGS AND OTHER PETS

Some people like keeping other animals in a run next to chickens, for instance rabbits and guinea pigs. On children's farms and in small animal parks this usually works out fine, mainly because there is sufficient space and it is possible to get away. However, chickens now and then actually tend to peck at these animals. Often this is done out of sheer curiosity, but sometimes they really intend to harm them. Neither rabbits – notably the smaller kinds and younger animals – nor guinea pigs are well able to defend themselves, with all the consequences this entails. In a small run of a couple of square meters (sq yards), one had better not keep rabbits or guinea pigs. For the same reason, you should not put any other defenseless creatures, like the smaller types of pheasant, quail, small ducks or even tortoises, in the run together with your chickens.

However, there is certainly some difference between the various chicken breeds in regards to their 'pecking behavior' among themselves and with other animals. More active and temperamental breeds, like Frisians and Twente Fowl, cause more problems in this respect than calm, good-natured ones like Wyandotte Bantams or Silkies. In regards to larger henhouses with many chickens, one is sometimes advised to keep an active rabbit in the coop. The rabbit's hopping and running provides the chickens with some diversion. In this way, it can sometimes prevent the chickens from feather-pecking out of boredom. However, it goes without saying that one should not keep a rabbit with very temperamental chickens, from the point of view of the rabbit's well-being, and that one should not place a dwarf rabbit together with a heavy chicken breed either. Do keep a close eye on the contacts between these different species, so that you can intervene, should this be necessary. Sometimes the aggression does not come from your chickens, but from the other animals. For instance, there are pheasant types with which your chickens are not safe, especially not during the pheasants' breeding season. If you have sufficient space, then you may very well keep chickens together with certain types of ducks, most

Orloff bantam, hen

Wyandotte bantams are among the most popular breeds.

kinds of geese and turkeys, and even with goats, sheep, pigs, horses and deer. However, always keep your eyes peeled. People who seriously intend to breed their chickens will very seldom house them together with other species. For it cannot be prevented in a coop that the different species get at one another's feed. The kinds of feed are usually very different, consequently neither these animals nor your chickens get a well-balanced diet.

Cock and hens enjoying the spring sun

A matter of pushing and shoving: Orpington chicks, over four weeks old, of all kinds of colors

The Groninger Meeuwen, a fairly placid Dutch breed

Dutch Crested Fowl, hen

3 Getting Chickens

Buying chickens: where to go

When you have settled on a particular breed you will have to go in search of a fancier rearing and selling these birds. Many breeders advertise in club newsletters and specialist journals. Some of these periodicals are available at newspaper stands, while others are only circulated by subscription. Apart from the professional press, one also regularly finds ads in local dailies, weeklies and advertiser papers. On the internet too there are countless 'chicken sites', where you can either offer animals for sale (free of charge or otherwise) or buy them. Also most specialist breeding societies, called breed clubs, are found on the internet. Next to info about breeds, shows and the like, you can usually also find an address where one can reliably purchase chickens of your particular breed. Otherwise you may inquire about addresses of breed clubs at the National Poultry Association in your country. This national body can also provide you with telephone numbers of local clubs in your neighborhood. In every district there is sure to be a poultry club, or some organization coordinating the activities of either poultry, pigeon or rabbit raisers living in the area. And you may often find them in your municipality's information brochure. You could also inquire when a poultry show is to be held somewhere near to you, or where and when there is going to be a major international poultry exhibition. All over the country, shows are held practically every week during the exhibition season (October to January). At the larger exhibitions you will usually find far more animals and also a greater variety of breeds than at the shows of local clubs. If you are looking for a rare breed, then it is usually more than worthwhile to visit a major international exhibition. A common breed like the Wyandotte Bantam or Barnevelder is often also seen at local exhibitions. At these shows, you can familiarize yourself with the various birds and can meet their owners and breeders. Often animals are also offered for sale there.

Buying chickens: where not to go

Lately, we see less animals being offered for sale at markets and fairs, but it still happens. However, purchasing animals at markets and the like is not without its risk. If you fetch the birds from a breeder's, you know in what circumstances they were reared, and you are able to make inquiries about the care and feeding of this specific breed. Usually a reliable breeder will not let you down at a later stage either, should you want to consult him about something. This is all out of the question when you buy your birds at a market. Many market vendors get animals left and right from fanciers and breeders in order to slaughter them or sell them to private individuals, so that a certain animal can only be traced if it has a sealed leg or wing band. If the animal is banded, this shows the year it was born, which otherwise is just guesswork. There is also the hazard that in

If you want a comparatively rare breed like the Ardenner Bantam, you will sometimes have to look around a bit longer.

Dutch Booted Bantams are popular, so there is always a breeder nearby.

If you read breeders' advertisements in magazines, they often seem to be phrased in a kind of 'secret language'. An advertisement that runs as follows *Orpington lrg. buff 0–7 + + Wyandotte bant. blk. 1–2 avail. '02* means that the breeder is offering large buff-colored Orpingtons for sale as well as black Wyandotte Bantams. There are seven Orpington hens, one Wyandotte hen. The animals on offer were bred in the year 2002.

Getting a breeding flock

If you interested in a rare breed, and is it not inconceivable that you are going to take your new animals to shows or even start breeding them then it is advisable to seriously study the breed of your choice beforehand, previous to purchasing the animals at a specialist breeder's. By all means go to shows and talk to the breed's various fanciers. In that way, you will learn what is going on with the different

Silver black spangled Owl Beard Bantam, hen

the marketplace you might buy animals from stocks that are bad layers, have problems with broodiness or are not up to expectation in some other way – the breeder has had his own reasons for giving them to a dealer, because dealers usually pay a lower price than serious fanciers do. Another disadvantage of markets and fairs is that animals from different breeders are usually put together without any consideration whatsoever. In that case, there is a serious possibility that diseases are transmitted. Still, this of course is not always the case, and it is also very well possible to get healthy, lively animals at a dealer's or at the market. However, if you want to be on the safe side, it is advisable to only purchase your birds at a serious fancier. Should you nevertheless decide to purchase chickens at a vendor's or the market, then make sure to ask for young animals. Also clearly state that you want hens or pullets. If you merely ask for 'chickens', you are not making a distinction between hens and cocks. The vendor might take advantage of this by selling you cocks or old birds. For you, being unfamiliar in this field, it is often impossible to tell the difference. Recouping your losses at a vendor is often out of the question, as he has simply complied with your demand for 'chickens'.

breeds, and what you therefore should focus on when getting a breeding flock. Also the Internet has lots of information in this field. If you don't have access to the Internet, then you could contact the breed club specializing in the breed of your choice. Usually such clubs have a newsletter or bulletin that will be sent to you upon request. As a rule, all breed clubs also have a breeders' day, where you will be very welcome as an interested person. The advantage of all this is that you will have done your homework and will eventually be able to make an informed choice about the breeder you get your birds from, or about a specific color variety or a particular type of fowl. Should you purchase these animals in order to start breeding them, then do see to it that they are not too closely related. Although one can make excellent use of double mating to secure certain desirable features, in the long run repeated inbreeding is not conducive to vitality. Together with desirable genes, undesirable ones may also get embedded in a strain. If you start out with closely related birds, you will very soon need one or more unrelated

The bare patches on the backs of these hens are due to the active cock's 'treading'.

animals ('new blood') to avoid problems of inbreeding.

A healthy chicken: what to look for

After looking around at a serious fancier's, there is not much risk of your returning home with diseased or otherwise defective chickens. A specialist breeder will usually sell you very healthy animals with a small flaw. Breeders

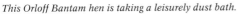

This Orloff Bantam hen is taking a leisurely dust bath.

Barred Wyandotte Bantams, hens

Healthy, vigorous chickens, like these Orpington Bantams, are always on the go.

usually keep the most promising animals to themselves to improve his breed to regularly enters his birds in shows. Still, it is always good to know how to tell a healthy animal. Healthy, vigorous chickens are constantly on the go, looking for food, taking a dust bath, scratching the dirt or preening their feathers. They do not react in panic when you go up to the henhouse together with the breeder, nor do they give an impression of apathy. Panic-stricken reactions in chickens can however be breed-related, because some pure breeds tend to be rather shy and may be a little scared when a stranger arrives at the coop. Check the skin under the feathers in order to find out whether an animal has parasites. The feathers around the vent must also be clean. The droppings you find in the coop should be fairly firm and in part white or yellowish. In healthy, adult and non-broody animals, the comb and wattles should be well saturated with blood

and therefore red. If a comb has a dull color, this is often a sign of a bad condition. The eyes should be clear and the feathers shiny and plentiful, without bare patches or lesions. During the mating season, damaged backs and necks are however more or less normal in hens, because the cock now and then tends to tread his hens a bit too fervently. When you hold a chicken, the bird should be firm to the touch. If you feel a sharp breastbone, the animal is too skinny. This may be a sign of bad care, but it usually indicates that the bird is troubled by some digestive disorder. Keep in mind that all this is true for fully developed adult animals. If you buy half-grown chickens or birds that are molting, the picture you get is somewhat different. A molting chicken does not feel fit and its feathers are rather unkempt. Also its comb and wattles tend to be a bit shriveled and pale at such a time. Semi-adult birds are often still molting and also have rather small combs.

Various strains

If you get standard-breed chickens, you more or less know what to expect both to the animals' appearance and their character. For character is hereditary too. Aggressiveness, pecking at one another's feathers and taking bad care of chicks may be basically determined by heredity, although no one will wittingly select his or her breeding animals with a view to such behavior. However, it of course happens occasionally within any breed that an individual is born with character traits untypical of the breed itself. If it is a good-looking animal, there is a chance that one will nevertheless mate it up, thus affecting the nature of its offspring. If a fancier of a gentle breed continues breeding from an aggressive rooster, then it is very likely that some of this cock's descendents will also be hard to get on with. Of course, the other way round is possible too: by selecting placid animals, a breeder can work miracles with a breed that is shy and by nature has a tendency to be flighty. Thus, it won't do any harm to keep an open eye and ear at the breeder's.

Character is not only related to breed, but also to stock, besides being influenced by the owner.

Transport boxes for chickens; they also come without the wire mesh, so that the birds remain calmer.

Transportation home

PREPARATION

Before fetching your animals, you should have their water ready and put grit and litter in the coop. Ask the person selling the chickens to give you some feed for the first couple of days. In that way, you can accustom your chickens slowly to the possibly different composition of the feed you have bought.

An old-fashioned transport basket for chickens

TRANSPORT BOXES AND BASKETS

It is best to transport your chickens in a special chicken basket or carrier. If you don't have one, then you can also take your birds in a box. In that case, see to it that such boxes are firmly closed, so that the chickens cannot get out. However, there should of course be enough ventilation holes. In order to prevent injuries in transit, it is better to transport one animal per box, with preferably a thick layer of hay or straw on the bottom. Underneath this, you should have a layer of newspapers to absorb moisture. The box should not be much bigger than the chicken itself. In a box that is too large, the animals will tend to slide to and fro during transport, and this causes a lot of stress. Chickens can stand the cold quite well, but they are not very 'heat-resistant'. Please keep this in mind when transporting birds in summer: never ever leave them behind in a car and never put their box or basket in the direct sun. If it is very hot and the journey takes over an hour, then it is advisable to stop on the way and give the animals a little lukewarm water to drink. On a real hot summer's day, it is not wise to transport chickens. If it can't be helped, then preferably do it in the early morning, or else in the evening when the sun is no longer blazing and it has cooled down a little.

Acclimatizing

Put your animals in the run or in the coop's inner section, and give them a chance to recover a bit from the journey and to acclimatize. If your henhouse does not have an outside run

During the first days in their new home, chickens will often be a bit ill at ease and noisy.

Newcomers are more readily accepted if you place them on the perch together with the other birds in the evening.

and the chickens are allowed to wander freely about the yard, then first keep them locked in the henhouse for a couple of days. This is usually enough to get them accustomed to the henhouse as their home base. On the third day you open the coop, but leave the chickens to find their way out by themselves. It is not a problem if this takes a couple of hours, and by doing so you may rest assured that they will also know how to get back in again.

Quarantine

If you already have chickens, it is better to house the newcomers separately for the time being. Maybe they have germs or parasites with which they could infect the other chickens. Keep the animals apart for at least two weeks, and in the meantime have the newcomers' droppings analyzed for potential pathogenic organisms. Your vet may possibly be able to do this himself, otherwise the droppings will

Breda Fowl rooster in the cuckoo color

Brahmas in the popular columbian color

than having all your chickens coming down with some health problem that might prove difficult to cure afterwards.

Introduction

If you already have a few chickens and want to introduce new ones to the flock, then this is preferably done at night when the animals are roosting and it is dark. Adding chickens to an established group in broad daylight is not a good idea. The 'old' animals may in fact start to attack the new ones, regarding them as intruders, usually with fatal results for the newcomers. As soon as it is dark, chickens are not active and accept newcomers more easily. Although a chicken does not have a highly developed sense of smell, it is nevertheless able to tell its roostmates by what they smell like. Therefore it actually helps to provide all of the chickens with the same smell. This is simply done by spraying the roosting chickens and newcomers with some water with a little vinegar in it, using a plant spray. By the time it gets light, the chickens are often already accustomed to one another, though one is advised to keep an eye on them at first. Minor skirmishes are unavoidable within such a group, as the social order has been disturbed. It takes a couple of days to determine a new order of precedence.

How fierce these fights between the birds are depends on the breed's character. If the run is an enclosed one, you should create possibilities for escape. An upside-down bucket or box onto which the chickens may withdraw for

have to be sent to a laboratory. This is a routine analysis and usually not very costly. Perhaps you may find it a bit of a rigmarole to have to go to such lengths over a few chickens. But please realize that it is better to invest a little time, attention and money in them now,

Brabant Country Fowl or Brabançonne, chick

35

a while will usually do fine. Still, it is better to add several chickens in one go to an estab-

Rheinlander cock

lished group than just adding a single one. A solitary hen sometimes has difficulty fitting in, and often the group does not really accept her.

Black white mottled Naked Neck hen

Taming

Certain breeds become tame more easily than others. It sometimes helps when a fancier of a rather shy breed accustoms chicks to the sound of a radio at an early age. Then they will not be so easily scared of all sorts of sounds. Furthermore, you can feed them something good from your hand. If you squat down quietly and keep on making the same little noises, then the chickens will get used to this and will after a while start feeding from your hand, coming to you when you make this familiar noise.

Some breeds take to this very readily, feeding from your hand the very same day and even sitting on your lap while they let themselves be stroked. Other breeds always remain a bit suspicious and never become so tame that they can be handled. In any case, you should regularly pick up the animals, getting them accustomed to this procedure. Always behave calmly when in the run, so that the chickens start to trust you. And never chase them!

Some breeds become very tame and are also suitable for kids.

These North Holland Bantams soon learn to feed from your hand.

Minorca Bantam

Leghorn Bantam, American type

See to it that your chickens have the benefit of the morning sun.

4 Housing

The roost

No matter what kind of breed you choose and what your plans are, all chickens need a roost where they can sleep in safety and shelter from cold, wind and rain.

LOCATION

When building a roost, you will have to take into account several things. First it is important that, whenever possible, the front of the roost should face the south-east. Thus, the chickens have the benefit of the morning sun, while at the hottest time of day the front is in the shade. The roost's front should not be in a place that is exposed to the sun all day long, as chickens cannot stand the heat very well. Also draft is disastrous, so the best thing is to place your roost in a sheltered spot. Before starting to build a henhouse, it is best to make inquiries at your town hall. As a rule, you do not need to apply for a building permit for small coops; sometimes it is enough just to report your

For this type of henhouse you don't need a building license but the occupants will have to be very small.

For keeping a few chickens, there are ready-made chicken runs with inner sections for sale.

plans, and often even that is unnecessary. For larger edifices, however, you will usually need a building permit.

CHOICE OF MATERIAL

Most henhouses are made of wood, but if you are very handy or have a bricklayer in the family then a stone henhouse is to be preferred. It is more durable and takes less maintenance. Preferably finish it by applying a layer of stucco to the masonry on the inside. After drying, this can be easily painted with concrete paint in some light color. As a base, a smooth concrete floor is the best choice. When building the coop, keep in mind that you will have to enter it regularly to clean it out and to provide water and feed so you should preferably be able to stand up straight in it and get into it easily. If your henhouse is a big one, see to a wide door, also enabling you to enter in an upright position and enter with a wheelbarrow which is very handy when cleaning the coop. In any case see to it that the henhouse is insulated well, so that frost and heat are kept out as much as possible. You can achieve this by applying insulation material to the inside of the place and covering this with chipboard or polythene sheeting. If you only intend to keep a few chickens, there are low, ready-made chicken runs with inner sections available ('bungalow style'). Also the larger rabbit hutches raised on legs will do fine for a few small bantams.

VENTILATION

Although the henhouse should be insulated well, ventilation is almost as important, if not more so. The easiest way of ventilating is having a window you can leave open night and day, only closing it when it freezes hard. Behind the open window you can place an insect screen of fine, yet strong wire gauze, preventing vermin from getting into the henhouse that way. If you are putting in several windows, keep in mind that it could become drafty, which may prove fatal to the chickens. In that case, place the windows in the top of the coop's roof so that the chickens are not in the draft. In a small henhouse with three or four birds, a few ventilation slides will suffice.

When constructing a coop, you have to make amends for the crowing of your rooster (as your neighbors won't appreciate this). Alongside good insulation, you might also consider

Open-fronted coop

some other form of ventilation. Perhaps having a mechanical exhaust system or bathroom fan in the roost could be a solution. If your garden is very sheltered and out of the wind, then it is sometimes not even necessary to have an inner section. In that case, you could make a kind of aviary in which only the sides, roof and back wall are of solid material. The front may then entirely consist of wire mesh. The ventilation in such open-fronted coops is optimal, which is conducive to the animals' vitality. Chickens are very well able to cope with frost, so that you don't have to be afraid of harming your birds in this way. However, an open-fronted coop must certainly be in a sheltered spot.

THE FINISHING

Try to avoid joints in the coop as much as possible, to avoid lurking parasites. Therefore, you should finish the interior with some kind of smooth (polythene) sheeting. Furthermore, you could whitewash the inside of the henhouse. The outside of a wooden henhouse can best be stained with a view to durability. It goes without saying that you should only let the animals into their accommodations after the strong paint smell has subsided, as this is in fact highly poisonous to birds and thus also to chickens. A slanting roof is best in order to prevent leakages, and preferably there should also be an eaves-gutter to drain off the rain.

LITTER

Wood flour, saw dust, clean 'sharp sand', or a mixture of these is best as litter. Hay is less suitable, because it easily gets twisted around the chickens' legs, thus endangering them. Also it tends to cake when contaminated with droppings. Straw on the other hand is fine, provided it is not too long, preferably chopped straw. When having straw, see to it that it remains airy and dry. This may be done by regularly working it over with a rake, but your chickens can also take care of this– if you scatter a little grain in the straw every day they will turn it over themselves. In general, straw and wood flour tend to cause more dust than 'sharp sand'.

Nails soiled by dried manure

HEATING AND LIGHT

In building a coop, it is sensible to install an electricity cable in order to provide artificial light for the chickens during the fall and winter months. That way you may lengthen the day for your birds, so that they continue to lay in winter. Furthermore, you can plug in what is known as a 'plate warmer' or heating pad. This is made of synthetic material and has a small heating element of about eight watts inside. When there is frost, you can put a plastic drinker on top of it so that the water will not freeze over. Such heating pads can be ordered at pet stores and are sold at the larger poultry exhibitions. It is certainly not necessary to heat the roost; as a rule, this will only harm the animals. Chickens are adapted

Open-fronted coop in a sheltered spot: the transparent corrugated roofing lets more light into the run.

very well to the cold, even to sharp frosty weather, provided that they can roost out of the wind in dry conditions. At night, chickens protect themselves by sticking their heads in between their warm plumage. Then they sag at the 'knees' a bit (or rather, at the hocks), so that also their legs and toes are enveloped in warm feathers. By somewhat ruffling up their feathers, a well-insulating air cushion is formed between plumage and skin. Moreover, chickens love huddling together on their perches, so that they only lose very little body heat. By heating the roost, your chickens would have to go out in the mornings from a very cozy and warm roost into a freezing run, and would almost certainly catch cold and fall ill. Consequently, there would be a serious risk of frozen wattles and combs.

THE 'POP-HOLE'
The pop-hole by which the birds go in and out should preferably be about 20 to 60cm (³/₄–2 ft) above ground level. That way you will prevent draft along the henhouse's floor. How big this opening will have to be of course depends on the size of the chickens you are go-

ing to keep. An average width is around 30cm (1 ft), with a height of about 40cm (1½ ft). For crested fowl, one must recommend making the opening a little higher than for other chickens of a similar size. In any case, it is not a good idea to have an opening that is too low as it is very likely that the animals will graze their backs against the pop-hole's top every time, subjecting their feathers to a lot of wear. With a small slide or hatch that you operate from outside the wire-mesh (with a bit of string or a chain), you can close the entrance when all of the chickens are in the roost at night. The advantage of this is that no vermin can get in by way of the pop-hole in the dark. Moreover, it prevents your hens and rooster from going out at the crack of dawn and perhaps annoying your neighbors with their noise. There are also electrical systems available, operated by a timer, and if you have irregular working hours one of those might be

Black mottled Houdan cock

a solution. It should be easy for the animals to get out when they are in, and in when they are out. For this, you can make a little 'duckboard' of some good quality wood, with small wooden slats every 10cm (4 ins) across it. See to it that there are no splinters or sharp edges on which the animals could hurt their legs here. Secure such duckboards well, so that they cannot slide away.

The perches

The perch diameter and the level at which to install it depend on the size of the breed you intend on keeping. A heavy chicken breed, for instance, benefits by perches that are no higher above the ground than about 1 foot, as such animals have a flying problem. For short-legged breeds like the Japanese Bantam, it is better to keep the perches close to the ground: 6 inches is an ideal level for them. For other breeds, the perches may be installed at around 2½ feet. It is better not to place perches at different heights, for chickens always want to sit as high as possible and will start pushing and shoving on the favorite highest perch and possibly get into scrapes. The distance between the perches and the walls should be adapted to your particular breed– if the birds are too close to the wall it may damage their tail feathers. Usually around 1 ft distance is sufficient. How many perches you install of course depends on the number and size of the animals you intend to

get. Normally, a single square yard (3½ ft) will accommodate four or five bantams, or two or three chickens of a heavier breed. It is handy if the perches can be taken down easily as this enables you to clean them well and disinfect them.

Good perches are not round, for this provides too little support. They should preferably be rectangular to oval in shape and for larger breeds they should have a width of around 2½ in. and be about deep 2 in. Medium heavy and light breeds can make do with a perch of as little as 2¼ in. wide and 1½ in. thick, and for bantams 1½ in. by 1¼ is usually sufficient. The broadest side should always be horizontal, enabling the animals to grip it with their toes, getting enough support. See to it that the perches are smooth and without any splinters or hard edges, for the birds must spend the entire night on them and might hurt their toes and legs if they are not good. Still, there are chickens that seldom use perches– Silkies, for instance, normally roost on the ground.

Finally, we also recommend having a 'droppings board' underneath that can be easily removed and on which the animals' manure will collect. You can take this board out of the henhouse twice a week to thoroughly clean and disinfect it, so that the floor of the coop gets less dirty and takes less work.

Phoenix Bantam, cock

The nest boxes

Nest boxes or laying-nests are among every henhouse's standard equipment. If you provide a suitable spot for laying in a henhouse, you will find the eggs there. If not, the hens will go in search of a spot themselves, perhaps in a place that is hard to get at or is inconvenient in some other way.

Laying an egg takes a while. On average, a chicken will be busy doing this for an hour and a half or even two hours a day. That is why the nest boxes should be absolutely comfortable and spacious for the birds. Moreover, as hens have a preference for quiet, dark or dusky spots put the nest boxes in a fairly dark corner of the inner section. A nest box should be enclosed on all sides, except for the front and the top, so that the hen has enough privacy. If you also want to close off the top, then this should be done at a steep slant. This prevents the chickens from sitting on it and covering it with their droppings. An approximately 1½ ft high nest box with a surface area

If nest boxes are fitted with a slanting roof, as seen here, the birds cannot sit on top and dirty it.

of 1 sq ft will suffice for a light breed. For bantams you may make the nest box a little smaller, and larger for the heavy and medium heavy breeds.

How many nest boxes you should have depends on the number of hens you've got. As a rule, it is sufficient to get one nest box for three hens. It is best to fix the nest boxes about 4 ins to 1½ ft above the ground. If you are going to provide several nest boxes, then you should see to it that they are all placed at the same level. If this is not the case, you will notice a strong preference for the nest box that is situated best. This will result in pushing and shoving, and too many chickens will want to squeeze themselves into the same nest. Due to this, newly laid eggs will break, making the nest box very dirty, while the outcome may also be that chickens get into the habit of eating their own eggs themselves.

Moisture-proof board or sheeting is a suitable material for the nest, as smooth and with as few joints as possible. Putting a layer of grit in the nest boxes is a good idea. If the hen has to lay, she can at the same time have a nibble of grit, containing the calcium she needs for the egg shell. Of course, you can also use straw or hay, provided this is changed regularly.

Feeders

There are many types of feeders and drinkers available, all of them with their advantages and disadvantages. If you don't have many chickens, then a heavy, glazed earthenware bowl, like the ones for dogs, will do. But by all means buy a feeder with an inward-bending rim and never fill it to the brim. Otherwise chickens will scatter their feed all over the place, as they tend to scratch about in it. Not only will this greatly contaminate the feed, but it will attract vermin like mice as well. You can also purchase a feeder of some other material, as long as you make sure that it is easy to clean. Lightweight bowls are unsuitable, as the birds will overturn them.

If you have several chickens or chicks, then more professional equipment is desirable.

Drinkers and feeders

Drinkers and feeders

At shows, one can often buy a lot of stuff that you will not readily find elsewhere.

There are specific elongated little stainless steel troughs that can be bought in various sizes and are easily cleaned with a disinfectant. These troughs should preferably be placed on a somewhat higher surface, so that the feed does not come into contact with the coop's litter. Also a small feed hopper (tube hopper) hanging in the middle of the coop, so that the chickens cannot scratch in it or sit on it, is a handy way of feeding. Naturally, you will have to see to it that the chickens have no problem reaching it. For green stuff you can get a special metal 'rack' or manger to hang up in the roost. From the point of hygiene, it is not very sensible to simply dump vegetable matter on the ground. Moreover, by hanging up this rack you provide the birds with a lot of diversion and exercise, especially if you hang the rack just a little out of your chickens' reach, so that they have to jump up to get at their greens.

In regards to drinkers, it is better not to place them on the ground, as there is then the possibility that they will be overturned or else contaminated by droppings. It is preferable to hang some 'reservoir' or jar waterer in the roost, or to place the drinker on a shelf along the coop's wall. The level depends on how tall your chickens are. The 'little tons' or jar waterers are good drinkers. They are available in measurements from 0.5 to 5 litres (1 pt to 1 gal) and are made of synthetic material so that they are easy to clean. The measurement should correspond with the amount of water your chickens drink in twenty-four hours.

Small cock of no standard breed

This Antwerp Belgian goes out for a breath of fresh air every day.

Orpington hen, black laced buff

Amrock Bantams

If you have chickens with lots of feathers on their heads (crests and/or beards), it is advisable to get them special feeders and drinkers. These are constructed to prevent a tuft or beard from getting dirty or wet when the chicken eats or drinks. Such equipment is often not found in pet shops or agricultural stores. However, at major poultry shows there are usually some stands of suppliers of this sort of stuff, and these people also advertise in the trade press.

Cornish, double laced hen

Brahma cock, columbian

Sulmtaler Bantam, hen

The outside run

It is always good to adapt the outside run to the sort of chickens you intend keeping. Thus, breeds with lots of feathers on their feet, like Booted Bantams, benefit from an entirely roofed-in run, where the roof has a great deal of overlap, preventing the rain from blowing in, so that the run remains dry. The same goes for crested breeds. For breeds that like to fly and are good at it, the outside run should always be entirely roofed over, either with wire mesh or with real roofing. For the heavy and medium heavy breeds that are not really good fliers, a fence of around 1.80m (6 ft) high is usually sufficient. Whatever the case may be, a roof is in fact always recommendable; it prevents the droppings of wild birds falling into the run and perhaps in that way infecting your animals with some kind of worm or microbe. Finally, a fully enclosed run is safer for the animals in connection with raptors and cats. One may also cast a concrete floor as the outside run's foundation, placing the fence on a wall a few stones high. Then the run will remain cleaner and no water will be able to find its way into it. Instead of a concrete floor, you could have a tile floor as a foundation. On this, one could spread a thick layer of clean sand, in which the chickens might grub and scratch. A layer of at least 20cm (8 ins) would do the job. If you are not going to put in a solid floor in your run, you should in any case see to it that the ground is underdrained well and preferably a bit higher than outside. As a rule, it is not really worthwhile to plant vegetation in a run– chickens are past masters at 'decimating' bushes and plants, certainly when this is the only fun to be had. As an 'occupational therapy' a couple of shrubs are however welcome. In that case, you should choose strong

bushes with leathery leaves, like cherry laurels, or else conifers and pines, and you should regularly replace them.

Dust box

All chickens have a need to 'wash' themselves with sand. For this purpose, you can make a special dust box of wood with a raised edge of about 8 in. How large this box should be depends on the size of the fowls using it. For bantams, the size will be 2x2 ft, while for the larger breeds you can increase this to $2^{1}/_{2}$–$3^{1}/_{2}$ ft. Fill this dust box up with clean white sand, and change it regularly. The box should definitely be in a dry place, so that the contents remain dry and clean. If you place this box in an outside run, choosing a sunny spot, your chickens will use it gladly and frequently.

Running free

If you have sufficient space around your home, you could let your chickens run free. For the chickens this is the most natural and pleasant way to live. They are able to look for food themselves, are free to choose where to have their dust bath and will be on the move all day long. Thus, the animals will remain in good condition and won't turn to fat. Moreover, chickens can 'scrape together' a great deal of their living in this way, polishing off many an insect, worm, slug or budding a little weed on the side.

Chickens love a dust bath

It goes without saying that you can only let your chickens run free if they are not a nuisance to others, so only if the garden is well fenced around. How high the fence should be depends very much on the breed you have. For large Brahmas a height of 2¼ ft is more than enough, but lightweight breeds like Frisians or Brakels very easily fly over a fence 6½ or even 10 ft high. If the space is large enough, however, and the animals are not scared or being chased, these light breeds will usually remain inside the fencing.

Letting your chickens run free does have a number of disadvantages. The birds are unprotected from potential menaces, like raptors and dogs. And you yourself may find it rather a nuisance if you are fond of a tidy garden. In that case, it is not a good idea to let your chickens roam about in it as chickens tend to scratch the dirt, take leisurely dust baths in your herbaceous borders and leave their droppings all over the place. Furthermore, it can sometimes be difficult to get your free-range chickens back into the roost in the evenings. When they have newly arrived, it helps to keep the chickens in their roost for the first couple of days before you set them

Brabant Farmyard Fowl or Brabançonne

free, so that they will start to regard it as their 'home base'. If you feed them in the evenings in their roost, your chickens will soon get the hang of this, returning to the henhouse every evening. Should they have difficulty finding the entrance, then just leave a narrow trail of grain leading from the outside inwards.

These Bassettes are allowed to run free.

This Antwerp Belgian is completely at ease with his owner.

5 Care

Hygiene

One of the main things to keep in mind when taking care of chickens is hygiene. If you observe the rules of hygiene and do not keep too many birds in a small area, there is very little risk of being confronted with diseases or parasites, for these only proliferate if there is stress due to overpopulation, or if the henhouse is not cleaned out often enough. Still, lice form an exception to this rule. You can't really prevent them spreading through sparrows and other wild birds, however well you take care of your chickens. If the chickens do not run free, but are kept in an enclosed run, then use wire mesh with a mesh width that sparrows and other birds cannot get through. A sound maxim in preventing contamination problems is to clean out run and roost not *when* this is necessary, but *before* this is the case.

Cleaning

It depends on the number of occupants how often you should clean out the henhouse. If you have few chickens and they run free, then this will be less of an effort than keeping a lot of animals in an enclosed area. Still, whatever number of chickens you have, you will need to scrape clean the droppings board, gather the eggs and change the water every day. Also you will have to clean out the drinkers daily, and the perches will have to be scoured once every two days to two weeks, depending on the number of chickens using them. The droppings in the henhouse's inner and outer section can be best raked together once every two days to once every month, also depending on how many birds there are. It is sensible to clean the droppings board and the perches between once a week and once a month with a disinfectant, and to thoroughly clean out the feeders and drinkers. In summer, it is best to disinfect the nest boxes once a month, and in winter about once every two months. Also put fresh straw or grit in the nest boxes once a month. The floor of the roost usually consists of sand or litter, or a mixture of these. If you have many birds, it is important to remove all of the litter every month, but if you only have a few chickens it is usually sufficient to do this once every four months. Then you can also clean the floor of the roost with a disinfectant. A good rule of thumb in changing the litter is that it should always feel dry to the touch, so if it is damp, get rid of it. If an outside run is not very big, it is sensible to dig out a layer of about 20cm (8 ins) once a year, replacing it with clean sand. There is no objection to spreading the dug-up dirty sand over your garden. Finally, you should whitewash the inside of the roost once a year.

Ventilation

Good ventilation is indispensable in keeping chickens healthy. In a well-ventilated henhouse with dry and clean litter, you are unable to smell the chickens. If you do, then you need to clean it out more often or do something about the ventilation. In that case, you could place a small fan in the roost. Fans can be bought at any D.I.Y. store and are easy to install.

One can easily pick up bantams, like this Sulmtaler Bantam.

Large breeds, like Orpingtons, can be quite heavy when carried.

Handling chickens

For people with no experience with chickens, it is often not easy to pick up and carry a chicken in the right way. The right way is to first put your hand on the animal from above. Usually the chicken will stand still at this. Maintain a slight pressure with your hand on the chicken's back. This will make it lie down, so that it is easier to lift. Then slide your other hand under the chicken, your fingers on either side its legs. Now you have index and pinkie on the outside of the legs and your two other fingers in between. With a little dexterity, using the thumb and pinkie of the same hand, you may now also press the wing tips against its body, while the other hand remains on the chicken's back. It is possible to pick up the chicken and carry it in this way without the animal panicking. Also, you can hold a very large chicken pressed against you, clasping its body under your forearm. At markets and in old photographs, we sometimes see chickens being grasped at the juncture of body and wings. That is an incorrect way of

Ancona hen

carrying them, for in this manner all of the weight strains on the wings. Never lift a chicken by its legs either.

Nails, spurs and beak

Most chickens are tough creatures requiring very little care. However, you should keep an eye on a number of things. Thus, it is not good for the animals if their nails grow too long. Check this regularly, and clip the nails when this is necessary with a good pair of special nail clippers. If you don't dare to do this yourself, then have your vet or a friendly fancier take care of it. If your chickens often have this problem, it is a sign that something is wrong with your coop. Provided the ground is hard, nails as a rule wear down naturally when chickens actively look for food. Chickens kept in henhouses with wooden floors sometimes tend to be bothered by nails that are too long. Therefore, it is better to have a concrete floor or concrete tiles in the roost.

Roosters generally have pointed horny protuberances called 'spurs' on the back of their legs. In some cocks, these spurs tend to get very long or grow back into the flesh of the legs. In that case, it is best to trim the spurs. Also the beak's upper mandible sometimes grows too long. This is not only a disfigurement, but may also impede the chicken when eating, so it is better to regularly trim such a beak. For this, you can also see an experienced chicken fancier or a vet.

Washing

In principle, one does not wash chickens, but sometimes it can be necessary. Chickens with a lot of feathers on their feet or with crests and chickens that have really made a mess of themselves or are infested with parasites (lice) sometimes benefit from a good wash. Fanciers often wash their animals before a show. A show is a beauty contest and a beautiful chicken with clean, shiny feathers will therefore always stand a better chance of favorable judgment than one that is at least as good, but has dirty legs and soiled feathers. You wash a chicken by carefully dunking it in water that is warm to the touch, stroking very gently against the 'grain' of the feathers, in that way thoroughly soaking the down. Subsequently wash the animal with baby shampoo and see to it that it does not swallow any of it. Then rinse out the shampoo well, again with lukewarm water. After rinsing it, use your hands to rub along the feather's grain in order to get as much water as possible out of the feathers. Subsequently dry the animal thoroughly with a towel, making sure before you put it back into the henhouse that it is completely dry. This can be achieved with a hair drier or by leaving the bird in a box next to the central heating for a couple of hours. Once the chicken is dry, you must gradually accustom it to the temperature in the henhouse– never send it straight from a heated bathroom, scullery or kitchen out into a cold coop. Remember that chickens are very susceptible to draft,

New Hampshire Bantam, blue marked cock

A case of abnormally growing nails as well as of scaly legs

Java Bantam, cock

takes a month or two. When a hen is molting, she usually does not lay eggs; she needs all her energy, certainly at the end of the molt, to grow a new plumage. Because the feathers she gets are brand new, it is possible that they will differ a bit as to structure or markings. For a smooth molting, good conditions are essen-

North Holland Blue, hen

and a wet chicken all the more so. As the protective film on the feathers has in part been dissolved by the washing, you should see to it that the animal does not go out into the rain for a week.

The molting season

Molting is an annually recurring process during which the chicken sheds its feathers one by one and grows new ones. Normally, this

Owl Beard Bantams, hens, white moor's head

tial. The best thing is when a chicken sheds its feathers very quickly, donning a new plumage just as fast. By this pattern, one can usually tell which hens are the best layers. A slow molt almost always indicates that the hen is not a good layer either. Molting is a real assault on a chicken's health. Comb and wattles shrivel up and the head looks pasty. Growing a new set of feathers takes a lot of energy and protein. Therefore, it is sensible to feed chickens a bit differently during the molting period than when they are in lay. You will find more about this in Chapter 6.

Holland Fowl

White Cochin cock

Dutch Crested Fowl, chick, blue

Nutritional needs vary according to a bird's size, age and activity.

6 Feeding

An omnivore

Chickens are omnivorous creatures. When free-range, they eat seeds, berries and other vegetable matter as well as insects, worms and slugs. Depending on the season and what is available, the animals are left to decide for themselves what else they need alongside the feed they are given. If chickens are kept in a henhouse with a run, they cannot gather their food themselves. Then it is up to their owner to provide them with a sensible, balanced nutrition. 'Sensible' does not only mean that the feed should be complete, but also that it should be of good quality. A fowl living in the wild will not of its own accord eat bad food, instinctively knowing what is edible and what not. Our domesticated chicken, however, has rather come a long way compared to its wild cousins and now lacks this instinct or only has it faintly. Also boredom can be a reason for chickens to start pecking at stuff that is unsuitable for them or even downright harmful.

Purchasing and storing feed

Always keep your grain and poultry pellets in a firmly closed bin as well as in a dry and cool place. Never leave this open, for then dust will get into the feed, the vitamins will degrade faster and it will moreover attract mice. These uninvited guests do not only send up your feed bill, they also contaminate the feed with their urine. When chickens take in such sullied feed, they very often get gastrointestinal complaints. If you have but few birds, it is better buying a small packaging of feed several times a year than a big sack only once. A larger quantity is relatively cheaper, but also has its disadvantages. For, what you cannot see is the quality of the vitamins the feed contains. The older the feed, the lower its vitamin content. As a rule of thumb, feed should be used up within three months of its production date.

Chickens are omnivorous.

Always get grain mixtures and layers' pellets at a busy store, and make sure that the seeds look shiny. They should not smell musty or be dusty. Greens should of course never be withered, bad or moldy.

Complete feed

Commercial chicken feed comes both in the form of pellets and of mash. Poultry or laying mash (also called 'layers' meal') contains the same nutrients as pellets, only it hasn't been compressed into pellet form. Mash can be given dry, and the advantage of this is that, compared to compressed feed, the birds need to make more of an effort to take in the same amount. They have to 'work for their living' and do not grow fat so quickly. Mash can also be mixed with water, and many chickens readily and eagerly eat the resulting soggy substance. When preparing the laying mash with water, it goes without saying that any leftovers must be removed from the coop within a couple of hours, as this feed tends to go off soon. The disadvantage of chickens rummaging through a bowl of mash is that much of the feed gets scattered. You can prevent this by only half filling the bowl and by using bowls with inward-turned edges. Spilling is the reason why some fanciers prefer giving their chickens pellets. Compared to mixed grains, an advantage of compressed

Poultry mash or laying mash

Poultry pellets or layers' pellets

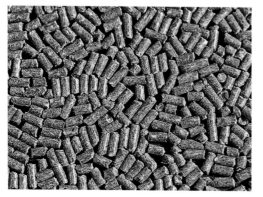

commercial pellets is that the chickens cannot pick out the tastiest bits, and therefore take in all necessary substances. For bearded and crested fowls, pellets are more suitable than mash. The latter tends to stick to their beards or topknots more easily, certainly if these are wet on account of the rain. Their sisters in the henhouse will get curious about this moving food source and start pecking at the soiled crest or beard. The result is that those features become spoiled. If you feed your chickens compressed pellets, you should see to it that your birds get the right pellet size. Small bantams for instance often have trouble eating standard layers' pellets, which are rather big for them. Manufacturers of commercial chicken feed take into account the various sizes of the standard breeds. Their assortment often also contains special small pellets for bantams.

Grain feed

Mixed grain usually contains wheat, oats, corn and barley, sometimes with the addition of small sunflower seeds. This should be provided as an additional feed, not as a main diet. If the chickens have little room and don't get much exercise, they very easily turn fat when getting too much extra grain. But you can put a broody hen on a diet of exclusively mixed grain if you want her to hatch her clutch of eggs – should she indeed feel like eating. Commercial chicken feed contains more calcium, which probably stimulates laying. An additional advantage of feeding grain to a broody hen is that her droppings (manure) become drier. Due to this, the chicken will not easily soil her clutch. If you have small chickens, just get a mixture of broken-up grain and corn, for whole grains are often too

Mixed grain for normal and large chickens

A blend of compressed pellets and mixed grain

Mixed grain for bantams

Mash for very young chicks

big for their little beaks. All chickens love grain, and it certainly is ideal feed for the animals to make them get used to you and tame them. Even after a few days, lots of breeds will try and eat some grain from your hand. If you keep this up, the birds of most breeds will get tame really easily.

Quantities

It is not easy however to indicate exactly how much complete feed chickens should get. It depends on their size, the degree to which they are taxed (exercise, brooding, laying) and the ambient temperature. In winter, a chicken needs more food to keep its body temperature up than during a hot summer. Adult chickens on average eat 30–100g (1–3½ oz) of feed every day. If your birds wander about freely, then our advice is to clamp down on additional feeding. It is better to give your free-range poultry their feed towards the evening, in their roost. In that way, you attract them to the place where they can roost safely at night.

Feed composition

Growing chickens need feed of a different composition than laying ones. A chicken that only lays eggs for consumption should not get the same feed as one laying a clutch to be hatched. This is because a hatching egg must offer an optimum nutritional basis for the

Growers' pellets

Additional feed for chicks

chick developing in it. That is why feed manufacturers have come up with different types of feed.

Give chicks a complete chick mash or special chick pellets (chick starter feed), with a bit of

Plymouth Rock chick

your animals greens that are fresh. If anything is left over in the coop, it must be cleared away the same day. This is not only sensible on account of your chickens' health, but any feed left lying around may attract vermin.

SUITABLE VEGETABLE MATTER
- Berries, e. g. blackberries, raspberries
- Greens, e. g. lettuce, broccoli and carrots; green matter from onions and chives (small quantities)
- Weeds, e. g. plantain, young nettles, chick weed, shepherd's purse, grass, dandelion
- Fruit, e. g. apples and pears

Flock of Araucanas with tails

chick crumbs on the side. This is a mixture of various broken-up grains and seeds, as chicks, like bantams, can only take in grains and seeds that are not too big. At around six weeks, chicks, which by then have feathers, should get special growers' pellets for older chicks. You should preferably go on giving growers' pellets until the hens lay their first eggs, when they are about five or six months old. Only then will it be possible to give the animals regular laying mash. If you want to start breeding them, you had better give them special feed for breeding flocks, which has a somewhat different composition than regular complete feed.

Green stuff

Apart from complete feed, chickens need fresh greens. You may give your animals a bit of these every day, preferably as varied as possible. You can grow them yourself in your garden, simply buy them at a greengrocer's or gather them out in the country. In the latter case, be careful not to pick plants in places that might be polluted by exhaust gases, pesticides, herbicides or deposits of smoke-stack industries. And of course you should only give

Animal protein

A chicken loves a bit of animal protein. If your chickens live in an enclosed run, then small bugs and grubs are few and far between. Gather some rain worms now and then for your birds, or get them mealworms at a pet store. Beetle larvae make good mealworms and you can buy them live. They can be kept for a long time, provided you leave them in a cool, dark place. If you keep this feed in a high-rimmed bowl, there is no need for a lid or cover. Also maggots can be stored that way, and most chickens are crazy about them. However, only give this feed as an extra, as it is very rich in calories.

Mixed grit and granite grit

Alongside of all this, chickens want mixed grit. Mixed grit consists of burned and ground oyster shell. The hens very much need the calcium this contains to produce egg shell. Moreover, there are also minerals in it which the birds certainly can do with.

Put a thin layer of grit in the nest boxes, so that the hens can peck at it when they feel the need. If you've got hay or straw in your nest boxes, you may offer the grit in a separate bowl.

Granite grit consists of tiny stones that are sharper than ground shell, and it has an important function in a chicken's digestive system. Chickens 'chew' their feed with granite grit, which – after the animals have swallowed it – lands in the gizzard. This granite grit has the same effect as millstones, as the tiny stones crush and grind the grains, making them more digestible.

You may also offer granite grit in a separate dish, or possibly mix it up with grit. If you make such a mixture, it is sensible to put a bit of fine charcoal through it. This counters digestive disorders and the animals can have some whenever they feel like it.

If your chickens run free, you should in any case regularly provide them with a handful of grit and granite grit, as these are not present in every garden.

Mixed grit and granite grit should always be available.

Drinking-water is indispensable– change it every day.

Drinking-water

Drinking-water is indispensable to any chicken and certainly to a laying hen. An egg consists largely of water, and a hen should be able to get this on top of the water her own body needs. If a hen has been unable to drink for only a day, her egg production may stop for a far longer period. The drinking-water you

Phoenix Bantam cock

Dutch Crested Fowl hen, black

molting is limited to a changing of the neck feathers and often occurs when a pullet just starts laying. The disadvantage of this semi-molt is that the chicken stops laying. Neck molt is caused by the fact that a hen has started laying too early. Her body is not yet fully grown and has basically not reached the stage of laying eggs yet, so that too much is required of the undeveloped bird. Usually the reason is that the pullet has been given layers' feed when it was still too young. That is why pullets should get growers' pellets until they are point-of-lay, which depends on how fast a particular breed grows.

Niederrheiner cock, silver birchen

provide must be changed every day. It is hard to indicate how much water a chicken needs. Among other things, this greatly depends on the ambient temperature and on the animal's size. You can see for yourself how much water your birds drink every twenty-four hours. Make sure that they never go to their drinker in vain.

Feeding during molting season

Molting is a true assault on a chicken's health. Its comb and wattles become smaller and its head looks pasty. The growing of a new set of feathers takes a lot of energy and protein, so it is sensible to feed your chickens a bit differently during the molting season than when they are laying. There is so-called maintenance feed available that is more suitable when molting than regular layers' feed.

Apart from the annually recurring molt that takes place in the summer or fall, chickens can also be inconvenienced by neck molt. This

Obesity

Most chickens prefer feed that is high in protein and fat. However, if you provide this without limit the birds will soon get fat, especially when they don't get much exercise, so the animals need enough to do. If you keep a placid breed in a small run, give them poultry mash instead of pellets. Furthermore, hang up a little rack with greens, so that the birds have to leap up to get at them. In that way, they really need to exert themselves to get something to eat, which is good for their condition.

When a hen grows too fat she stops laying and obese cocks usually have fertility problems. If you have never kept any chickens, it is not easy to determine whether your poultry is too skinny or over-fat. Pick them up regularly and feel along their breastbone, which should be fleshy, but not too much so. If a breastbone feels sharp, the animal is certainly too skinny. Perhaps the bird eats enough, but has some

intestinal trouble or worms. At the pet store or the vet's, one can get medication to control this. You can easily pick out a bird that is too fat by its broad backside, and if you pinch this softly, it should be possible to feel the fat.

If your chickens are too fat, you should see to it that they get more exercise and have more to do, and you should go slow on the food. Obesity can always be prevented by not feeding them too much. This means that it is not necessary at all to keep the feeder filled all day. Ideally, your chickens should get a certain quantity of feed in the mornings that is finished in the evenings when they come home to roost. How much feed you should precisely give them is a matter of experience and of always using the same measuring cup. In the beginning, you will just have to work it out, but within a week it should be clear what the correct amount is for your batch of chickens.

7 Laying

Why does a chicken lay eggs?

Chickens, some quail and a number of domesticated breeds of geese and ducks have a strange characteristic. They want to reproduce and thus lay eggs, even when there is no male bird present. Moreover, for the average chicken, laying eggs is not limited to a particular season, like for other birds. This phenomenon is based on a hereditary factor. In the course of time, one has by selection more or less eliminated the characteristic that birds only lay eggs after having mated up in the mating season. This is the outcome of a focused selection. Real layers, notably the egg hybrids that we are not looking into in this book for fanciers, can lay three hundred eggs a year or more. But there are also a number of original breeds that are close to 'primeval chickens', like the Sumatras. Such pure breeds often lay far less eggs, while laying usually remains limited to spring and summer.

About the chicken and the egg

Even at birth, a hen chick has a number of rudimentary egg cells ('yolks-to-be') in her ovaries. The number of these cells is the same as the maximum number of eggs that a hen can produce in her entire life. When and at what pace the egg cells are used up to form eggs depends very much upon the breed, feed, hygiene and housing. Pullets are sometimes already able to lay eggs at the early age of four or five months. Hens of this age are often said to be at 'point-of-lay' when their head furnishings start getting bigger and redder. Another striking feature of point-of-lay hens is that they start 'talking'. This refers to the very soft muttering noises the hens make. A hen lays most eggs during her first laying season. After this, she renews her set of feathers and starts laying again. During her second laying season, a hen will lay fewer eggs, but these are usually bigger than in the first season. When multiplying the number of eggs by their weight, it appears that the amount of kilos a hen lays per season remains more or less the same. As soon as a hen is about five or six years old, she will start producing less eggs or stop laying altogether. Then an egg becomes an incidental event that may occur up to a ripe old age. Thus, there are chickens still laying an egg now and then after they are ten years old but once the egg cells every hen has in a rudimentary form run out, she is finally finished laying. If you want to increase the egg production by providing artificial light in

The size of a chicken does not say much about the size of its egg; here we see an egg of a Welsummer (right) and of a Welsummer Bantam (left).

Pullets between five and six months old are 'point-of-lay'.

winter, the hens' supply will run out sooner. This reduces the number of potential laying seasons.

It is striking that there is absolutely no relation between the size of the chicken and that of the egg. Thus, a relatively small egg hybrid can lay very large eggs. A Brahma, called 'the giant among chickens', lays eggs that are about as big as those of a bantam. Within the breeds, there is often a lot of difference between a large chicken's size and body weight and that of its bantam counterpart. However, the difference between these breeds in regards to egg size is often relatively small.

Stimulating laying

Most chickens lay the majority of their eggs in spring and summer. Real layers also continue throughout winter, though usually their egg production is a lot lower then. This is only to a limited extent caused by the ambient temperature. The main reason is that there are less hours of light in fall and winter. So, it is very easy to stimulate hens to keep on laying in winter by artificially lengthening the number of light hours. If in the late fall and winter, you lengthen the day to at least ten hours, then with most egg breeds you are sure to get eggs during the winter months. Laying is however also influenced by feed. 'Layers' pellets', sometimes called poultry pellets, stimulate laying. And hens should also have water available all day long, because if they have to

do without for a day, it is very likely that they will stop producing eggs during the following days and maybe even for a week.

The egg's color

Eggs do not only vary in size and shape, but also in color. The color may range from snow-white to dark brown, with all shades of beige, brown and gingerish in between, and with or without dark specks. Also there are hens that lay light green, light blue or light pinkish eggs, like the South American Araucana. But normally the egg's color is related to that of the ears. Thus, chickens with white ears lay white eggs, while those with red ears as a rule have eggs of a brownish color.

The egg shell acquires its color in the oviduct. This is the last stage of an egg's formation. The process starts when a 'ripe' egg yolk is released from the ovary. Egg white or albumen forms round this yolk, covered by a membrane. The egg white contains the so-called 'chalazas'. These are beady protein structures linking the yolk with the pellicle or membrane on the inside of the shell. The purpose of the chalazas is to keep the yolk in position. The egg travels through the body with a rotating movement and in this way acquires its definitive shape. During the last hours of the process, the shell is formed and the pigment is deposited as well. This is found in the shell's outside layers. If you break a dark brown egg and compare the color on the shell's inside with that on the outside, then you will see straight away what we mean by this. The amount of pigmentation deposited is not consistent, so that all the time there are differences in color, also during the laying season. If the hen starts with a very dark brown egg and she is a good layer, then in the course of the laying season the color of the eggs will fade, becoming a light instead of a dark brown.

Araucana egg: its color is greenish blue, but the shade and the intensity may vary.

Fertilized or unfertilized

If you run a cock with your hens, the eggs you gather are likely to be fertilized. However, if you collect the eggs on the day they are laid and they have not been sat on, no difference can be detected or tasted between a fertilized and an unfertilized egg. So fertilized eggs can be eaten normally, within a couple of weeks after gathering. Only when a fertilized egg has actually been sat on by a broody hen, will it

The Maranses are known for their eggs of a dark reddish brown.

Araucana with tail

Welsummer cock

Welsummer cock

There is a lot of variety in the 'annual yield' of the various breeds.

can be difficult to take them away from her. The best thing is to lift her from her eggs and

Holland Fowl

develop rapidly and you will find, even after just a few days, blood vessels all over the yolk. Sometimes you may find a little blood in an egg. However, this does not indicate whether or not the egg has been fertilized. These small specks of blood can come about when a blood vessel bursts in the hen's ovaries. If this happens at the moment an egg cell is released, there is a chance of a little blood being enclosed in the egg.

Stopping broodiness

Chickens that are broody remain sitting on their eggs and stop laying for this period. If you do not intend to have the clutch hatched, then broodiness is undesirable. A number of breeds are known for the fact that they get broody at the drop of a hat while others are hardly ever broody at all. Broodiness usually lasts for three weeks, but may take longer in persistent hens when their (unfertilized) eggs do not hatch. Most hens stop eating when broody, or just have very little. A broody hen usually fanatically guards her eggs, so that it

let her 'cool down' for a couple of days in a separate space, where there is no opportunity for brooding. If you also give her a bit of company, for instance a rooster or some other hen, then usually the broodiness subsides for the time being. Certainly see to it that she

Leghorn cock

Should your chickens already have acquired this bad habit, then there is a trick which sometimes – though unfortunately not always – helps to cure them. For this, you should get an egg from the henhouse and make a small hole in it. Let the contents run out and fill the egg again with some liquid, of course non-poisonous, which chickens hate, mustard with pepper for instance. Put this egg back into the coop, so that the chickens are able to eat it – and they will find the taste dreadful. You might have to keep this up for a couple of days or a week or so, before the birds have learnt that no good comes from eating eggs.

If all of this does not help, then as a last expedient you could use what are known as 'roll-out nests'. These nests can be bought, but you can also make them yourself. They are nest boxes with a double bottom, in which the first bottom slopes towards the back, leaving a gap at the foot of the back wall. Due to this, the freshly laid egg rolls to the back and then drops a few inches onto the second bottom. This is covered with soft material, so that the egg does not break when dropping. Remember to make sure the eggs are gone before the hen gets a chance to peck them open.

has water and layers' pellets during this period. With broody hens that are not all that persistent, it is sometimes sufficient to lift the birds off their clutch twice a day, taking away the eggs, while in the meantime giving her something to eat and to drink outside the henhouse.

Egg eating

Once a hen has tasted an egg, she will probably appreciate the flavor so much that afterwards she will peck at every freshly laid egg in order to devour its contents. Preventing this behavior, called egg eating or egg pecking, is better than having to remedy it. If you gather the eggs every day, this prevents them from breaking when trodden on accidentally or falling out of the laying-nest. Several nest boxes at the same level stops a favorite nest from being visited by too many chickens, which would also increase the risk of broken eggs.

Brabanter hen

Abnormal eggs

One might find an egg in the coop that is different from normal. Usually this is a sign of poor nutrition, but not always. What we call a 'soft-shelled egg' is an egg that has a membrane, but does not have a shell. Quite a number of hens that have just started laying tend to produce such eggs. Also the last egg at the end of the laying period can be a soft-shelled egg.

Don't worry about a strange egg once in a while. However, if it tends to occur regularly, or if such eggs are laid by a hen with an egg production that is in full swing, then there may be various reasons for this. It could be a question of a calcium deficiency. In that case, feeding additional grit is necessary. An inflammation of the oviduct may also be the culprit, and in fact not much can be done about this. The chicken is not ill, but laying soft-shelled eggs could become chronic in such a case. Eggs with a soft or extremely thin shell can also come from a hen that is unable to ingest enough calcium, although sometimes it may also be the result of too much stress. Double-yolked eggs can arise when two yolks are released into the oviduct instead of one. This phenomenon occurs regularly and does not influence the taste or quality of the egg.

Laying problems

Chickens have a flexible, open pelvis which they need when laying eggs. In some breeds the eggs are relatively big and usually such birds are built accordingly. In spite of this, it may occasionally go wrong if a hen lays eggs that are in fact too big for her physically. As a result of too much straining, the oviduct can start to sag, so that you can see part of it hanging out of the chicken. In that case, you will have to react quickly, as other chickens usually start pecking at the unprotected oviduct. Separate this bird from the others as soon as possible. Take out the egg and clean the protruding innards thoroughly. This is best done with lukewarm water that has been boiled. After this, the oviduct should be pushed back carefully. The problem is that this is mostly – though fortunately not always – only a temporary solution, so that the gut starts pro-

Being egg-bound is a serious problem.

truding again the same day or after a couple of days. Perhaps the vet can help the chicken, but also for him or her this is a difficult problem. If the gut keeps on protruding, the only thing to do is to put the hen out of her misery. Sometimes it may happen that a hen becomes egg-bound. The animal spends a lot of time in the nest box, but simply does not lay an egg. Mostly it is a question of a pullet having to lay her first egg. Administering some medicinal liquid paraffin to the vent could be of help, and also putting some paraffin ointment around the cloaca. Also cooking oil may be used for this purpose. Subsequently, separate the animal from the others, preferably in fairly warm surroundings (20–25 degrees centigrade; 68–77 degrees Fahrenheit). And usually the hen will 'lose her egg' the same day or else the following day.

71

Shamo, cock

8 Diseases, Abnormalities and Parasites

Prevention is better than cure

Many of the diseases found in chickens can be prevented with the right medication, yet this is unfortunately not true of many others. That is why you had better do your utmost to prevent your animals from falling ill. In order to achieve this, you should adhere to the following rules:

- See to sufficient ventilation in the henhouse (no draft, but not stuffy either);
- Give them a well-balanced diet;
- Take perishable food that has not been eaten out of the coop the same day;
- Keep the feed in a well-closed bin and in a dry, cool place;
- Keep the henhouse and the run clean, and clean them out *before* it becomes necessary;
- Prevent your animals from getting stressed (too many birds fighting) for this reduces resistance;
- Do not keep growers and chicks in the same coop as adults;
- Leave new animals in quarantine for a while and have their droppings tested;
- Worm the birds in time and have them vaccinated against incurable diseases.

Symptoms of diseases

Someone who is frequently in contact with animals will soon recognize abnormal behavior that might indicate a disease. A few symptoms of diseases or parasites are:
- Itchiness
- Bare patches
- Loss of weight
- Diarrhea
- Symptoms of paralysis
- Swollen legs with the scales standing up
- Laying is stopped
- Sitting hunched up with ruffled feathers

Lethargic behavior often indicates an underlying problem.

- Droppings of an abnormal color
- Refusing to eat

Getting help

If you as yet are inexperienced as far as chickens go and suspect that your animals are ill, then the best thing to do is to get into contact with an experienced chicken breeder. Because of his many years of practical experience, he will usually be able to tell you what the problem is and what the best thing is for you to do. Should this breeder also have no clue as to what is wrong with your birds, see a vet. Preferably choose a doctor known for his ability in treating chickens, for most vets only see cats and dogs during surgery hours. Due to this, the average vet's ready knowledge and experience in regards to chickens is not very great.

The points of this cock's comb have frozen off.

The points of this cock's comb have frozen off.

Brahma

Here we are unable to look into all the diseases and abnormalities prevalent in chickens, but the following sums up a number of familiar and common diseases and abnormalities, so that you may recognize these if your chickens contract them.

Frozen head furnishings

During hard frost, a chicken's featherless parts can become frozen. This results in a dark discoloration of the parts that have been frozen and in the entire comb and wattles, or sections of these, dying off. In cocks, this phenomenon may even cause infertility in spring. Animals with smaller combs and with what are known as 'rose combs' do not often have this trouble. Thus the problem more or less exclusively occurs in birds with large combs. The reason is too much atmospheric humidity, in combination with frost. The air gets more humid when animals roost in an insulated, heated space. If they then go out in frosty weather again in the mornings, frozen wattles and combs can be the result. Therefore, the best advice is to ventilate the roost well. Of course it should not be drafty either, but the ventilation should be really effective. For instance, an open window or two (with a slight current of air between them) in the top of the roost's roof sees to lots of fresh air and gets rid of condensation. Apart from this, you can protect large combs and wattles by putting a little acid-free vaseline on them.

DIARRHEA

A healthy chicken's normal droppings are of a greenish brown color with a little white in it. Moreover, the texture of such droppings is rather dry. If chickens have diarrhea, then this is a sign that something is wrong. At mild signs of diarrhea, you can give your animals ground charcoal to eat. If the diarrhea is very watery and even contains a bit of blood, and your chickens lose weight and are listless, they may possibly have coccidiosis (see page 81). However, worms can also cause diarrhea.

WORMS

Chickens can contract various types of worms. Sometimes you can find them in your animals' faeces, but sometimes you will only notice your birds losing weight or having diarrhea. A worm infection can be prevented or clamped down on by worming the animals every six months, preferably once in spring and once in the fall. As it can occasionally be difficult to administer the worming agent to the chickens, this medication is usually available in powder form, which can be mixed through the moistened laying mash. There is also a worming agent you can put in the drinking-water. The medication is available at specialized shops and at the vet's. Worms are extremely contagious and can spread via the droppings. So always clean out the coop well and regularly disinfect it. Remember that after visiting the henhouse of someone with infected chickens, you should always change your shoes before going into your own coop.

RED MITE

This parasite (*Dermanyssus gallinae*) has eight legs, is an arachnoid and therefore related to spiders, and is easily visible with the naked eye.

A study of the head of a white Dutch Booted cock

Crested fowl are more sensitive to mites than breeds without a topknot.

However, a chicken fancier seldom gets to see it, because during the day it keeps a low profile in the nooks and crannies of the roost. Red mites are active at night and react to body heat. They only appear when your chickens are roosting. Then they get onto the skin of your birds, drinking their blood. Although red mites are rather common, these parasites are far from harmless. For, they can be carriers of diseases like Newcastle disease, fowl cholera and avian diphtheria or fowl pox. Moreover, they are an assault on your chickens' condition.

To prevent your coop from being visited by mites or even permanently housing them, you should see to it that the inside of the henhouse is as smooth and even as possible, subsequently whitewashing it or treating it with fruit-tree carbolineum, available at agricultural stores. A likely place to find red mite is at the bottom side of the perches. That is why you should always see to it that the perch can be taken down, so that you can easily check and clean it. If a henhouse contains many red mites, experts can sometimes smell them and tell their presence by the light gray 'dust' in the coop, which is the cast-off skin of the mites.

There are preparations available against red mite that can be used on both the chickens and their surroundings. A single treatment is seldom effective–often you have to treat your animals and their living quarters several times

in a row. Please keep in mind that these parasites are very persistent and can survive for a long time without food. If you get a second-hand henhouse, then the best thing to do is to treat it preventively against red mite.

This bird is infected with northern fowl mite.

COMMON FOWL LOUSE

Alongside red mites, the common fowl louse (*Menopon gallinae*) is a frequent disease in birds. Lice are among the greatest pests and also one of the most common parasites found on chickens. They can be seen with the naked eye. Chickens troubled by these parasites often get very itchy. This becomes obvious as they scratch and peck themselves, causing bare patches. There are various medications available against lice, the instructions of which you should meticulously follow. Usually it is necessary to repeat the treatment again in three weeks' time, in order to prevent a recurrence. Some breeders put tobacco stems in the nest boxes, as lice detest the smell of this.

Common fowl lice is the most common type of louse. There are about six different varieties. Each of them has a specific preference for certain areas of the skin. The most common types we find in the tufts of crested fowl and around the vent or cloaca. Lice tend to reproduce very rapidly, depositing clusters of eggs (nits) onto the feathers. If you look amongst the feathers, then you will see the lice moving about, while the eggs and nits are to be found on the feather's shaft. The chickens get very restless as the wriggling of the lice makes them itchy.

It can be treated fast and effectively by a powder or spray. This medication is available at any pet store. After ten days, a follow-up treatment is necessary in order to control the new generation of lice.

Feather mite

Holland Fowl, rooster

Orpington cock, buff

Plymouth Rock

NORTHERN FOWL MITE

Feathers can be damaged due to pecking or too small a pop-hole between henhouse and run, or sharp edges along the fencing. However, the damage can also be caused by the northern fowl mite (*Ornythonyssus sylviarum*). The tail and sometimes also the wings of animals infected by northern fowl mite often look as if they have been gnawed at. Northern fowl mite preferably settles in these places, where it hides in the feather's follicle.

It is not easy to control northern fowl mite, and it should be tackled at two levels. First, you will have to take all of the chickens out of the coop and house them elsewhere for a while. Second, you must meticulously clean out the henhouse, preferably applying a fruit-tree carbolineum solution to it all over. Then you should make a mixture of ten parts of methylated spirits, one part camphorated spirits, and a little bit of cooking oil (olive oil), and thoroughly soak the infected animals' tails with this and if necessary their

Langshan hens

Sebright

wings. See to it that these areas are really dripping with the stuff. This treatment should be repeated every week, until the animals are free of this parasite (not visible to the naked eye). As a rule, this is to be done preventively, for once northern fowl mites have settled in the feathers they are very difficult to get rid of. Do not return the treated animals to their roost or henhouse before the smell of carbolineum has totally subsided, as carbolineum fumes are poisonous.

Ardenner cock

Silkie

Dutch Crested Bantam hen

Phoenix Bantam

paler, certainly when hen fleas are numerous and the chickens have lost a great deal of blood due to this. As fleas thrive in damp, humid conditions, the problem usually arises in summer. Because most of the flea population is not found on the animals themselves, but in their environment (in the form of eggs, pupae and larvae), treatment should focus on the animals' living quarters. Like mites, hen fleas belong to the ectoparasites. These pests can be controlled on the birds' bodies with a flea powder or a spray. Use the same method to disinfect the henhouse as for red mite.

SCALY LEGS

When a chicken is troubled by swollen, itchy legs that give the impression of being somewhat calcified or horn-like, then we refer to this as scaly legs. If the animal has had this trouble for some time, the 'leg segments' ('scales') start to stand out from the legs, while gray crusts form

HEN FLEA

Most people are familiar with the fact that cats and dogs can have fleas, but chickens can also serve as hosts to these parasites. Hen fleas (*Echidnophaga gallinacea*) are easily visible to the naked eye. Unlike to red mites, which are also visible, they have six instead of eight legs, and they usually take a big hop when discovered. If your chickens are bothered by fleas, this may be revealed by the fact that they are itchy, sometimes resulting in bare patches and weight loss. Often the combs and wattles are

Scaly legs

79

in between, consisting of the mites' excreta. Under the skin, the legs of seriously affected animals are usually inflamed and often also bleeding. In a later development of the disease, the birds have difficulty walking. All this is caused by an itchy mite, known as the scaly-leg mite (*Cnemidocoptes mutans*). This is a parasite we cannot see and which settles between the scales of the legs.

If one of your birds has this trouble, treatment is most certainly necessary. First remove all of the scabs and crusts on the legs. If you do this without any precaution, they will start to bleed; so, therefore you initially need to soak them by applying fruit-tree carbolineum, soft soap or glycerin to the legs. Let this absorb for a couple of days. After a few days, carefully clean the legs with a little brush and lukewarm water. Then apply a special scabies medication to the legs. This is available at most veterinarians and should be designed for use after soaking and removing the scabs. To prevent a recurrence, the henhouse will also need to be treated with an agent against parasites or a good disinfectant.

Scaly-leg mites are transmitted by the chickens themselves and cannot be spread by people or other animals. As this mite thrives in damp conditions, it will be clear that ventilating the coop well is a preventive measure. Often the chicks are infected at a very early age. Therefore it is imperative to give a hen preventive treatment, before she hatches her eggs.

INFECTIOUS CORYZA

Coryza is a bacterial infection. Birds infected with coryza give the impression of having a severe cold. Their breathing is heavy and wheezy, they have swollen eyelids and their nostrils are runny. Also the animals tend to sneeze a lot. The disease spreads rapidly through the coop, infecting all of your birds. However, treating them with antibiotics is effective and soon cures the complaint.

THE COMMON COLD

It is impossible to confuse a common cold with coryza. For, in the former, the eyelids are not swollen, though the animals do tend to have a 'runny nose'. Sometimes they have their beaks open, as they are unable to breathe through their nose due to accumulated slime. The common cold often occurs in animals that don't get optimum care: for instance, they live in a far too damp coop that is exposed to draft. Also, sudden fluctuations in temperature may cause them to catch a cold. This is perhaps the case when, from a heated inner section, the birds go out into the chilly air in the mornings. The common cold is usually easy to cure. Both the vet and the pet store have a wide assortment of remedies for this.

CHRONIC RESPIRATORY DISEASE (CRD)

A third respiratory complaint that is fairly common is chronic respiratory bronchitis. Infected animals are huddled up in the henhouse, making hawking or humming noises. This disease is very dangerous and usually even fatal in young chicks. Adult chickens are more resistant and seldom die of it. There is no good

Langshan cock

80

Owl Beard Bantam, hen, golden moor's head

cure. However, it is possible to have your animals vaccinated preventively.

FEATHER-PECKING AND PECKING BEHAVIOR

That chickens tend to peck at one another is a well-known fact. Chickens have a strict hierarchy or 'pecking order'. The bird that ranks highest in this order only pecks others, the one ranking lowest is constantly pecked by the rest of the group. Under normal circumstances, in which the animals have enough to do and sufficient room, this pecking behavior will seldom escalate into a fight or in actually injuring a fellow creature.

Chickens can start pecking one another excessively for various reasons. With temperamental animals, the reason is usually boredom or overstocking. By giving these birds more to do and more room, this pecking behavior can be prevented or cured. It is less commonly known that glaring white artificial light also causes pecking in chickens. If this is the reason and a softer light is installed, it usually takes care of the pecking behavior. Also when the animals get too hot, they occasionally tend to lapse into this undesirable manner, and in that case good ventilation may be salutary as well. Once in a blue moon, even a different litter might solve the problem. Should all of this be to no avail, then it may have become a habit with the animals. That is a nuisance, as they sometimes even tend to pluck the feathers out of one another's bodies, and in some cases, certainly when blood flows, they may seriously injure one another and fight to the death.

There is a very effective agent available that you spray on frequent victims of pecking. The stuff smells and tastes horrid, so that the chickens will stop their assaults almost instantly. Also preparations to stop pigs and piglets gnawing at one another's tails can be successful. Still, feather pecking can be in part hereditary, so it is sensible not to breed from animals that show this behavior frequently.

COCCIDIOSIS

Coccidiosis is a complaint that arises when a chicken is infected with coccidiae, tiny single-cell organisms (protozoans) seriously affecting the chicken's intestines. Coccidiosis usually raises its ugly head during hot weather, often with fatal results for young birds. Also damp, bad hygiene and too little ventilation can stimulate an outbreak of these harmful, single-cell organisms. The disease has many different symptoms that may occur alongside of one another, but sometimes there are not many symptoms or none at all. Symptoms include: chickens sitting hunched up with ruf-

Neglect and disease often go hand in hand.

fled feathers, becoming emaciated, a decline in laying, bloody diarrhea, yawning and paralysis. If you suspect one of your birds to be infected, you should have its droppings analyzed as to the presence of coccidiosis. The vet can provide you with various preparations to control this disease.

Coccidiosis spreads through droppings, so it goes without saying that you must keep your coop spic and span and disinfect your shoes (or wear protective plastic 'slip-overs') when going from an infected coop to another henhouse. Coccidiae are however very tough, and in practice you will see that a regular disinfecting of the coop will get you nowhere. The only effective way of getting them out of your henhouse is scattering lime on the coop's floor. Then bind this slaked lime with an ammonia solution, so that the coccidiae are encapsulat-

ed in plaster, after which you can remove them from the henhouse's floor.

MAREK'S DISEASE

A fatal, sporadically occurring illness is Marek's paralysis or Marek's disease, a kind of herpes virus. Infected animals show symptoms of paralysis that often go hand in hand with a contraction of the toes, with legs stretching either forwards or backwards. Sometimes it may take a couple of weeks or so, but fowl with this disease always die as there is no remedy. However, young birds can be vaccinated preventively against Marek's disease. It is striking that some breeds are more susceptible to Marek's than others. Thus, for instance Sebrights and Barnevelders have a bad name as far as unvaccinated chicks go. Other breeds, like the Marans and the Suma-

Cuckoo-colored Java Bantam cock

Brahma cock, silver partridge

abbreviation NCD. Newcastle disease is a viral complaint. A combination of green droppings and total paralysis indicates that the animal is infected. Other symptoms are breathing difficulties and sitting hunched up with ruffled feathers.

Unfortunately, there is no cure for Newcastle disease. The only thing you can do is have your birds vaccinated. As Newcastle disease is very contagious and moreover fatal, it is compulsory for breeders in most countries to have their animals vaccinated before entering them at exhibitions.

To treat this, one might recommend contacting a local chicken breeder who is a member of an association for breeders of small livestock. Through their club, breeders are usually able to join a collective vaccination program, which is cheaper than going to the vet on your own with a couple of chickens. This vaccination provides your animals with good protection and is effective for about three months.

Kraienkoppe or Breda Fowl hen

tra, never or hardly ever come down with this disease. So a selection as to natural resistance appears very well possible.

FOWL POX AND/OR AVIAN DIPHTHERIA

Pox manifest themselves as dark lumps on the head and they are caused by various viruses. If the grayish black ulcers are only found on the skin, the disease is called pox. If they also occur in the oral cavity, then we call it avian diphtheria. It is essentially the same infection, unlike the illness in mammals. Bites of insects like mosquitoes are usually responsible for transmitting this disease. That is why outbreaks of the pox usually occur during an Indian summer, when there are many mosquitoes. Vaccination is the best prevention. During an outbreak, it is a good idea to carefully treat the ulcers with tincture of iodine.

NEWCASTLE DISEASE

Newcastle disease is a much feared malady with a deadly outcome. It is also known by its

9   Reproduction

Have you got what it takes to be a breeder?

Many people who like chickens love having little chicks around, and this is certainly tempting if you have a breed that is often broody. But although it is a beautiful thing to let your hen hatch her own clutch of eggs and watch the chicks grow up, breeding also has its drawbacks. Normally, about half of the chicks will be of the male sex, while the other half are females. If you have enough room, you might keep these hens yourself or otherwise they will usually find their way to fanciers. However, with the cocks it is a different matter. As a rule, it is in practice very hard to find roosters a good home. Perhaps you might find someone wanting the odd rooster, but getting a place for several cocks is very difficult in practice. Most small animal parks or children's farms have more than their share of cocks, and most caretakers have no qualms about giving illegally dumped cockerels to wholesale buyers or simply slaughtering them. If you live in a crowded residential area, you certainly cannot keep all the cockerels yourself, as they are very noisy. Moreover, at a certain point they can become aggressive towards one another, especially the roosters of the temperamental breeds, which is no fun either. In that case, the only thing to do is to offer the animals to a dealer, after which the odd cock might land at a fancier, while the majority of the birds will end on somebody's plate. If you find this painful, then you had better not start breeding. Having the 'surplus' cocks slaughtered or doing this yourself is simply all in the breeding game. Also in the wilds, there is a substantial depletion of male birds. Through their brighter coloring, they are more conspicuous than their female counterparts and their longer feathers see to it that they cannot escape as easily. So, as a breeder you will have to realize that you now and then need to get rid of your surplus cocks or have them taken away, knowing that they will be slaughtered.

Breeding flocks

If you would like your chickens to have offspring, you will have to assemble a breeding flock of promising birds, usually consisting of one cock and a couple of hens. Several hens are run with one cock because a cock mates several times a day. This is called 'treading'. Running one hen with one cock usually makes her life a misery, especially when the cock is active. Standard breeds have remained 'close to nature', like Sumatras and a number

A bare patch on the back as a result of an active cock

Tiny chicks grow up.

Four day old Orpington chicks

of the game breeds, can best be kept in pairs: one cock with one hen. Often these animals remain faithful to each other for life. Also other breeds are sometimes kept as pairs. Occasionally this works out fine, but sometimes it does not. By observing the animals, you can find out whether breeding 'one-to-one' is possible with your breed.

The maximum number of hens you can run with a single cock depends on the breed you've got. With placid breeds like Orpingtons, you might have between two and five hens, while with a highly active, slender breed you could run a cock with ten hens. Some cocks are such ardent treaders that they damage the feathers on the hen's head and back. The feathers of the neck and head offer the cock a grip, so that during mating his feet can remain on the hen's saddle feathers. When using a cock several years old in the

A week old Owl Beard

It is possible that the ear-lobes shrivel up somewhat during the breeding season.

flock, it is important that its spurs do not grow too long and the same goes for its nails. Due to their weight, heavy breeds have more difficulty here than light ones. If treading the hens results in completely bare, featherless patches, it is worth considering to house the cock separately for a while, giving the hens some rest, or else to introduce more hens into the flock.

The number of hens is not only important in connection with the amount of attention a cock gives a hen, but also as to the eggs. For the eggs must be fertilized, and if a cock of some placid breed has ten hens or more, then by far not all of the hens' eggs will be. However, for a successful fertilization, one needs no more than one or two successful matings a week. So, the number of times a cock treads his hens is no indication of his success as a 'begetter'.

It is not sensible to keep several cocks together, certainly if there are also hens in the same coop. This way, you get no idea of the breeding qualities of the individual cocks – no rooster leaves his name tag on eggs – and animals are also likely to start fighting. With very placid, gentle breeds, it is sometimes possible to keep several cocks together, provided there is sufficient space and you have enough time to observe the birds. Then you can step in when you see that the animals are at one another's throats. In commercial breeding, one tends to work with several cocks, but in that case there are also hundreds of birds together in a large space.

Age

Whatever you do – if you want to breed, always select hens that are at least a year old and entirely adult. Cocks are reasonably fertile from the age of seven months, and by that time they no longer let themselves be dominated by hens. Both cocks and hens are on average fertile up to an age of five or six, although the number of eggs a hen lays tends to drop somewhat annually. How long a cock remains fertile and a hen goes on laying not only depends on an individual bird's condition, but also on the breed. In general, the lighter country fowl types can be used for breeding for a longer period than heavier chickens. It goes without saying that in a breeding flock you only keep birds that are one hundred percent healthy, besides also being up to scratch appearance-wise.

Sulmtaler chicks; notice the tiny tufts on their heads.

Fertilization

After putting together a breeding flock, the eggs that the hens lay are not fertilized straight away. The animals need time to get used to one another. By far not every hen immediately accepts a strange rooster, so one should allow for a brief period of habituation. Leave the animals alone as much as possible and take good care of them, giving them good feed. If you keep to this rule, it is highly probable that after about two weeks most of the eggs your hens lay will in fact be fertilized, provided the cock is fertile. Infertility in cocks, whether they are yearlings or several years old, is usually temporary. The problem may simply be that the rooster is too fat and therefore not in good condition. Also the time of the year plays a part. Some cocks, notably older ones, only get fertile when spring is truly in the air, but throw in the towel in wintertime.

Treading

Breda Fowl chick; the leg feathers are already present in a young chick.

Chick of a Dutch Crested Fowl, in which the skull is clearly higher.

In chickens, fertilization takes place when the animals bring their sex openings (cloacae) together. To do this, the cock must mount the hen, usually gripping her neck with his beak. That is why frequently trodden hens tend to have bare patches in their necks. Both animals subsequently get their tail feathers out of the way, so that their sex openings can be joined and the sperm can be received. At just one treading, lots of eggs can be fertilized, as the sperm can remain alive for more than ten days. This means that the hen, after being separated from the cock, can go on laying fertilized eggs for ten days in a row.

Broodiness

Laymen sometimes tend to confuse a broody hen with a sick one. A real 'broody' can however be recognized by the following symptoms:

- The hen stays on the nest for long periods of time, and sometimes even refuses to leave it;
- At the start of the breeding season, head and comb still have a fresh red color, later on this fades;
- Certain parts of the abdomen and breast become featherless ('brood patches');
- The hen makes clucking or plaintive noises;
- Usually the hen will be less sociable, taking a threatening attitude towards other hens or becoming aggressive towards her minder.

When precisely a hen becomes broody for the first time varies. Many hens of the so-called egg breeds are non-sitters. Other breeds, for instance Silkies, Sussex and Wyandottes, can get broody for the first time at a very early age, sometimes even when they are only six months old. However, at that stage they are mentally not up to hatching yet, nor to looking after chicks. If you have such a broody hen, you had better separate her from her fellow chickens and take care of her as described under the heading *Stopping broodiness* in Chapter 7. Most adult hens get broody in early spring, under the influence of the lengthening of the days. Also, it may be of help not to gather the eggs the hens have laid, but to just leave them. However, because hatching eggs are perishable and there is the risk of stepping on the eggs and breaking them, it is better to decide to collect the eggs the hens have laid and put some crock eggs in the nest boxes.

Note the date and other particulars on the egg in pencil, so that later on you know where it came from.

Broody Orpington on her nest

Hatching eggs

As soon as you notice your hens getting broody, or perhaps even before that, you can start collecting the eggs they have laid. These are the fertilized eggs, which you later on can put under your hens, when some of them are good and broody and refuse to get off their nests.

Not all eggs are suitable for incubation, so only collect flawless eggs that have a normal shape. Very heavy eggs, possibly double-yolked, are better not kept as hatching eggs either and also eggs with a thick ridge on the shell or with a shell that looks marbled are unsuitable. But these you can eat. If you have a lot of eggs to choose from, then you can decide to only keep the eggs that are unsoiled or

A week old North Holland Blue

else you can scrape off any possible manure. Do not wash the eggs, for by washing them you remove the natural protective film on the outside of the shell. This gives bacteria the opportunity to penetrate the egg and increases the probability of the young life within dying. Also here, it is true that prevention is better than a remedy. If you see to it that the nest boxes are clean, the chickens will not contaminate their clutch.

The best thing is to mark the eggs. In that way you know exactly when they were laid and, should you be saving eggs from various breeding flocks, from which birds they come. Always use pencil to mark them. Other writing materials can be poisonous and this may affect the chick in the making due to the porous shell. Store the hatching eggs at a temperature of around 12 degrees centigrade (54 degrees Fahrenheit) in a place where the atmosphere is sufficiently humid, and see to it that their position is changed every day. A cool cellar is the ideal place for storing them. By turning the eggs, you will prevent the yolk from sagging to one side, which will prevent the chick from developing normally.

One should always turn them along their longitudinal axis. The first day the egg stands tip down in the egg rack or box; the next day the tip points upwards. In this way you can keep your eggs for up to two weeks. After that, the vitality of the germ cells declines considerably. Still, it does happen that eggs of several weeks old – four to five weeks even – are successfully hatched.

If you have a breed that is often broody, you can also let these birds hatch the eggs of other breeds.

Rheinlander Bantam hen, blue

wrapped in some other way, so that they cannot crack on the way back. Before putting the eggs under the broody hen, first leave them to 'rest' for a full day in some cool place.

Natural brooding

As mentioned just now, it is possible to get the eggs hatched by a hen of a breed known for its broodiness. Many hens, notably of the egg breeds, are non-sitters or not reliable in this respect, so that your efforts will seldom be rewarded. Very good broodies are found among the Wyandottes, Cochins, Sussex and Silkies.

The hens of the Sussex breed are known for being broody often.

Breeding without a cock

It is also possible to enjoy chicks growing up in your yard, without having a cock. For this, you need a breed that gets broody rather easily, the hens of which are known to be reliable brooders. Then you can buy hatching eggs at a breeder's of the kind of chicken and/or color variety you want. Hatching eggs are cheaper than chicks or adult animals, and sometimes you can even get them for free, but the breeder is of course not able to guarantee that all of them are fertilized and will hatch. Also, he cannot tell you whether the chicks will be male or female, and in what proportion this will be the case. So, these hatching eggs are basically more or less surprise packages. By the time one of your hens is really broody, remaining on her nest for several days and refusing to leave, you can inquire at breeders if there are any hatching eggs available. Preferably take the eggs home in an egg box, or certainly very well

Brahma

Chick in the egg, 10th day of incubation

This goes for both the large breeds and the bantams. If one of your hens is good and broody, you can set her apart from the others. This is necessary, as too much diversion can cause stress, which seldom leads to successful rearing. In order to prevent fleas and mites, you can treat a broody hen before she sits on the clutch with some agent against parasites. Subsequently move the hen to a nest box made specially for this purpose, in a quiet, rather dusky space. If the hen is real broody, she will usually remain on the nest, certainly if you put her there at night when it is dark.

Usually a small wooden crate or a strong cardboard box is very suitable as a nest. Put a big piece of turf or sod upside down on the bottom of this crate, preferably moistening it somewhat beforehand. This will prevent the clutch from drying out. However, make sure that there are no stones in the sod, for this may cause the eggs to break. Make a comfortable nest on the upturned sod of straw or hay, with possibly some dried tobacco stems in it. These stems are available from a pet shop or a store selling agricultural stuff, and tend to keep away lice. Then place a number of crock eggs in the nest, as you first have to make sure that the hen is really broody. If she is not, it is very likely she will give up sitting after a day, while the eggs have started to develop. Only when your hen remains on the crock eggs for a full day, can you replace them by hatching eggs.

How many hatching eggs you are able to put under the hen depends on her size and of course also on the size of the eggs; on average, hens of bantam breeds are very well able to hatch six or seven eggs, while the larger breeds

Chick in the egg, 15th day of incubation

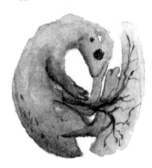

Chick in the egg, 20th day of incubation

can accommodate up to about eleven. The hen arranges the clutch around her heat source, i.e. the naked breastbone. In this way, you get an oval or egg-shaped grouping of the clutch. It is easier to achieve this formation with an odd number of eggs than with an even one. If there is always one egg or more outside the nest, it usually means that you have given the hen too many eggs for her size. Take these eggs away, as otherwise not much will come of the brood. For, as the brood hen or broody constantly goes on turning her eggs, there will always be one left outside of the nest, in the cold.

Taking care of a broody hen

Normally, a hen does not eat and drink much when brooding. Put down food and water at some distance from the nest, so that she will be forced to leave it if she wants to eat or drink. Upon leaving the nest, defecation usually follows, so you prevent her from doing this in the nest and soiling the clutch.

Give the hen only mixed grains to eat. These provide a lot of energy, which the hen can certainly use during this period. An additional advantage is that the manure becomes a bit more compact and drier. Due to this, there is less risk of the eggs getting soiled. If you have a hen that is a very persistent brooder and she absolutely refuses to leave the nest, she is wearing herself out unduly. In that case it is up to you to take the bird from the nest once a day and offer her some feed and water. If there are no droppings outside the nest and the feed remains uneaten, you clearly need to

do this. When taking a hen off the nest, don't give her a chance to return to it for twenty to thirty minutes. This is in fact better for the eggs. Leave the animal in peace to rest as much as possible.

The hatching process

Hens keep on sitting on their clutch until the eggs have hatched, which under normal circumstances takes about 21 days, large eggs taking a bit longer than small ones. So a bantam hen may already have chicks after brooding for 20 days. This has to do with the egg's mass. A big, heavy egg needs more time to warm through all the way than a small egg does. This you also see when you boil eggs in order to eat them. Small eggs are hard sooner than larger ones. It is a good idea to moisten the eggs a bit once, when they have been sat on for about 18

Newly hatched chicks are wet, but they soon dry.

A box filled with little bundles of joy

days. This is preferably done with a plant spray. Thus, you make it easier for the chicks to get out of the egg later on.

By Day Twenty you may hear some cheeping, although there are no chicks to be seen. This is because the chicks, right before actually breaking the shell, are first pecking through the egg's air space. This air space is found at the 'blunt' side of the egg, as you will know from your boiled eggs. By cheeping, a chick makes contact with its mother. They recognize each another by the noises they make.

Around the twenty-first day, the chicks will leave the egg. They will break the shell themselves by piercing it with the egg tooth on the tip of their upper mandible. Upon leaving the egg, the chicks are at first still a bit wet, but they soon dry to become fluffy little balls that are able to run around straight away and can cheep, eat and drink. They need their mother for the warmth of her body and to protect them against the rain and other menaces. What is more, the mother takes the lead and serves as an example to them.

As soon as most of the chicks have hatched, the hen's behavior changes, and from now on she is a fussy mother, moving around with her chicks in tow. In case of danger, cold or rain, the young chicks can snuggle up under their mum, safe and sheltered within her warm down. With very placid and tolerant breeds, the mother hen and her chicks can be put with the other birds, but in many cases it is better to house the animals separately.

Helping or not?

The eggs that have not hatched on the twenty-second day are either infertile or contain dead chicks. Therefore, it is best to take these eggs away as soon as possible. Sometimes one is advised against helping chicks that have difficulty in getting out of the egg by themselves. However, this goes against the grain with many fanciers, and as such there is no reason why you should not help an individual chick, as long as you realize that there is usually something wrong with these birds. For, if the hen has done a good job, a healthy and energetic chick will in fact always be able to get out of the shell without help.

Therefore there is probably something the matter with chicks that need a helping hand, as they may possibly be handicapped and so will take a lot of extra care. In any case, they will not be as hardy and vigorous as the others. That is why it is not sensible to breed from such 'backward' chicks.

Feeding and taking care of young chicks

Young chicks need warmth. If the hen does not abandon her task, they will be able to go in between their mother's warm down when it gets too cold for them. It may be a good idea to hang up a heat lamp if it is still very cold. These lamps come with either white or red

Some chicks have difficulty getting out of the egg by themselves.

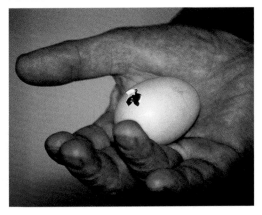

light, and the red ones are to be preferred. Also 'dull emitters' (an enclosed ceramic holder containing a heating element, but not spreading any light) or heating pads are very suitable. As they don't produce any light, the latter two are more natural for chicks. In this way, the animals keep a normal daily routine. When there is light, feed is actually taken in

Chicks can go to their mother for warmth.

Soon after hatching, young chicks no longer need help eating and drinking.

Orpington chick of about six weeks old

around the clock, while a chick or an adult chicken normally rests when it is dark.

Put down special chick crumbs for the chicks, offering this feed in very low bowls or on a plate, so that the animals can easily get at it. However, they often only start eating when they are two or three days old. Before that, they still have enough nutritional reserve from the egg yolk. Preferably offer drinking-water in waterers (little water towers) that are placed on the ground. Whether in saucer or dish form, drinkers should always be so shallow and narrow that the chicks can only drink from it, not step into it. For wet chicks fall ill easily and can even drown in a little water. The mother hen will lead her chicks to the feed, urging them to eat and drink. You can go on giving complete chick feed – preferably mash or pellets, possibly supplemented with some fine chick crumbs – until the animals are six weeks old. At that age, most chicks are more or less entirely feathered, so that you can offer them growers' pellets for bigger chicks. Only when the animals are four to five months old can you give them feed for adult chickens.

If you have a very calm and tolerant breed, a mother hen with chicks starting from the age of one or two weeks can be run with the other birds. However, in many cases it is preferable to house them in a separate space, until the chicks are better able to defend themselves, at about the age of five months. For there is the risk that the established flock will start pecking at the chicks, causing casualties. By putting them elsewhere, you will also prevent your chicks from contracting contagious diseases to which they as yet are not really resistant.

Cock or hen?

For someone without any training with chickens, it is impossible to tell whether day-old chicks are cocks or hens. Only when the animals start growing up does the physical difference become clear. The tails of cocks are often held a little higher, and sometimes cocks are a bit bigger than hens. Moreover, in most breeds the cocks get their feathers somewhat later than their sisters do. As soon as they are about three months old, many cocks already start to crow, while the secondary sexual characteristics stand out more. They get ornamental feathers which the hens lack and often have more pronounced and larger head furnishings. Also the behavior of cockerels is different. Among themselves, they will start determining order of precedence by sham fights. So, it may take a while before you find out how many hens and cocks your mother hen has hatched.

'Autosexing' chicks form an exception here. These are chicks of breeds in which the coloring is sex-related, like in the Bielefelder. Also in partridge-colored chicks one can tell the difference straight away. The males have a dark stripe running from the corner of the eye, while the female chicks often have a self-colored yellow head. However, one should not go by this unquestioningly, for there are known exceptions to this rule.

Older chicks

Normally speaking, the mother will be prepared to watch over her chicks until they are six or seven weeks old. Often she will be laying again when her chicks are that age. So, the best thing for you to do when the chicks are six weeks old is to get the hen accustomed to the breeding flock again, leaving the chicks in their own coop.

When chicks are around three months old, it actually starts to dawn upon the cocks that they are 'different'. In what way is not entirely clear to them, but this awareness is strong enough for them to keep on chasing their sisters all day long. This causes a lot of unrest in the henhouse and interferes with growth, as the animals are wasting their energy. Therefore, the best thing to do is to set the cocks apart from the hens at this point. If the unrest continues within the group of young cocks, called cockerels, because they are constantly getting into fights with one another, then the solution is to place the breeding cock within this group. He will be lord and master right away, and due to his natural authority he will suppress the fighting between the young birds. Keep the pullets separate until they are point-of-lay. Depending on the breed, the pullets will then be between four and five months old. At that age, you may also get your animals to switch from growers' pellets to layers' feed and can possibly run them with the adult hens.

Partridge-colored day-old chicks, hen (left) and cock (right)

In these Anconas, the cock (right) is starting to show secondary sexual characteristics.

Six week old Malay chicks

A band helps you to individually monitor your chicks.

Slide up the band a bit higher when the cocks start developing spurs; this cock is aggravated by his band.

Poultry bands

Chicken breeders usually provide their animals with an identification mark indicating the chicken's descent. These are poultry bands of some synthetic material or aluminum that one fixes on the leg and, alongside of the year of birth, also shows a serial number. Such bands one slides around a chicken's leg when the bird is about eight weeks old, which at that age is easy to do. If the animal is older, the leg will be thicker, so that the band can no longer slide off. This band is only necessary if you want to take your chickens to shows, as birds without an official band are excluded from participation. However, it is also convenient if you, as a breeder, know how old your birds are and which individual you are talking about. In this way, selection as to behavior, laying and age is easier. If you don't intend to exhibit your chickens anyway, you can band them with the colored plastic bands available at pet stores. But first inquire at your poultry club what size band your breed needs, so that you don't use a band that is either too big or too small for your animals. Bands that are too big are a nuisance, because the birds can get caught on branches and the like; bands that are too small can become ingrown in the leg as the animals get bigger. In practice, it is often better to fit your birds with official bands. The non-official bands are in fact usually only available in a limited number of sizes, so that it is likely that you will not be able to find a size to fit your breed. As the animals will be wearing these bands for the rest of their lives, one that fits well is the best choice.

Artificial incubation

There are many breeds in which broodiness and the care for clutch and brood has been eliminated by selection (non-sitters). Well-known examples of this are the various chickens bred as layers, like the Barnevelder or the Leghorn. If you have chickens of such breeds, the chances are very slim that one of your hens will get broody. If you nevertheless want your chickens to have offspring, you will have to get a hen of some other breed to sit on the hatching eggs or otherwise use an incubator. Incubators come in all types and sizes, and are usually not cheap. If you only want to have a few eggs hatched, perhaps a breeder with an incubator can accommodate you. There are also professional hatcheries or hobby firms specializing in hatching eggs for

Incubators

On the 21st day the clutch hatches

fanciers. Your local poultry club will have addresses of these firms. Then you take your eggs there and after three weeks' time you can go and fetch your chicks. Chicks that have been hatched in an incubator need a lot of warmth, as they do not have a mother hen to cuddle up to. That is why such young chicks should be transported in a closed box and must not be exposed to either draft, damp or cold.

Taking care of artificially hatched chicks

Upon arriving home, put your chicks in a separate space above which you hang an infrared lamp or where you have placed a 'dull emitter' or heating pads. The temperature that the animals need during the first week of their life is around 35 degrees centigrade (91 degrees Fahrenheit). After that, you can let the temperature drop by 2 degrees centigrade (3 degrees Fahrenheit) each week by gradually raising the heat lamp a little. It is often hard to find out whether the temperature is all right for the chicks. However, from measuring it with a thermometer, the chicks' behavior is a perfect indication. If the birds are lying in a small circle under the lamp with their heads pointing outwards, the temperature is optimal. If they throng together under the heat source's center with their heads reaching upwards, they are cold and the lamp is too high. And if they are lying in the corners of the coop with their beaks open, it is far too hot. In their initial dwelling, it is sensible to enable the chick to move to an unheated part of the coop. For this purpose, you can put up a partition in the coop with an opening in it. This mimics conditions when they are reared by their mother, when the chicks also have the choice whether or not to snuggle up between her warm down. In this way, the chicks grow up a bit more natural, developing a better resistance.

Until the age of about six weeks, chicks need a heat source. After that, their plumage has usually developed sufficiently, and an ambient temperature of 20 to 25 degrees centigrade (68–77 degrees Fahrenheit) is enough. Do not take away the heat source abruptly, for the animals must be given the opportunity to get used to a lower temperature. By using a time clock, you can at first switch off the lamp in the middle of the day, during the warmest hours, then only have heating during cold nights, finally getting rid of it altogether. Chicks that have just been deprived of their heat source tend to huddle together when they are cold. This might cause some of them to get smothered. That is why breeders let their chicks spend the night on a grid of wire mesh or slats from the age of six weeks onwards. In that case there is a current of fresh air under the chicks, preventing them from 'overheating', or even worse: from suffocation.

This crate has a hole in it so that the chicks can have both a cool place and a warm one.

10 Anatomy and Plumage

Flying

Chicken belong to the class of Birds (*Aves*). Aside from a few exceptions (penguins, ostriches, kiwis), the capacity to fly is one of the features of the animals in this class, though chickens usually get about by walking. The fact that many breeds never or hardly ever fly has much to do with being selected as a placid, tame nature and with the fact that many chickens have become increasingly large and massive in the course of the domestication process. Due to this, the body is now too heavy for the wings to lift. Just think of a plane that is too heavily loaded: the heavier the load, the longer the runway will have to be for the plane to take off. Most chicken breeds only fly when necessary. This phenomenon is also seen in wild jungle fowl, which prefer grubbing about on the ground amongst bushes and undergrowth. Because of predators on the ground, they look for a safe and high roosting place at night. In domestic chickens, this behavior is still present: instinctively, the birds seek a perch high-up in order to roost.

Skeleton

Like most other bird varieties, chickens have a light skeleton, consisting of hollow bones. Fortunately broken bones are very rare in chickens, for these hollow bones rarely heal. A chicken has fourteen neck vertebra that are small and highly flexible. With this it can turn its head a 180 degrees and is also able to move it vertically and horizontally. A chicken's shape is very much determined by its breastbone. Depending on the breed, the muscles are either normally or highly developed there. The build can be correspondingly either broader or more delicate. Also the breastbone's length varies from breed to breed. For example, the typical build of the Old English Game Bantam is the result of a short breastbone.

Skull

The shape of a chicken's skull also depends on the breed. This is why game fowls usually have a short, broad skull with a 'beetling brow', while the skull of country fowl breeds is somewhat longer and narrower in shape. Crested fowls, like the Dutch Bearded Bantam and the

Old-English Game Bantam, silver partridge

Shamo Bantam

Houdan, have a lump of bone on the crown of their skull, called the crest knob. This enlarges the skull's surface area, so that there is more room for feathers, resulting in a crest.

Legs and feet

If you look at a chicken's legs, you see a hinging joint where the feathered thighbone becomes the clean shank or tarsus. This joint is called the 'hock', and you can compare it to your own ankle. The actual knee is much higher up at the top of the thigh bone. If you pick up a chicken and carefully move its leg to and fro and up and down, you can clearly feel this. At the bottom of the shank there are the toes. In most chickens there are four of them, three of which point forward and are well spread, while the fourth toe points backwards. On account of this, you get a surface area that offers good support. Some breeds, like the Dorking, the Houdan and the Faverolles, have a fifth toe as a special feature. This toe is not functional, for it is positioned on the inside of the shank, above the fourth toe, pointing upwards at a slant. However, it does not bother the animals. This feature has arisen, like many other specific standard features, during the domestication process and is the result of a mutation. A chicken's shanks and feet can also be covered in feathers. Maranses are a breed with only few feathers on their feet and with sparsely feathered legs.

Breeds with fully feathered feet and profuse feathering on their legs also tend to have long,

Dutch Booted Bantam

An old cock's spurs

stiff feathers on their heels, especially if their plumage is somewhat hard. This phenomenon is called 'vulture hocks' and is a feature of standard breeds, such as the Dutch Booted Bantam and the Breda Fowl or Kraienkoppe.

Spurs

Somewhat higher up along the shank, mainly in cocks, we find the spurs. These spurs are a male feature and should in fact only occur in roosters, but once every so often they are also seen in hens. The spur is a pointed cone of horn on the inside of the shanks. Cocks use their spurs in fights to determine their order of rank. Usually, a spur is blunt at its tip, so that no deep flesh-wounds can be dealt when fighting. At cockfights in the olden days, spurs were made into lethal weapons by filing them until they were sharp, or by attaching sharp metal blades to them. Throughout a cock's life, its spurs keep on growing and may get so long that they can become a nuisance to older cocks when walking and mating. If a spur grows too long, it is the best thing for the animal's well-being to shorten it yourself or get this done. This does not hurt, as spurs consist of dead tissue, with only a small live core at their juncture with the shanks. Clipping spurs can therefore be compared to clipping nails. If you don't like to do this yourself, then go to an experienced chicken fancier, who will usually be prepared to show you how to go about it.

The color of the skin and the legs

The flesh-clad skeleton is enveloped in skin and the color of this skin may vary per breed. Thus, we have white-skinned breeds like the North Holland Blue and the Faverolles, and yellow-skinned ones like the Cochin. There are also dark-skinned breeds, in which the skin's pigmentation ranges from very dark to almost black. Examples of this are the Ardenner and the Silkie. Breeds that originally were bred as table birds are almost all white-skinned, because in the consumer's opinion this looks tastier. Yellow-skinned breeds have a yellow pigment in their epidermis, by which we also recognise in the yellow or green color of the legs. Green legs are the optical outcome of a combination of yellow and blue. The dermis of these breeds contains a blue color and the epidermis a yellow one. Examples of breeds with green legs are the Modern

Ardenner Bantam, silver necked

English Game Fowl, the Araucana and the Sumatra.

Head furnishings

Chickens are characterized by all sorts of protuberances on their heads that are called head furnishings. Thus, under the beak we see the wattles, which may be either short or long, depending on the breed. At the side of the head there are the ear-lobes (formerly called 'deaf

Silkie

ears'), protecting the auditory duct. These ear-lobes can be red, bluish or white, and again their size depends on the breed. Game fowl have small red ear-lobes, while both the Minorca and the Java Bantam have very large white ones. Under the beak, between the wattles, we find in some breeds a fold of skin called the 'dewlap', for instance in the Brahma and the Shamo. The skin around a chicken's eyes is naked. In a chicken that is in good condition its skin is well saturated with blood. If an animal's head is pale, this indicates bad blood circulation in the skin of the head, which is a sign of reduced resistance.

Types of comb

On top of the head, there is the comb. The comb can have various shapes, the most common ones being:

• The single comb, as for instance found in the Brakel and the Leghorn. This comb stands in an upright position on the head and has a number of serrations. In this way, the comb's points arise. These are called 'spikes' in some English-speaking countries. Depending on the breed, particularly in laying hens with a single comb that is a bit bigger, the back part of the comb tends to become droopy or lopped;

- The rose comb, a comb type found in the Wyandotte, among others. This is a low and broad comb without points. Towards the

Frisian Bantam cock with a single comb

back, the comb tapers off into what is known as a 'spike', which is also call 'leader' in certain countries. Depending on the breed, this spike may either follow the neck line or point straight backwards;

- The V-shaped or horn comb is found in a number of crested fowl breeds or breeds akin to these. Here, the comb consists of two either vertical or backwards slanting little horns. A breed known for this comb shape is the French La Flèche, also referred to as the 'devil-headed chicken';

- The walnut comb gets its name from the fact that it resembles half a walnut. It has no leader. The comb is placed on the front of the head.

Rheinlander cock with a rose comb

Twenthe fowl

- The pea comb or three-ridged comb is found in a number of game fowl breeds and in the Brahma. In its pure form, this comb consists of a single base with three low lengthwise ridges and pea-like points. The middle ridge is a bit higher than the ones on the outside. This comb type is related to the single comb;

- The buttercup comb, leaf comb or cup comb is akin to both the single and the V-shaped comb and is formed by two single combs. In the buttercup comb these have grown together at the front as well as the back. If the combs are only fused in front, it is called a leaf comb. The buttercup comb is for instance found in the Sicilian Buttercup; the leaf comb we see in the French Houdan.

- The cross comb is a variant, seen in a number of Spanish breeds, of the single comb. At the back of the comb, on the comb's blade, there are two fleshy bits that are at right angles to the blade. If you look at this from behind, then, together with the comb's blade, these two protuberances form a cross.

The feathers

'Clothes do not make the man' as the saying goes, but feathers certainly do make the chicken. Not only a chicken's color, but also its shape is to a great extent determined by its feathers. Thus, breeds with feathered legs look different from those with naked ones. Not all breeds have the same amount of feathering. There is a big difference between a Sultan with crest, beard and leg as well as foot plumage, and the Naked Neck, which has no feathers on its neck at all. Depending on the part of the body where they are found and on the chicken's sex, feathers have different shapes. Thus, the primaries or flight feathers ('flights') are elongated, broad in shape and their structure is stiff, on account of their lifting capacity when flying. On the other hand, down feathers are short, broad and loosely structured, as their purpose is to insulate the body. The amount of down feathers very much depends on the breed. The feathers of game fowl have

Cornish Bantam with a game fowl's typical tight feathering

very little fluff, and in specialist terminology this is called 'hard-feathered' or 'tight-feathered'. Cochins and Wyandottes have a lot of down, which makes them look as if their plumage is very profuse and as if they are heavier than is actually the case. Tail feathers have a firm structure, and can be either short or long, depending on the breed. Thus Orpingtons have short and rather soft flights and main tail feathers, while the tail feathers of a Leghorn are long and hard. The feathers on the breast, back and wing shoulder are fairly short, broad and well rounded. They cover one another like roof tiles do, so that the down remains dry when it rains. Hackles or neck feathers have a soft texture and are long and narrow in shape.

FEATHER STRUCTURE

Due to their typical structure, feathers are closely knitted normally speaking. A feather consists of an axis or shaft with what are called 'vanes' on both sides. These feather vanes branch out twice into what are called barbs and barbules, which have outgrowths with tiny

Orpingtons have many down feathers.

Silkie Bantam

chickens are a well-known variant. In the feathers of these breeds, the barbicels have a different shape and do not interlock to form a web. Therefore the feather vanes are not smooth and united, but rather resemble hairs. These feathers we find in the Silkie and the silk-feathered Japanese Bantam. The outcome of another mutation is that the feather's shaft is no longer straight but twisted, so that the feathers curl back and upwards. This mutation we see in frizzle-feathered Crested Fowl and frizzle-feathered Japanese.

ORNAMENTAL FEATHERS IN THE COCK
Apart from the feathers mentioned, male birds also have ornamental feathers or sex feathers. They are found in the neck, the wing shoulders, the tail and on the back and the saddle. The ornamental feathers in the neck and on the saddle have a softer texture and a narrow, elongated shape, and are very shiny. A cock's feathers on shoulders and back are somewhat triangular. In the middle of the wing, separating wing shoulder and bow from the flights, there are two rows of short, broad and well-rounded feathers forming a bar called the 'wing bar'. On each side of the cock's tail, we find the main and lesser sickles, which are fairly broad and long. They protrude well beyond the tail feathers, and are usually nicely

Ancona cock, blue white mottled

hooks (barbicels). These hooks cling together, so that the vanes constitute a 'web'.
By mutation, various plumage varieties have come about in chickens. The silk-feathered

Dutch Bearded Bantam, hen

Dutch Bearded Bantam, cock

curved. Apart from main sickles, a cock has a number of lesser, short and narrow sickles covering the tail feathers. The Malay cock has very few of them, and these are very narrow and short, while the Yokohama has many extremely long ones.

Crests, beards and muffs

Erect feathers on a chicken's head are called a crest, tuft or topknot. In a cock, crest feathers have the same shape as hackles, i.e. long and narrow. In a hen, these feathers are a little shorter and broader. The shape of a cock's crest is narrower and inclines more backwards than a hen's does. Dutch Crested Fowls have big, full topknots growing from a knob on the skull, while the Sulmtaler has a tiny and rather narrow tuft called a 'tassel' and lacks the skull knob. Chickens can also have 'beards' – a group of feathers growing under the beak. Bearded breeds have no wattles or else these are very small. Some also have side-whiskers called 'muffs' or 'muffles'.

11 Colors and Marking Patterns

Different colors and markings

There is an enormous variety in the colors and markings of chickens. Some colors and marking patterns are connected with a single breed, others are found in many. In order to familiarize you somewhat with this vast range of colors, marking patterns and their variants, we have segmented them into groups. This classification is not complete, for there are countless varieties possible, but the best known and most common ones are dealt with here. In the breed descriptions, you will find possible breed-related particulars in regards to colors and color patterns (as marking patterns are also called). The classification of the color groups is based on what you see when looking at the chickens.

PARTRIDGE, PARTRIDGE MOTTLED AND WHEATEN

The markings and basic color of the partridge category and its variants most closely resemble those of the wild Red Jungle Fowl. To many, the partridge variety is the color in which they first and foremost picture a rooster, and such a cock's coloring is very striking and handsome indeed. Its breast and tail are pitch black with a green sheen. The hackles and saddle are orange-red, with a grayish black lengthwise marking along the feather's shaft. Its wing bows and back are a rich brilliant red. Across the middle of the wing runs a glossy greenish black bar.

The edge of the wing that is carried well tucked against the body, is of a warm brown. This color continues to where the wing bar starts. The coloring and markings of the partridge-colored hen are less spectacular. She is more of a bay color, with a deeply salmon-pink breast. Her back, shoulders and saddle are a brownish gray. The bay feather is finely sprinkled with little grayish black dots ('peppering'). The black in the partridge variety may also be either blue, pearl-gray (also called 'lavender'), white or cuckoo-colored. The brown feather parts can be bred in white, yellow or reddish brown as well. In this way all sorts of color combinations arise, like for instance blue partridge, silver partridge, yellow partridge and cuckoo partridge. It is also possible to breed a mottling factor into the partridge color. By doing so one gets small white specks on the feathers, which is called 'partridge mottled'. If, by selective breeding, the black markings on the neck and saddle are gotten rid of in both sexes, and also the peppering in the hen has been eliminated through selection, the result is a color pattern called 'wheaten'. Color variants may be bred in this wheaten too, by substituting the black by either blue, lavender, white or cuckoo. Apart from the standard partridge color and partridge mottled, there is yet another variety: laced partridge or Asiatic partridge, in which the partridge color's peppering is no longer spread across the entire feather but forms a little strip running along the feather's edge. This color we see in

Twente Fowl hens, partridge

Wyandotte hens, partridge, multiple penciled

the Brahmas, the Wyandottes and the Cochins, among others.

THE QUAIL COLOR
The quail color is typical of Belgian breeds. Genetically, it is related to the partridge color. The quail-colored cock is a golden auburn or maroon, with almost black hackles and a black tail. The saddle feathers are of a velvety black, with a golden brown lacing along the edge. The wing shoulders and wings are a golden brown, with a warmer shade on the shoulders. When the animal spreads its wings, the black markings on their primaries become visible. The breast of the quail-colored hen has a warm golden brown color. The feathers on back and wing shoulders are of a velvety black and have a tiny golden brown edging. The shaft of these feathers is also golden brown, while the feather tips are velvet black again. The neck feathers in quail-colored hens are marked in a similar way. As in the partridge color, the black markings may have different variants, for instance black, blue, white or lavender. The golden brown can be substituted by either white or lemon yellow. In this way, new colors arise, such as blue quail, silver quail, white quail, lavender silver quail and white lemon quail. The quail markings are very popular in the Antwerp Belgian, but also breeds like the Belgian Bearded d'Uccle Bantam, the Bassette and the Brabançonne are bred in this color.

Bassette hen, quail

Brabançonne or Brabant Farmyard Fowl, silver quail

Sulmtaler hen, wheaten

ers with a tiny black lacing) and silver blue laced (white feathers with a tiny blue lacing).

COLUMBIAN, BELTED AND BLACK TAILED WHITE

Formerly, the columbian marking was also called 'ermine', due to the fact that it reminded one somewhat of the ermine skins in the 'royal robe'. The basic color is white with a black marking at the body's extremities. Thus the tail feathers are black and the hackles white with black lacing. When there is more black in the hackles, so that they almost become pure black, we get what is known as a 'belted' marking, which we see in the Dutch-German breed called Lakenvelder. If breeders do not select with a view to increasing the black in the hackles, one gets animals with an entirely white neck and black tail feathers. These birds are then called 'black tailed white', a coloring we for instance find in Japanese Bantams. In the columbian as well as in the belted marking and in the black tailed white, the primaries are

LACING

A number of breeds, like Sebright Bantams, Barnevelders and Wyandottes are frequently bred with a pattern of markings called laced or double laced. A golden black laced hen has golden brown feathers, with a bit of black lacing running neatly along the feather's edge. The cock's breast and wing bars also show this marking. His ornamental feathers in the wing shoulder are of a golden brown color. The hackles and saddle are black with a golden brown lacing. If there is not only lacing around the feather's edge, but also a second lacing within the feather, then this is called double laced. This color is not only found in the Barnevelder, but also in the Cornish or Indian Game Fowl. Also in this color group, the golden brown and the black come in countless varieties. There are also silver black laced (silvery white feathers with a tiny black lacing), golden blue laced (golden brown feathers with a tiny bluish gray lacing), yellow white laced (yellowish brown feathers with a small white lacing), lemon black laced (light yellow feath-

marked black and white ('black white'). However, this is only visible when the animals spread their wings; closed wings simply appear to be white. As is the case with other color patterns, columbian, black tailed white and belted can be found in various colors.

The parts that are normally white can also be of a golden yellow hue, i.e. buff columbian, or golden belted. The black marking can be substituted by blue. By combining various traits, colors can arise like columbian with blue markings, buff columbian with blue markings, blue tailed yellow and blue belted.

BIRCHEN AND SILVER NECKED

Akin to the columbian marking is a variant that can be best described as 'reversed columbian'. The parts that are white in columbian are black in this color variety. However, the tail and neck have no white markings; the tail's color is similar to the ground color, in this case black. The marking is only found in the neck, where the black feathers are laced with a small white edging. The shoulders and saddle of the cock are a silvery white. This color variety, called 'silver necked', is found in the Ardenner for instance. A variant of silver necked has black breast feathers laced with silvery white. This color pattern is called 'birchen', and is found in the Modern English Game Bantams. If the silvery

Silver necked rumpless Ardenner hen

white is replaced by a golden yellow, one gets colors like golden birchen and golden necked. Black substituted by bluish gray produces blue golden necked or blue birchen. In the Marans we find a variant of the golden necked color, in which the gold is of a deeper shade and has rather a brassy hue called 'brassy black'.

PORCELAIN, SPANGLED AND HALF-MOON SPANGLED

The color porcelain is highly popular in a number of breeds, like the Sussex, Orloff, Dutch Booted Bantam and Antwerp Belgian. The basic feature of porcelain is that the feathers are three-colored. The feather's ground color is a brownish yellow or bay. At the tip of the feather, there is a rather large, rounded black spot, known as a 'spangle'. Within this black

Dutch Booted Bantam, porcelain

Brabanter hen, silver black half-moon spangled

a golden white spangled or yellow white spangled marking pattern.

PENCILED

Penciled markings are found in a whole series of old country fowl breeds, and they take their name from the markings in the hen. A striking feature is the presence of a number of little black spots on the feathers of breast, back and wing shoulders. Between two and five pairs are always found on either side of the feather's shaft. This is what we call 'penciling'. Still, it always depends on how you look at things: what is referred to in the American standard of perfection as 'multiple penciled' – usually called 'penciled' – is sometimes known in the United Kingdom as 'triple laced'. Not only the number, but also the shape of these pencilings may vary by breed. Thus Frisians have tiny spots that are detached from one another, shaped like grains of wheat. In the Groninger Meeuwen, there are two or three pairs of pencilings of a rather squarish shape. In the Brakel, the pencilings are linked with one another across the feather's shaft, forming small crosswise bars.

spangle, we find a small round speck at the feather's tip, which some people call the 'pearl'. In the main tail feathers and primaries, this marking seems different, but this is due to the feathers being a lot longer there. In porcelain, it is possible to replace both the bay ground color and the black marking by other colors. If the parts that are normally black have become blue, this is called 'blue porcelain', a color pattern found in the Dutch Booted Bantam. If the basic color is white, the animal is called 'silver porcelain'. The feathers of spangled birds are similar to those of porcelain ones, only the white pearl is lacking. Golden black spangled is a color variety that one frequently sees in a Holland Fowl. A variant of spangled is half-moon spangled. Here, the spangles are not of a neat round shape, but more crescentic. The color pattern golden black half-moon spangled is found in the Brabanter, among others. Of course, there are also variants possible as regards this marking. Silver black spangled was, for instance, bred by replacing the basic bay color by white. If the black spangle in golden black spangled is replaced by a white one, then we get either

Holland Fowl hen, lemon penciled

Cocks have virtually no penciling. As a rule, they have only the basic feather color. The cock's tail is black, with or without lacing on the main sickles. If the basic color or ground color is a golden brown and the penciling is black, then this is called golden penciled. If it is silvery white, this is called silver penciled. The penciling's color can also be something else than black, for instance blue or white. Thus, colors arise like golden blue penciling and yellow white penciling. The latter is mainly a question of an optical effect. A golden brown ground color combined with black markings seems to be darker than the same ground color with white markings. That is why the color is called 'yellow white penciled' instead of 'golden white penciled'.

CUCKOO, STRIPING AND BARRING
One calls a color pattern 'cuckoo' or 'creole' if black has receded into crosswise stripes, so that dark gray and light gray stripes alternate on the same feather. These stripes are not clearly defined, and they run crosswise over the width of the feather. In the North Holland

Barred Wyandotte bantams, hen and cock

112

Cochin hen, buff

Belgian Bearded de Watermaal Bantam, laceless, blue

Fowl the dark gray is lighter than in other breeds, so that when seen at a distance one gets the idea of a bluish gray color. This breed therefore also used to be called the North Holland Blue. As a result of selecting for more contrast between the dark and the light stripes,

Splashed

the striping is now narrower and more sharply defined in some breeds. It has in fact become a barred marking. This marking can even be seen on the fluff at the feather's base. A breed known for its barred markings is the Amrock.

SELF-COLORED OR SELF
Colors that have no markings, or hardly any, fall into this category; they have often been referred to as basic colors in the above. Self colors are colors like black, white, lavender gray, buff and blue. In chickens, blue is a grayish blue that is a 'dilution' of black. This is bred both with and without a dark edging along the feather, called lacing. The blue color is passed down intermediately, meaning that when blue is bred to blue, about half of the chicks will have their parents' color, while the other half has color defects. Those with defective coloring are black, or otherwise white with small, irregular dark blotches. This white variant is called 'splashed'. If a splashed individual is mated with a black one, all of the chicks are blue. Lavender gray, like blue, is a dilution of black and is a very light and delicate color. Buff bears no relation to either black or white. Here, it is a question of a yellowish brown in which originally some black markings were found on the

tail and the wings. Through a focused selection, the black has been almost entirely eliminated and the animal looks a self-colored light yellowy brown. Genetically regarded, buff is therefore not a self color, but rather a variant of the columbian factor. This color is very popular in Orpingtons, among others.

Color and chicks

There is a lot of difference between the color and markings a chick shows in its first and second feathering and an adult chicken's eventual set of feathers. Thus, chicks of very many color varieties have white in their feathering, which often disappears entirely after the second molt. When they are chicks, buff-colored animals for instance have a great deal of white in their primaries, while in the adult birds this has disappeared entirely. Also the degree of pigmentation is of influence on a chick's color and its first plumage. Thus, chicks of dusky-legged black chickens are usually pure black in color too. Chicks of black chickens with yellow legs on the other hand are black with white spots, and have lots of white feathers in their first feathering.

Lakenvelder chick, three weeks old

Upon reaching adulthood, these usually disappear entirely.

Color and sex

Another factor influencing the juvenile plumage of chicks is their sex. Very young cocks look rather like hens. This is because, when they are young, they do not have their ornamental feathers yet. These ornamental feathers only appear after the second molt, changing a cockerel into a clearly masculine specimen. In their juvenile apparel, cockerels of most marked color patterns have markings like hens. Thus young partridge-colored cocks have the same markings on their wing shoulders as the hens do, to wit 'peppered' feathers, while on their breast the coloring is rather mottled. Only upon reaching adulthood do the carmine red wing shoulders appear and does the breast become pure black. The cocks keep this color and marking throughout their life, although the plumage tends to get less abundant as they grow older. Thus the sickles of the partridge-colored Holland Bantam cock return more briefly after molting at the age of one. Also the cock does not get as many lesser sickles, so that its tail becomes more sparsely feathered.

Color and age

In many animal species, one can tell by the color whether a creature is fairly young or getting on, though this is less obvious in chickens. However, certain color groups are definitely influenced by a chicken's age. This is seen in all of the color patterns that have a mottling factor, like porcelain and black white mottled. The first set of feathers in young birds of these colors usually contains very few tiny white specks, and sometimes none at all. After juvenile molting, these young animals have a few more small white spots, though usually not all that many yet. Each year, after the annual molt in the fall, the white spots become a bit bigger and also more numerous. Due to this, the animals seem to

get whiter after every molting. Other colors that change when birds grow older are buff and blue. However, the change here is not a permanent one, for it is caused by wear and tear and the influences of the weather, so that after the annual molt these colors regain their original shades again. Due to the influence of the sun, the animals' delicate pigmentation tends to fade, which one can clearly see, as the color is no longer even. The feathers that are formed later on are richer in color than the older ones. If the animals have been out in the rain and then go into the sun after that, discoloration takes place even faster. Drops of water on the feathers in fact have the effect of a burning glass. They refract the sunlight, forming a color spectrum, so that a wet feather rapidly discolors. Adapted housing can slow down this temporary fading. The colors buff and blue will not fade as soon if you keep your chickens in the shade instead of in the blazing sunlight or rain.

Ancona hen, black white mottled

Dutch Crested Fowl, buff; this color variety is still being developed.

12 Exhibitions

Exhibitions and clubs

Many chicken buffs get enjoyment out of keeping chickens by simply taking care of them every day. Other poultry lovers, however, mainly find pleasure in breeding beautiful chickens regarding build, color and markings or the laying of neatly shaped and colored eggs meeting a well-defined breed's standard. These chicken fanciers have formed small livestock societies or breed clubs. The aim is to have regular contact with other chicken fanciers and to organize shows. At these shows, one can be awarded prizes, but this is not the most important thing. The prizes are usually modest, thereby guaranteeing a convivially competitive atmosphere among the group of fanciers. The real aim of such shows is to exhibit to an interested public the various handsome, charming breeds, colors and egg shapes, and to compare these birds and eggs with one another.

Dutch Bantam cock, white

Judges

Comparing the animals is the principal thing at shows. In order to acquire an impression of a chicken's standard-breed qualities that is as objective as possible, judges are appointed. They go through long and thorough training, in view of which examinations are held every year. Upon successfully concluding a round of exams, the judge is qualified to judge a breed. During this evaluation, a chicken is compared with the breed's recorded standards of perfection and well-defined color standard. The judge's final opinion is written down on a score card, concluding with a predicate. This is a gradation of value or scale of points. With small differences, this system is used in most countries. The greatest difference is found in the way the judges acquire their authority. In countries like the Netherlands, Germany and Belgium, training courses, practice sessions and exams are held. In other countries, any breeder with a lot of experience can be appointed judge without having to do an exam.

Judging

For chicken breeders, judging is often the highlight of the season. After putting togeth-

The much coveted cup is what every breeder works towards.

birds, being six or seven months at the time, are only just full-grown, while yearlings have recently acquired their new plumage in October or November.

Local, national and international shows

From the beginning of October to the beginning of February, almost every local club has its show. Alongside various chickens, one can usually also admire rabbits, guinea pigs, small rodents and pigeons at these shows. Furthermore, there are a few special organizations arranging the major national shows and international exhibitions or world poultry fairs. At these shows, one can often admire thousands of animals. If you want to get an impression of what there is to be seen in the field of chickens, you should in fact go to the larger exhibitions. Here, often the breed clubs also have information about their breed. Moreover, usually there are suppliers of feed, incubators, reading material and things like feeders and drinkers present at the show.

er a breeding flock and carefully rearing chicks, there is the tension of whether the bred animals are indeed up to the breed's standard of perfection. This is also the opportunity to compare one's 'home-bred' animals with the results of fellow breeders. This collective competition, the judge's commentary and the final predicate have seen to it that most old chicken breeds are still of good quality. For the breeders, these exhibitions are the highlight of the year. The period during which such chicken shows are held has been keyed to the time that the chickens are at their best: in the fall and winter. For then the young

Also decorating eggs is a hobby in itself.

Belgian Bearded de Watermaal Bantam hen, cuckoo

Grooming

When chickens are put on show, it is in fact a beauty contest. For the breeders, it is essential to groom their chickens as well as possible for the judging. This cannot be managed by merely giving attention to the birds a couple of days before the show. One must work throughout the year towards the show season. By good care and housing, the breeder sees to it that the feathers are in perfect condition and undamaged. If the set of feathers is not entirely clean, then this is meticulously washed a few days before exhibiting. With a bit of extra nourishment, one manages to get the combs nice and red and, for instance, the legs of the Wyandotte bantam bright yellow.

Breeders also take into account when an animal is to be born in order to be able to successfully participate in a particular show. Thus a Leghorn hen will have to have her lopped or droopy comb. This is regarded as a standard feature. However, pullets that are not in lay still have a comb that is too small and erect. The breeder will therefore plan the brooding period in such a way that all of his animals have just started laying when the important shows are due.

Exhibiting the eggs

Until a couple of years ago, everything at the shows described here was focused on a breed's standard qualities. Due to present-day urban housing, it is however no longer possible for many people to keep a rooster with their hens. So, due to this, breeding and exhibiting chickens is out of the question for this category of fanciers. To nevertheless draw

Judging the eggs

these people into the poultry fancy, some countries organize 'egg judgings'. In that case, not the animals, but the eggs are entered for judgment at shows. Upon scrutinizing your own chickens and their eggs, you will see that the daily eggs quite clearly tend to vary. This difference is not merely limited to the color, but is also evident in the shape. Also for eggs, standards have been developed. These lay down what – in an egg of a certain breed – the shape, color and shell's texture should be like. By perfect nutrition and selection within a group of chickens, the exhibitors try to come up with hens laying the most handsome eggs. The exhibits consist of a few eggs, threesomes or half-a-dozens. In the first group, basically what is at stake is the perfect egg. In the second and third group, apart from the perfect egg, it is also a question of the uniformity of the different eggs. This new type of hobby is suited to fanciers who are able to keep hens but not cocks.

Judging the eggs

A meeting point where all your questions are answered

In general, it is true that at these shows the mutual contacts between breeders form a source of knowledge and experience. Most breeders are prepared to exchange their experience in keeping, housing, breeding and taking care of chickens. If you really want to know more about chickens, it is a good idea to join a club and visit a couple of exhibitions.

Besides well-known breeds, rare ones are also to be seen at world poultry fairs.

Part two:
The Large Breeds

Buff Orpington hen

13 Layer Breeds

Old and new breeds

The notion of 'good layers' should not be taken too strictly with some poultry breeds. A breed known as an excellent layer in the nineteenth century, at that time tended to lay far less eggs than a modern egg hybrid nowadays. Modern egg hybrids have been specifically selected to 'lay themselves silly', on as little feed and with as little living space possible. In practice, this boils down to an egg practically every day during the initial laying period. After this period, their egg production declines, and in commercial farming these chickens are then sold to a wholesale buyer. As the word 'hybrids' indicates, modern layers are not of any specific breed, being the 'end product' of various highly inbred strains merged into a cross. The standard-bred chickens discussed in this book fail to meet the production requirements that large-scale factory farming makes upon egg hybrids. On the other hand, they are no doubt far more attractive to look at. That they lay less eggs is something no one

Rhode Island cock

is going to worry about: for most people, the main objective in keeping chickens is to create a 'homey atmosphere' and not to get as many eggs as possible.

In the group of layers, there are old breeds developed as early as the eighteenth and nineteenth century, and younger breeds created during the last century. The latter group as a rule tends to lay more and also larger eggs than the former one.

A study of a Brakel hen's head, golden

Leghorns, American type

Qualities

Often layers are the somewhat lighter breeds of the country fowl type. Given a chance, they will diligently scratch and dig. Because they are light and not within the larger breed category, they are usually good flyers. So, in constructing a run or raising a fence, you will have to keep this aspect in mind. If you provide artificial lighting in the roost, thereby lengthening the day to ten or twelve hours during fall and winter, you may look forward to a considerable number of eggs in wintertime. As to their nature, these breeds are usually shyer and in the main tend to keep a bit more aloof from their minders than most other purebreds. This means it will take more of an effort to tame your chickens, though usually this is no problem if you approach them in a relaxed way.

As broodiness is not really appreciated in layer breeds, the urge to get broody has been eliminated by selection. The result is that most of these breeds seldom or never get broody ('non-sitters'). If you want to raise a standard layer breed, you will have to take this fact into account. It can be simply solved by placing the eggs under a 'borrowed' broody or getting them hatched in an incubator. If it is important to you that your birds lay a lot of eggs, you must select them as to this feature, certainly if you intend to replace some of your older egg-layers by young ones every year. There are a number of qualities by which you can easily tell whether a chicken is a good layer or not: chickens with yellow legs use the pigment present in their body to color the yolks yellow. At the end of the laying season, a good layer has almost white legs, while a bad layer's legs are a faded yellow. An example of a yellow-legged breed is the Leghorn. As to chickens laying dark brown eggs, for instance the Welsummer and the Barnevelder, it is true that the amount of pigment produced by the body is insufficient to make the eggs a dark brown color. A hen that lays well soon starts producing eggs of a lighter brown, while a bad layer goes on laying dark brown eggs for a very long time. Furthermore, you also have to keep an eye on the feathers. Notably, hens spending a lot of time in their nest boxes tend to subject their tail feathers to wear by 'tossing and turning' on their nests. A chicken which is still

Leghorn, partridge

Black white mottled Ancona rooster with rose comb

very nicely feathered at the end of the season is not a good layer.

Standard breed descriptions

Ancona

COUNTY OF ORIGIN
Italy

ORIGIN
The breed has been named after the Italian town of Ancona. From this town, the British took these black-and-white country fowl with their strikingly yellow legs back home halfway through the nineteenth century. From Britain, this layer breed was exported to other countries, including the United States.

APPEARANCE
The Ancona's type bears a marked resemblance to that of the Leghorn. The Ancona is clearly of a country fowl type, with a somewhat elongated build giving a slender impression. Its back is long and smoothly in line with a tail carried medium high. The tail itself is made up of long and broad main tail feathers that are well spread. The cock's tail has rich ornamental feathering. The shanks are of a normal length and yellow in color, preferably with some dark mottling. The head has enamel white ear-lobes and reddish bay eyes. Most Anconas have a fairly large single comb, which in laying hens tends to lop at the back. There is also a rose comb variety, which is less common.

Blue white mottled Ancona rooster, single-combed

COLORS AND MARKING PATTERNS
This breed's original color is black white mottled. Later on a 'diluted' variant, blue white mottled, was added. The latter is not recognized in all countries.

QUALITIES
Anconas are active animals that are busy all day long. If they are well taken care of and get good treatment the birds do tend to become trusting, though they can never really be 'trained to the hand'. As representatives of the group of country fowl, Anconas are excellent

Black white mottled Ancona cock, single-combed

Blue white mottled Ancona hen, single-combed

125

Blue white mottled Ancona chick

Blue white mottled Ancona chick

Black white mottled Ancona hen with a rose comb

flyers, so if you let them wander about freely you will have to put up a high fence. The hens lay quite a number of white-shelled eggs annually. Their black and white mottling tends to change: after every molt, the white spots become bigger. So, a young Ancona is mainly black with tiny white tips on its feathers. Animals of a few years old are much whiter.

PARTICULARS

The qualified comb shapes in this breed, the single comb and the rose comb, are quite frequently interbred. In such crosses the rose comb is dominant. It is impossible to tell from the appearance of a rose-combed Ancona

whether it will breed true as regards its comb or not. So if you mate up an individual, it is very well possible that single-combed chicks will be the outcome.

Araucana

COUNTRY OF ORIGIN
South America

ORIGIN
The name of the Araucana breed was taken from the Chilean Arauca Indians, who we know kept this breed, or its predecessors, for

Black white mottled Ancona cock with rose comb

Black white mottled Ancona hen, rose-combed

many centuries. Araucanas, as well as their various sub-breeds that arose in the course of time in Chile and neighboring countries, were a rarity for a long time. Taking into account an Araucana's appearance, one wonders whether this breed might not have different forbears than most other chickens. Practically nothing has been recorded in writing about the Araucana's origin and ancestors, so its history is obscure. Only after the sixties of the last century did the breed become popular among poultry breeders and fanciers.

APPEARANCE

The Araucana, as we know it in Europe, is a rare thing. In most countries, the breed, both with and without a tail, can be seen at exhibitions, but in the Netherlands only the rumpless variety is accepted. One can tell from the animals carriage that they are akin to the game fowl. This is seen not only in their comparatively upright attitude but also in their fairly short, well-rounded and broad skull. The birds have a certain feature that makes the breed special: on either side of their head, where normally the ear-lobes are found, there are wartlike skin folds or plicae

Rumpless Araucana hen

with feathers growing on them, resulting in two bunches of feathers called 'ear-tufts'. Ideally, these ear-tufts slant backwards.

Araucanas have a pea comb of irregular shape, often a bit twisted. The color of the shank is green. In England a different Araucana is bred, which is best described as a large

Araucana hen with tail

version of the Belgian Bearded deWatermaal Bantam. This variant has neither a tail (rumpless) nor ear-tufts, but it does sport a full beard.

COLORS AND MARKING PATTERNS

In Scandinavia this breed is only recognized in three colors: black, self blue and a kind of 'fawn'. Other countries are more lenient in admitting colors. Germany, where this breed has a large following, is the country with most colors. Colors in which the Araucana is bred include partridge, silver partridge, blue partridge, yellow partridge, fawn, wheaten, white, black, golden necked, silver necked black and cuckoo. However, in judging the physical features of this breed, one does not worry very much about colors and markings. It is already a great feat if one succeeds in capturing the type and the spirit of this breed's appearance.

QUALITIES

It is perfectly possible to either keep these birds in a run or let them roam about. Their character is fairly placid and they are one of the most vigorous and hardy breeds. Arau-

Araucana cock with tail

Araucana eggs are greenish blue, the shade of which may vary.

canas are famed for laying eggs in different remarkable colors, ranging from blue to green in various shades. Also, certain strains have been reported to lay eggs of a pinkish hue. This remarkable quality has resulted in the bird being nicknamed 'Easter Egg Layer' in the United States and Great Britain. That the chickens lay blue to olive-green eggs is a trait which, according to some researchers, is connected with a lower cholesterol level. Moreover, the factor ruling the laying of 'diversely colored' eggs is dominant when handing down the genes. In crosses, use is made of this. However, a cross between an Araucana and a breed laying brown eggs has a different outcome than a cross with a layer of white eggs. In the first case the offspring will lay green eggs, in the second the eggs are blue. As this feature is hereditary, a number of hybrid breeds have been bred by way of the Araucana. The eggs of these hybrids are offered by a few supermarket chains as specialties; not only because of their color, but also because they are lower in cholesterol and therefore healthier. Recent research has shown, however, that eggs in any case do not send up one's cholesterol level.

PARTICULARS
- The peculiarities of this breed are the color of their eggs, their ear-tufts and the fact that they also come in a rumpless variety, i.e. without a tail. Due to the various ways in which these qualities are passed on, it is not easy to breed an Araucana having all of these features. Some books maintain that

the hereditary material carrying the ear-tufts gene is lethal, but this is nonsense. Still, the problem with this factor is that it is not passed on consistently, so that we find animals with a single tuft, with both a big and a small tuft, or with the one tuft pointing forwards and the other backwards. Apart from ear-tufts, most birds have a small beard. Alongside of 'ideal' birds, raising Araucanas without tails also tends to result in animals with the mentioned anomalous ear-tufts and in those that indeed have tails.

Ardenner

COUNTRY OF ORIGIN
Belgium

ORIGIN
Historically regarded, the Ardenner is the oldest Belgian breed, originating in the Belgian Ar-

Araucana cock

dennes and the neighboring region in France. It is not known how it came to be there and what fowls were the ancestors of this vigorous and rare creature. As a hardy country fowl, the Ardenner has always had a certain renown in Belgium, yet after the First World War it was unable to keep going as a commercial breed. There are Ardenner fanciers in various European countries, but their number is small.

APPEARANCE

The breed belongs to the country fowl, being slender and graceful in type. Its head has a single comb, while the color of the ear-lobes and the face ranges from dark red to purple. The wattles also have this typical purple color. The body is elongated, with wings carried well-tucked. The eyes are very dark brown with almost black rims. The tail is well developed and is carried semi-spread. Next to the Ardenner with a tail, there is also one without ('rumpless'). The two varieties are sometimes referred to as 'Wallikiki', being a corruption of the Flemish 'Walen Kieken' ('Walloon chicken'), to wit a chicken from the Walloon part of Belgium. The color of the Ardenner's shanks ranges from very dusky to rather blackish.

COLORS AND MARKING PATTERNS

Ardenners are found in the colors partridge, silver partridge, white, black, golden necked black, silver necked black and golden salmon and silver salmon. Most frequently seen are the colors golden and silver necked, which come both with and without breast markings, due to which they are also entered in shows as golden and silver birchen.

QUALITIES

Ardenners are extremely active and lively animals that should certainly run free. They do not have the right 'mentality' to be locked up. They are excellent flyers and if you offer them total liberty, they will prefer to look for some high spot in a tree to roost in. They are vigorous and tough, and are to a certain extent able to 'scrape a living' for themselves. Ardenners are quite rare and have an unusual appearance, among other things due to their dark pigmentation. All in all, this is a suitable breed for

Rumpless Ardenner hen

people who are looking for something special and want their chickens to run free in their yard. An egg breed in origin, the Ardenner was selected for its laying qualities at the outset of

Rumpless Ardenner cock, silver necked

the twentieth century. The highest score any hen of this breed in Belgium has ever attained was 170 eggs a year. Compared with a modern egg hybrid that is rather mediocre, but for a hobby breed it is certainly not bad.

Rumpless Ardenner hen, black

PARTICULARS

The color of the head's naked skin gives the Ardenner an outstanding appearance. In most chickens, the color of head, comb and wattles is a lively red. In the Ardenner, it is more purplish, a color which in Belgium is compared to

Ardenner hens

that of a ripe blackberry, so a kind of dark bluish black. There is a rather charming explanation given by some books as to the rumpless Ardenner's origin. It allegedly owes its existence to the fact that foxes were unable to get hold of these chickens, as they had no tail. Whether there is any truth in this story is doubtful, but it is a fact that there are many rumpless variants among the national breeds of Belgium.

Assendelfter or Assendelft Fowl

COUNTRY OF ORIGIN
The Netherlands

ORIGIN
The Assendelfter is a country fowl originating in the region called *Zaanstreek* in the province of North Holland. Its precise origin is unknown. For centuries, this breed has been kept there, and it is highly probable that it is at the basis of various other breeds known for their penciled markings, including the Holland Fowl.

A study of the head of an Ardenner cock, silver necked

APPEARANCE

The Assendelfter's type is very similar to that of the Frisians. It is a slender bird of slight build with a tail that is carried somewhat above the horizontal. The tail is held spread and has well curved sickles in the cock. The wings are carried well tucked against the body. The head sports a rather crude rose comb, with fairly large rounded points. The spike or leader can be either shorter or longer, and may point backwards or else follow the neck line. In this breed, it is important that the comb is fairly crude, so not overcultivated. The small earlobes are white and the color of the eyes is a reddish bay.

COLORS AND MARKING PATTERNS

The breed is raised in merely two colors, silver penciled and yellow penciled. Some still tend to call yellow penciled 'golden penciled', but that is no longer the official name. This is because the basic or ground color is a golden yellow, which is far lighter than the golden brown of the Frisian fowl. Like its rather crude comb shape and the fact that country fowl are uncultivated, the Assendelfter's penciling is crude and not very clearly delineated, which is perfectly in line with the breed. The penciling consists of two or three pairs of penciled markings that have a somewhat elongated shape.

QUALITIES

Due to their active personalities, these strong, vigorous creatures need quite a bit of care. Therefore you had better not keep them in runs that are too small. Scratching around looking for food is their second nature. As is

Assendelfter cock, yellow penciled

befitting to what in origin is an egg breed, the hens are fairly good layers. The lightly colored eggs are not very big; their average weight is between 40 and 50g (1½–1¾ oz). Inherent in their laying capacity is the fact that they are seldom broody.

PARTICULARS

- For a long time, this breed was quite rare. But after some media attention, perhaps due to an inclination towards things nostalgic, a revival is in evidence.
- With this breed, the Dutch in the olden days proved their sound business acumen. By mating a golden penciled cock with silver penciled hens, one got chicks of various colors. The ones of a yellowish brown were the hen chicks, while those that were yellow-white in color were the cocks. One kept the far more expensive hens oneself and took the cockerels to market. Because normally the difference in sex cannot be detected by the untrained, the buyers were under the impression that both sexes were represented in the chicks they purchased.

A study of the head of an Assendelfter cock

In this way, merchants were able to make more money on the cockerels. The deceit did not last long: eventually it became apparent that the purchased chicks were always male only.

Assendelfter hen, yellow penciled

Assendelfter hen, yellow penciled

Australorp

COUNTRY OF ORIGIN
Australia

ORIGIN
In the 1920s, the Australorp came about in Australia. It is not known from what breeds it was developed. However, it is certain that the Orpington was an important progenitor. As a utility breed, the Australorp soon found its way to other countries and nowadays it is known almost all over the world. In many countries, it is highly popular among fanciers breeding with a view to exhibitions, not only because it is pleasant to raise and to show, but also because it has many commercial qualities.

APPEARANCE
The Australorp is a lively, medium heavy breed. Its body is fairly broad and deep and has a plump build. Its back is averagely long, ending with a continuous sweep in the tail, which is held semi-erect. The tail itself consists of broad main tail feathers that are well spread. The cock has an abundance of broad main and lesser sickles. These almost cover the cock's tail feathers entirely. The shanks range in color from dark slate to blackish. The soles of the feet are pinkish white. The Australorp's head is rather small in proportion to the body. The single comb is of medium size and is nicely and regularly serrated. The points (sometimes called spikes) are broadly structured. The ear-lobes are red, as is the face's featherless skin. The color of the eyes is dark brown to brownish black.

COLORS AND MARKING PATTERNS
Australorps are found in black, white and laced blue.

QUALITIES
Australorps were originally bred both for their meat and their eggs. They are fast growers and the hens already start laying eggs round about the age of five months. As a layer, the Australorp is one of the most productive breeds.

Australorp hens

Australorp hens are generally non-sitters. They are friendly and also serene creatures that are rather easily tamed. For little kids the animals are too heavy to pick up: an adult Australorp rooster can weigh 3.5kg (7¾ lbs). However, a diminutive form of this breed has been developed, and these animals are of course easier to handle. It is possible to house them in closed runs, but they also thrive wandering about a spacious yard. They are certainly not

Australorp hens, six weeks old

keen flyers, so that a fencing of around 1.50m (5 ft) is enough. Among themselves, the birds are quite tolerant. Raising young cockerels within a breeding flock is therefore certainly possible, so there is no need to separate them.

PARTICULARS

The color that is most frequently bred is black. This should be a deep kind of black with a beautiful beetle-green sheen. Young black animals often tend to have a few white feathers, which is entirely normal. As to the white version, there is a difference of opinion about the shank's correct coloring. In Germany, the legs of an Australorp have to be bluish gray. This requirement makes it possible to improve the (rare) white color by way of the black Australorp. In the Netherlands, one assumes the Australorp was bred by way of the Orpington. White Orpingtons have pinkish white legs, so in the Netherlands white is a requirement for the legs. Due to this, improving the color by way of black Australorps is a longer and far more difficult process.

Australorp chicks, four weeks old

Barnevelder

COUNTRY OF ORIGIN
The Netherlands

ORIGIN
In this is about the only chicken breed that people who are not interested in poultry know about. They often erroneously call any brown egg hybrid a 'Barnevelder', which has however nothing to do with reality. This well-known and popular breed was created in the vicinity of the Dutch town of Barneveld, a place with a reputation to keep up worldwide when it is a question of chickens. The breed arose from local layers that were mated up with large Asiatic breeds. History has it that these were Cochins, Langshans and Brahmas. In the last century, at the beginning of the twenties, the first animals were exported to England, among other places. At that time, and even earlier, there was a great deal of commotion about the Barnevelder's coloring and markings. Due to the cross with the breeds just mentioned, there was a range of colors available. Eventually, next to self-colored birds, the double laced Barnevelder was preferred, so that all other colors hatched were kept out of the breeding program.

APPEARANCE
The Barnevelder is an averagely heavy chicken. Its back is of medium length and hollow, ending with a continuous concave sweep in the tail. The breast is well rounded and broad. Its head is adorned by a single medium-sized comb, preferably having four to five broad

points, though in practice this is often unattainable. The ear-lobes are red and the color of the eye is a reddish bay. The wings are well tucked and closely folded. The tail section is carried semi-high and not entirely spread. The cock's main and lesser sickles must be broad and should almost entirely cover the main tail feathers. In the cock, the color of the leg is dark yellow. In the hen, the scales on the front of their yellow legs are tinged with a reddish hue.

COLORS AND MARKING PATTERNS

The breed is found in black, white, double laced and blue double laced. The double laced

variety is recognized in most countries. In Germany, apart from these colors, there is also blue and dark brown.

QUALITIES

Barnevelders are famed for their excellent qualities as layers and notably for the color of their eggs, which are dark brown. The Barnevelder is a robust breed that will feel at home almost anywhere. You can either let them go about freely or keep them in a run. Barnevelders are poor flyers. A garden fence of medium height is usually effective in keeping them on your premises. Moreover, the animals are of a placid nature and can be easily tamed. A disadvantage of this breed is that it is susceptible to Marek's disease. A serious breeder will take this into account and have his day-old chicks vaccinated against this. When purchasing chicks, always inquire whether they are vaccinated, so that you won't be disappointed.

PARTICULARS

• When it comes to the color of the eggs, Barnevelders have little competition. The Maranses are in fact the only breed laying an egg of a similar dark brown. Still, this

A study of the head of a Barnevelder cock

Barnevelder hen, double laced

color is not consistent. At the beginning of her laying period, a Barnevelder hen that is a good layer will produce nice dark brown eggs, but after a couple of weeks their color will get lighter.

- The double laced variety turns the Barnevelder into something special. A white or a black Barnevelder is less outstanding. The white Barnevelder closely resembles the white New Hampshire. Double lacing is at its most beautiful when the ground color is a warm golden brown, in which a black lacing spectacularly flashes a green luster.

Brabançonne

COUNTRY OF ORIGIN
Belgium

ORIGIN
Officially, the Brabançonne or Brabant Farmyard Fowl has only existed as a breed since the beginning of the last century, although birds closely resembling the Brabançonne in appearance are seen in paintings from the seventeenth and eighteenth century. Like so many other breeds, this one also stems from

Barnevelder cock, double laced

Day-old Barnevelder chick

the crested fowl found in Europe, probably mixed with local farm poultry. At the outset of the twentieth century, the breed was reasonably popular as an egg-layer in the Flemish part of the province of Brabant. There are records of hens laying around 200 eggs a year, of no less than 65 to 70g ($2\frac{1}{4}$–$2\frac{1}{2}$ oz). After the rise of such breeds as the Leghorns, which were more remunerative as commercial layers, it was due to the fanciers that the breed was preserved.

APPEARANCE
Brabançonnes are country fowl of a rather slight build and with a fairly long body. In the hens, a full and deep backside is the sign of a good layer. The hens weigh around 2kg ($4\frac{1}{2}$ lbs). The breed's fairly long back slopes downwards, ending at a rather sharp angle in a tail that is carried high. The tail is not fully spread, but somewhat folded. The cocks have an abundance of ornamental feathers, with long, broad and nicely curved sickles. The wings are carried well tucked. The legs are clean and slate blue in color. The Brabançonne is a representative of the crested fowl category. The crest or topknot is not very big and should certainly never grow upon what is known as a 'skull knob'. The crest's base is almost similar to the skull's width and follows the shape of the skull towards the back. As the cock's head feathers are more elongated and narrower, his crest is also longer and less broad than the hen's. In front of the crest there is a medium-sized comb, the blade of which is

Brabançonne cock, silver quail

slightly raised. Due to this, the cock's comb protrudes above the crest. In the hen, the comb's anterior has a double S-shaped twist. The ear-lobes are small and white. In this

Quail-colored Brabançonne, cock

breed, the color of the eyes ranges between dark brown and brownish black.

COLORS AND MARKING PATTERNS

This breed, as a typical Belgian representative, is usually raised in the quail coloring or in some variant of this. Recognized colors include quail, silver quail, blue quail, columbian, buff columbian, white, black, buff and blue. The latter may be bred both with and without lacing (self blue).

QUALITIES

Brabançonnes are lively chickens and excellent flyers due to their being light and having rather large wings. The animals have an active nature and diligently go in search of food. That is why they are best given the freedom to wander about, or otherwise they should have a spacious run. A run will have to be enclosed by netting or wire mesh in order to prevent them from flying. By temperament, they are not much inclined to become 'close', so their minder will have to make an effort to gain their trust. However, with a lot of patience and a handful of grain much can be achieved. As a layer this breed is a good choice. Their white eggs weigh about 65g (2¼ oz) and the birds tend to lay quite a lot. These chickens do not go broody easily. Originally they are late developers, meaning that the first eggs are only laid when they are six to seven months old. Unfortunately, this breed has few fanciers, so the basis for breeding them is rather a small one. Due to this, one occasionally encounters

Quail-colored Brabançonnes, hens

skeletal abnormalities in the breed. A dent or a twist in the breastbone is the most frequently found defect. When raising chicks, one should take this into account. By giving the

Silver quail Brabançonne hen

animals sufficient calcium through their feed and seeing to it that even at an early age they roost on perches, you may in part prevent this ailment.

- The breed has various names. As mentioned above, it is known under the name Brabançonne, but also as Brabant Farmyard Fowl. However, in Belgium it is also called 'Topman' or 'Houpette'. The name Brabant Farmyard Fowl is quite often confused with the 'Brabanter'. These are however two totally different breeds.

Brakel

COUNTRY OF ORIGIN
Belgium

ORIGIN
The Brakel is one of the oldest chicken breeds. The birds originated from the country fowl that existed for centuries in the western part of Europe. Possibly these chickens arrived in Western Europe via Turkey in the sixteenth century. Also kinship with the French Bresse could be likely. In the past, there have been several types of Brakels. The Brakel from the Kempen

White Brabançonnes round about 1900

region was an example of this, but is by now practically extinct. The chickens from Chaam (the Netherlands) are also akin to the Brakels. In Belgium itself, there also arose a number of variants, like the Zottegem Fowl, which is sometimes called the *Zwartkop Brakel* ('Black-headed Brakel').

APPEARANCE

The Brakel is a elongated country fowl with a fairly deep, well-rounded breast. Everything shows that the hens are good layers: their backside (stern) is deep and full, while the fairly large comb lops to one side. Striking in this breed is the presence of dark pigmentation in the head. Due to this, the eyes are of a very dark brown, practically black, while the eye rims are melanistic. Part of the hen's comb is very heavily pigmented too, so that the comb's base is purple. The ear-lobes are white. The tail is fairly long, is carried in a nicely spread manner and is full-feathered. The legs are a dark slate blue.

COLORS AND MARKING PATTERNS

The original colors are golden and silver, and these are therefore recognized in all the countries where the breed is found. Apart from this, the color yellow white barred (also called 'chamois') turns up in many countries. In Germany and Belgium, the breed is raised in far more colors, including blue, black, white and white mottled.

QUALITIES

Brakels are tough, highly active and vigorous animals. The hens lays quite a lot of white eggs.

Day-old silver Brakel chick

Brakels, silver

A number of 180 eggs a year should not be a problem for a Brakel hen that is taken care of well. The eggs are rather big and weigh around 65g (2¼ oz). A broody hen is an exception, so eggs are usually hatched in an incubator or by a hen of some other breed. These chickens are best left to wander about freely, or else they should have a large run with lots of diversion. They are excellent flyers, which you should take into account if you live in a residential area. Brakels tend to grow fast,

Brakel cock, golden

and the hens start laying at an early age, usually when they are four and a half months old. By nature, Brakels are rather shy chickens. Their behavior largely depends upon the per-

A study of the head of a Brakel cock

Brakel hen, golden

are rather broad and are alternated by white ones that are narrower: this is known as 'barred penciling' or 'striped penciling'. In the hens, these markings are found on the back, the wing shoulders and the breast. The 'cape' is pure white or golden brown without any markings, which makes for a fine contrast.

Brakel hen, chamois

son taking care of them, but no matter how much trouble you take over them, you will usually not be able to tame them entirely.

PARTICULARS
- As Brakels are tough and vigorous and are able to forage for themselves, the breed has been put to service as a 'compost processor'. This experiment was very successful in Belgium, so that nowadays quite a number of households there use Brakels to get rid of their kitchen waste.
- Another specialty is the Brakel's pattern of markings, being a variant of the penciled markings. In this breed, the penciling continues on both sides of the feather's shaft or axis, forming a straight line. The pencilings

Drenthe fowl

COUNTRY OF ORIGIN
The Netherlands

ORIGIN
The Drenthe Fowl ('Drenth') has been found for centuries in the Dutch province of Drenthe. Not much is known about this breed's origin, but as to type, toughness and its rather shy character, it still closely resembles the Red Combed Fowl. In the Netherlands, the Drenth is one of the oldest breeds. In the nineteenth century, the birds ran free around the small farms of Drenthe. As the region was rather isolated, hardly any other standard breeds were imported. Thus, by the inbreeding of a mishmash of chickens, a handsome breed, developed which is now found in many colors. Under similar circumstances, local breeds closely resembling the Drenth arose in other European countries, examples being the Danish Country Fowl and the Czech Country Fowl.

APPEARANCE
The Drenth is a typical representative of the country fowl type. The main feature of country fowl is a fairly slight build, good flying capacities, white ear-lobes and gray-bluish legs. The Drenth has a medium-sized single comb and its eyes are a reddish bay. The rooster has a beautiful, copiously feathered ornamental tail, carried spread. A variant of this breed, sometimes popularly termed 'Clog Fowl' or 'Wooden Shoe Chicken', is the Rumpless Drenth. Due to the absence of a tail, the birds

Yellow partridge-colored rumpless Drenthe Fowl, hen

have a more erect carriage. Their remaining features are quite the same as those of the 'ordinary' Drenth. An old popular belief has it that rumpless chickens are better able to withstand attacks by foxes, as a fox cannot get a grip on them as there is no tail.

COLORS AND MARKING PATTERNS
In its region of origin, the following colors have been standardized: laced partridge, laced silver partridge, laced yellow partridge, laced blue partridge, laced silver blue partridge, partridge, blue partridge, silver partridge, yellow partridge, silver blue partridge, cuckoo partridge, silver necked black, silver necked blue, golden necked blue, bloodwing white and bloodwing silver partridge. In Germany, only partridge and silver partridge are recognized. On top of this extensive list of colorings, in the rumpless birds also the colors blue, white, black, silver penciled, golden penciled, yellow white penciled, lemon penciled and red penciled are recognized.

QUALITIES
This breed thrives best in spacious conditions. The animals are lively, active and usually a bit shy, so that they rarely become tame. However, they are truly tough and vigorous, so that they manage well when having a free run, be-

Frisian Fowl

COUNTRY OF ORIGIN
The Netherlands (Friesland)

ORIGIN
Nothing is known about the origin of the Frisian (sometimes also spelled 'Friesian'). For centuries, the breed was a familiar figure in the farmyards of Friesland, during which period it was never subjected to influences of foreign breeds. One assumes that this country fowl has the same, or partly the same origin as the Drenth, and therefore has some wild European fowl as its progenitor. The kinship with the Drenthe Fowl is clearly visible when you compare the Frisian's profile or silhouette with that of the Drenth. There is hardly any difference. This is the reason that Frisians are only recognized in what we call the penciled colors and in a few other colorings, while Drenths are found in the partridge varieties. One has made this choice in order to prevent too much intermingling of these breeds. In the distant past, there were also rumpless Frisians and short-legged ones known as 'crawlers' (*kruipers*). However, these two varieties have been lost. In the twentieth century, Frisians have been regularly mated up with Hollands.

APPEARANCE
The Frisian belongs to the country fowl group and is fairly small in size. The birds have a single comb and white ear-lobes. The tail is carried somewhat above the horizontal and is well spread. The eyes of Frisians are a lively red-

---

ing indifferent to weather conditions. The hens have a considerable laying capacity of eggs that are not all that big. However, they do not lay in winter, or hardly so. In origin, Drenthe hens are excellent sitters and mothers, and most animals still have these qualities. Possibly because they are an ancient breed that has been subject to a great deal of inbreeding, they tend to remain small. At present, attempts are made by way of Danish and Czech Country Fowl to bring them up to size again.

PARTICULARS
- The breed is especially popular in the Netherlands and in various other countries on the European continent. It is very rare in Great Britain.
- The laced partridge variety is a unique color only found in the Drenthe Fowl. In the 'normal' partridge color, the hen's saddle feathers are brownish gray and evenly sprinkled with tiny grayish black dots ('peppering'). Laced Drenths lack this peppering, but we do see little dull black serrated lines following the feather's shape. The feathers have several of these lacings and they are also encountered on the hen's breast. This distinguishes the color from the 'normal' partridge category, in which the hen's breast is a self-colored salmon.

The Frisian has hardly changed in a century; this image dates back to the beginning of the 20th century.

dish bay. The legs are clean and slate blue in color. The breast is well rounded and is carried middling high.

COLORS AND MARKING PATTERNS

The colors found most frequently in this breed are golden penciled, silver penciled and yellow

Frisian Fowl hen, yellow white penciled

white penciled. Alongside this, there are many other color patterns, including red penciled, lemon penciled, self blue, red mottled, cuckoo, black, black mottled and white. In the year 2001, a new variety was added to this list. This is called 'sandy yellow' and is a self-colored light yellowish brown. The color is best compared to that of 'paving sand' (sand used as underlayment for paved roads). The penciling we see in the Frisians is a variant of what is known as 'penciled patterns'. This is a marking in which golden penciled hens have small black specks on a golden brown ground color. Since time immemorial, these markings have frequently been found in country fowl along the eastern coasts of the North sea, for instance in the Belgian Brakel. However, this penciling's shape (the blacks specks) varies according to the breed, the Frisian having between three and five pairs of specks on each feather, which are unattached and have the shape of a grain of wheat. In the cocks of these penciled Frisians, a lacing around the main sickles is required.

Frisian hen, silver penciled

142

Frisians are active and lively birds. They are very similar to Drenths. Both breeds are at their best wandering freely around a yard. Frisians are good flyers, and given the chance, they will prefer to spend the night outside in a tree instead of in a roost. Frisian Fowl can nevertheless also be kept in a closed run, as long as they have sufficient space and diversion. The breed is not only strong and fairly resistant to diseases, it is also very fertile. The hens lay relatively large eggs with a white shell. Some hens go broody. They are good mothers, fiercely defending their chicks against any attacker.

PARTICULARS

The breed is popular among fanciers of Old Dutch breeds. However, most registered breeders are found in Friesland. Outside the Netherlands, this breed is not raised very often. Only in Germany do we see a considerable and even growing group of breeders. Frisians are also known in various other European countries and even in South Africa, though there are few breeders there.

Frisian hen, yellow white penciled

Groninger Meeuwen and East Frisian Meeuwen

COUNTRY OF ORIGIN
The Netherlands and Germany

ORIGIN
In the eighteenth century, one usually had farmyard fowl of no particular breed on the farms in the province of Groningen and in the east of Friesland. These chickens often had penciled markings and resembled the Frisian Fowl. However, at that time, the name Groninger Meeuwen was not yet in use for a breed. At the outset of the twentieth century, a breeder from Groningen entered in a show a number of Frisians that stood out because they were considerably larger and heavier than the original Frisian Fowls. From these, the Groninger Meeuwen arose, the name meaning 'Groningen Gull'. English uses the plural form of the Dutch 'meeuw'(singular) to denote one individual bird. However, the breed was lost, and only in the seventies and eighties of the last century did a few breeders decide to 'reconstruct' it. As the Groninger Meeuwen perhaps has the same origin as the East Frisian Meeuwen, the latter was also used in this process, for of these there was sufficient breed-

Frisian, yellow white penciled

ing stock available. Nowadays both breeds have a small but very enthusiastic following, mainly in the Netherlands. They are also raised in Belgium, France and Germany but are quite unknown in other countries.

APPEARANCE

There is very little difference between the East Frisian Meeuwen and the Groninger Meeuwen. In theory, they are slightly different as to body weight and eye color. The Groninger Meeuwen has dark brown eyes, while those of the East Frisian Meeuwen are reddish brown. The remaining physical features of these breeds are similar. In the country fowl category, both breeds are conspicuous because of their fairly heavy and powerful build. Their body is a bit more sturdy than that of the Holland for instance. The tail is large and full, and it is carried well spread at medium height. In both breeds, the single comb is medium-sized. In laying hens, the back part of the comb lops over. The ear-lobes are white, and the leg color is slate blue.

COLORS AND MARKING PATTERNS

Two colors are recognized in both breeds: golden penciled and silver penciled. The penciling is different in shape from that of, for instance, Frisians. In these breeds, the feathers only have two or three pairs of penciling marks that are rather large and squarish in shape. One is at present working on a third variety of these chickens: lemon penciled. This color has already been recognized in the Groningen Meeuwen Bantams. By crossing golden penciled with silver penciled, it is possible that an extra color gene appears. This gene will 'dilute' the ground color (basic color) to a lemon shade, while the penciling remains black. The result is lemon penciled.

QUALITIES

Like all country fowl, these breeds are vigorous, active and rather stand-offish towards their owners. However, they are a bit more subdued than Frisians, possibly due to the fact that their build is somewhat heavier. With a good calm approach, they can become reasonably tame. The chickens are suitable for

East Frisian Meeuwen round about 1900

144

A study of the head of a Groninger Meeuwen, cock

Golden penciled Frisian Meeuwen hen

keeping in a spacious run as well as letting them roam about freely. In the latter case, they are good foragers, gathering at least part of their nourishment themselves. They are good flyers, so in establishing the height of the fence around their territory, you should keep this trait in mind. Both breeds lay white eggs of a considerable size. They do not get broody often.

PARTICULARS

Diminutive forms have been bred of the Groninger Meeuwen as well as the East Frisian Meeuwen, though these are not described in this encyclopedia. Apart from the size, their qualities are the same as those of their big counterparts.

Holland Fowl or Hamburg

COUNTRY OF ORIGIN

The United Kingdom, the Netherlands and Germany

ORIGIN

Various countries claim to have created the Hollands, the origin of which we are in fact no longer able to trace. This breed's precursors were already known in Germany and the United Kingdom by the name of 'Hamburg' at the beginning of the eighteenth century, but at that time it was not a question yet of a purebred or standard breed. Hamburgs are animals with extremely beautiful markings (spangled), and were mainly kept for their utility as layers. Later on, one started to concentrate more on their elegant appearance, purposefully crossing them with other breeds. According to tradition, the self-colored variant of the Hollands

Golden penciled Frisian Meeuwen cock

arose in England. The Netherlands are mentioned as the country of origin of the penciled varieties. Do not confuse this Holland and Hamburg with the two distinct American breeds of Hollands and Hamburgs.

APPEARANCE

Apart from the three various colors, three different sizes can be distinguished within this breed, the penciled varieties being the ones that are smallest and most delicately built. The Holland has a long shape, the back line of which tends to slope somewhat in the cock. The self-colored birds and spangled varieties also have this shape, but their build is a little cruder. The head is rather elongated and has a rose comb of which the spike (leader) is well rounded, projecting straight backwards. In highly pigmented birds, the eyes are of a brownish red, while in lighter ones they are a reddish bay. The ear color is white. The ears themselves (sometimes called 'deaf ears') are almost round and of medium size, so that they are conspicuous. The cock's tail is carried well spread and is richly feathered. The legs are slate blue.

COLORS AND MARKING PATTERNS

There are three color groups within this breed. The best known is the one with spangled mark-

Holland Fowl cock, golden penciled

ings in the colors golden black spangled and silver black spangled. The penciled varieties are also frequently encountered, like golden penciled, silver penciled, yellow white penciled, lemon penciled and golden blue penciled. To attain the ideal image of markings in the hens, one breeds with 'hen-feathered' cocks in this category. In their feathering, these roosters lack a 'real' cock's features, not having any main and lesser sickles, also lacking the elegant ornamental feathers in hackles and saddle. Because of this different feathering, their markings resemble those of hens. In a third variety, we find the cuckoo-colored, self blue, white and black birds, though these are relatively rare.

Holland Fowl, silver black spangled

Holland hen, golden penciled

Holland hen, lemon penciled

QUALITIES

Hollands are very lively, active birds. They are hardy and thrive when running free around the yard. However, you may house them in a run, as long as this provides sufficient space for the animals to move about in. Also, you will have to see to sufficient diversion, because otherwise Hollands will soon get bored and start to direct their activities towards one another, resulting in injuries. They are not easy to tame, but they certainly can tell the difference between their minder and strangers. The hens lay white eggs

A study of the head of a Holland cock

of around 55g (2 oz) each. Broodiness does not occur often in these non-sitters.

PARTICULARS

When comparing the golden black spangled birds with the silver black spangled ones, you will notice that there is a big difference in the markings of the tail. Animals with a golden ground color have a totally black tail. The tail of silver black spangled birds is white, with a big black spangle at the tip of the feather. For some years now, in the golden black variety, breeders have been concentrating on tails with markings. The difficulty is to retain the markings without losing any of the color. The animals that do have markings in their tail in fact have a ground color that is too light.

Lakenvelder

COUNTRY OF ORIGIN
The Netherlands and Germany

ORIGIN
As to the origin of the Lakenvelder (also spelled 'Lakenfelder'), various stories are told.

One version has it that the Lakenvelder originated in the Netherlands at the outset of the eighteenth century, in the Utrecht hamlet of Lakervelt, situated between the villages of Meerkerk and Lexmond. Another version maintains that the breed was developed both in the German federal state of Westphalia and in the Netherlands and that it was named for its resemblance to the Lakenvelder cow. There are also people who point out that the name Lakenvelder comes from *lakenvel* meaning 'sheet skin', as the white of their bodies resembles a sheet. In English, we call this marking 'belted'.

APPEARANCE
The Lakenvelder is among the oldest standardized breeds and has a elongated body of slight build. The head sports a medium-sized single comb and has white ear-lobes. The color of the eye is orange-red to reddish brown. The wings are carried well tucked, pointing slightly downwards. The tail feathers are long, the tail is spread and carried fairly high. The cock has long, broad and well-curved sickles. The legs are slate blue.

COLORS AND MARKING PATTERNS
In all countries, the Lakenvelder is only recognized with the belted i.e. contrasting or framing color so specific to this breed. The contrast is usually black, but it also comes in a 'diluted' black, being a bluish gray called 'blue marked'.

QUALITIES
The Lakenvelder is a very attractive bird that moves about a great deal and can fly high. These animals come into their own when they are given free run in a farmyard or a field. A flock of Lakenvelders on a green lawn or in a meadow is a beautiful sight. These animals seldom feel at home in aviaries and chicken coops, shown by the fact that they get 'jumpy'. They are quite good layers, the eggs being white, and they are typical non-sitters. The animals are fast growers and very vigorous.

Lakenvelder hens

PARTICULARS
- Its belted marking makes this breed something special. In the whole of Europe, we find types of animals with similar markings and a similar name (there are belted or *lakenvelder* mice, cows and goats). What is called the 'Hollander marking' in guinea pigs and rabbits is also a belted marking. As said, the Netherlands do not have the exclusive rights to this marking type, and in Great Britain we find it in cows.

Lakenvelders

Lakenvelder hens

Week-old Lakenvelder chick

- Young Lakenvelder chickens do not have the right markings straight away. Only after the third molting do these birds acquire their definitive markings, in which there is a lot of variety. Many animals have a few black or mottled feathers in the patch of white plumage on their backs

Leghorn

COUNTRY OF ORIGIN

Originally Italy, but the development of the breed's various present forms took place in a number of countries.

A study of the head of a Lakenvelder rooster

ORIGIN

The Leghorn is descended from a country fowl originating in Italy. Leghorn is the German name of the city of Livorno. As these Italian birds were layers of renown, they were exported all over the world. In this way, different types came about in different countries, all stemming from the same initial material.

APPEARANCE

The Leghorn is bred in a number of types. There are certainly great differences between the various breeding directions, but there are also a few similarities. Thus, all of these directions are of an elongated country fowl type. The difference in shape is notably caused by the tail's carriage. The Dutch-German type has a large, full-feathered tail that is carried a bit below the horizontal and is not totally spread. The chickens of the American breeding direction carry their tail at the same level as the Dutch Leghorns, but they spread their tails entirely. In American cocks, the tail is very richly feathered. The chickens in the British breeding direction have theirs fairly low and almost completely folded. In the latter breeding direction, the stature and length of the legs is considerably higher here than in the other two directions. Furthermore, the English Leghorn has an enormous comb and very long wattles. In the hen, this comb is entirely lopped. The Dutch-German and American Leghorns also have large combs, of which only the posterior part is lopped in laying hens. Alongside of

Leghorn cock, American type

149

these, rose-combed Leghorns are also recognized in the United States. All Leghorns have white ear-lobes and yellow shanks. The eye color is reddish bay. In the Dutch-German breeding direction, we also find a rose-combed variant. This comb is rather broad and tapers off into a spike or leader, projecting backwards almost horizontally. However, rose-combed Leghorns are not often seen.

COLORS AND MARKING PATTERNS

Not all types are recognized in the same colors, while moreover the recognition of the colors per type varies greatly in the different countries. In spite of this, all of these different colors and breeding directions are called 'Leghorn', to which one adds the description of breeding direction or type. The animals in the Dutch-German breeding direction form an exception here, as in various countries they have not been named after the Leghorn, but the breed's name instead refers to Italy, its country of origin, e.g. *Italiener* (Germany), *Italiana* (Spain and Italy) and *Italienne* (France). The American type with its richly feathered tail section is found in

Partridge-colored Leghorn cock of the Dutch-German type

Partridge-colored Leghorn cock of the Dutch-German type

white (the 'standard color'), black, red, columbian, partridge, brown partridge, silver partridge and black tailed red. However, in most countries only white is recognized. The German or Dutch type is found in a variety of colors, including white, black, buff, self blue and laced blue, red, partridge, silver partridge, blue partridge, yellow partridge, brown par-

Leghorn hens, exchequer

tridge, cuckoo partridge, partridge gold flitter, partridge silver flitter, bloodwing silver partridge, blue mottled, golden black laced, golden blue laced, golden white laced, bloodwing white, barred, porcelain, columbian, columbian blue marked, lavender, silver necked, golden necked, golden necked blue, silver black spangled and exchequer. The English type with its remarkable head piece is found in white, which is the only recognized color in most countries. In Great Britain itself, this type is however also bred and exhibited in black, buff, self blue, partridge, silver partridge, multiple penciled partridge ('triple laced'), bloodwing, black mottled, exchequer and cuckoo.

QUALITIES
This breed was tremendously popular until the beginning of the 1960s, mainly due to its laying capacity. The hens lay around two hundred eggs annually, which in that day and age was quite a lot. The commercial sector therefore frequently turned to it as a utility fowl. Later on, the Leghorn shifted to being a show bird. Previous to this, the breed contributed towards the creation of the various egg hybrids. In spite of the refining of the different varieties, the present Leghorn is still an excellent layer, usually laying on during the winter months. The egg shell is white.
Leghorns hardly ever become broody, which is inherent in their original purpose. The breed has vitality, matures early and are fast growers. Leghorns can be left to roam about,

Leghorn chick, over two weeks old

Partridge-colored Leghorn hen of the Dutch-German type

but can also be kept in a run. If one approaches them calmly, they can become reasonably tame, though never tame enough to be picked up and most of them remain rather stand-offish and mistrusting. Should you choose the large-combed variety, then please keep in mind that these animals need extra care during the winter months. During frosty weather, one should put some acid-free vaseline on the comb and wattles to prevent them from freezing and thus in part dying off.

PARTICULARS
- In Germany, there are also Leghorns that are black white mottled. These markings correspond with the Ancona's. As the Ancona's type closely resembles that of the Leghorn, Anconas are not recognized in Germany. Others countries, including the Netherlands, have solved this problem by indeed recognizing the Ancona, but not the black white mottled Leghorn.
- The category called 'exchequer' is a black and white stippled or mottled animal. This variety is found in the English direction and in the Dutch-German type, though there are

Leghorn cock, exchequer

Marans hen, brassy black

a indeed a few differences as regards the desired color distribution. The exchequer of the Dutch-German type leans more towards the British breeding direction, and is therefore often bred separately.

Marans

COUNTRY OF ORIGIN
France

ORIGIN
The Marans originated at the outset of the last century in the French fishing village of the same name. The breed was developed as a layer. It is not know precisely which breeds were involved in the creation of the Marans, but possibly these include the Faverolles and the Croad Langshan, among others.

APPEARANCE
The Marans is a fairly sizeable fowl with a characteristic, elongated body shape. The animals have white legs of medium length, which are feathered on the outside. The outside toe also has some feathers, though not so many that the feet might be called completely feathered. The breed has a single comb and red ear-

lobes. The eyes are lively and orange-red. The carriage of the tail is medium high and well-spread. The breed has two breeding directions. The English type distinguishes itself from the French by the lack of feathering on the outside of the feet. Moreover, English Maranses are of a somewhat shorter build.

COLORS AND MARKING PATTERNS
The breed is found in various varieties, including brassy black, cuckoo, golden cuckoo, black, silver cuckoo, white, columbian and self black.
Apart from these colors, in France one also finds the color *fauve*. This can be best described as a somewhat reddish wheaten. The favorite color is without doubt brassy black, along with cuckoo. The brassy black has as its special feature that the feather's black parts are only allowed a moderate luster. This is unlike other chicken breeds, where black is usually required to have a green sheen. Brassy black is essentially a variant of golden necked black, in which the gold has been replaced by a brassy color.

QUALITIES
If the animals are taken care of well and approached calmly, they are fairly 'chummy' by

nature. However, they only very rarely allow themselves to be touched. Usually they are friendly creatures, and seldom or never aggressive. Maranses are suitable for wandering about the yard freely as well as for the run. The advantage of their only slightly feathered legs is that there is no objection to giving them the free run during bad weather.

One of the most remarkable qualities of this breed is the very dark reddish brown to brown color of their eggs. Without any doubt, this is the Marans' hallmark. In the past, this feature

Marans hen, silver black

Marans cock, brassy black

- It is not simple to retain the quality of laying very dark brown eggs in chickens. When this is the objective of commercial chicken farming, it always tends to detract from the Marans' appearance. Thus many birds from 'laying stocks' have a wrong leg color, badly shaped comb and mediocre markings. Birds with excellent physical features in fact usually do not lay the desired dark brown egg.
- Breeding the right leg color (white) can be difficult as this gene has a linkage to the sex chromosome. Due to this, raising cocks

was used to bring more vitality to the Barnevelder. Maranses are strong and robust birds that are good layers and rapid growers. Some hens become broody, though this quality is not generally present in the breed.

PARTICULARS
- According to the French Ministry of Agriculture, no salmonella bacteria are found in the eggs of Maranses. The reason for this is perhaps that the egg's pores are smaller than those of other eggs, while the membrane is also very thick and has a less open texture.

The eggs of the Marans are a very dark reddish brown.

with white shanks is easier than breeding beautiful brassy black hens with white legs. The solution to this problem lies in breeding from a cock that has down of a very light color. Notably on the saddle, the down should be almost white.

- Next to brassy black, both silver cuckoo and golden cuckoo are typical Marans colors. In fact golden cuckoo is the same as brassy black, in which the black in the feathers has been substituted by cuckoo. In silver cuckoo, the gold has moreover become silvery white. An additional advantage of chickens of these two colors is that, due to the fading of the black, they do have wonderfully white legs.

New Hampshire

COUNTRY OF ORIGIN
The United States of America

Day-old chick, Marans

ORIGIN
This breed originated at the beginning of the twentieth century in the State of New Hampshire in the United States. The Rhode Island formed the basis for the development of this chicken, which was mainly bred for its eggs, but in the second place has also come to be appreciated as a table fowl. In the United States, it became incredibly popular as a utility breed. In spite of this, it was not until the forties before any interest was shown from Europe. In countries like the Netherlands and Germany, this breed has now a large following, though in other countries, including Great Britain, it is very rare.

APPEARANCE
The 'Hamps' is a big, broadly built chicken. With a continuous hollow sweep, the bird's back ends in the tail. They have a single comb and reddish bay eyes, while their ear-lobes are red and the color of the legs is yellow. The tail section is not all that long and is carried well spread. A close feathering, with feathers of a broad, firm structure, is characteristic of the breed.

COLORS AND MARKING PATTERNS
New Hampshires are found in chestnut red, chestnut red blue marked and in white. Chestnut red is regarded as the original color and has been well developed in this breed to a beautifully warm reddish brown. The blue marked variety distinguishes itself from the chestnut red one by the fact that the black has faded to a bluish gray. This variety was developed in the Netherlands from a cross between a New Hampshire and an egg hybrid that had the factor for the blue markings. White is not

New Hampshire hen, chestnut red

New Hampshire cock, chestnut red

New Hampshire cock, chestnut red

accepted in the Netherlands, as the animals of this color are practically identical in appearance to the white Barnevelder.

QUALITIES

The breed was originally raised for both its meat and its eggs. Thus the birds are fast growers and the hens lay well, the eggs being brown. New Hampshires have a placid and friendly nature and are easily tamed. It is a vigorous and fertile breed, thriving whether kept in a run or wandering about the yard. As their body weight is considerable, these chickens are not really great flyers. The advantage of this is that a fence around their territory need not be any higher than 1.50m (5 ft). Among themselves, they are tolerant creatures and not very aggressive. Broodiness does occur, but the tendency is not strong in this breed.

PARTICULARS

The chestnut red coloring makes the Hamps an attractive figure. The cocks are required to be what is known as three-colored, meaning that they should have three different shades of reddish brown. The lightest shade is seen in the neck hackles (golden bay), the medium shade is found in the saddle hackles (deep

chestnut red), while the darkest one is on the saddle (lustrous dark golden bay). Apart from this coloring, the animals have brown primaries (flights) marked with black and a black tail. The hen has a bit of black marking in the neck. The way the color of the hens is influenced by outdoor life and laying is remarkable. When molting is done, a young hen has a fairly even reddish brown color. After one or two months, the color becomes lighter and more patchy under the influence of laying and of

Day-old chick, New Hampshire

New Hampshire chick, six weeks old

Blue laced Orpington cock

sunlight, so that at the end of the laying season, her color does not look anything like it did at the start.

Orpington

COUNTRY OF ORIGIN
The United Kingdom

ORIGIN
This breed was developed at the end of the nineteenth century by the Englishman William Cook from the village of Orpington. Involved in its creation were, among others, Croad Langshans, Minorcas, Langshans and Plymouth Rocks. Notably the Langshan set its stamp on this new breed, the first Orpingtons still looking very much like Langshans. The original breeding objective was to come up with a chicken with excellent laying capacities, and this was entirely successful. The literature from that period mentions some of these birds' enormous annual production of even up to 340 eggs. Whether this production was really so high :s dubious. However, it is

certain that these chickens stood out as superb layers at that time. The first Orpingtons were black, followed at the end of the eigh-

Orpington cock, buff black laced

mals stand so low that their down touches the ground. The head is broad and has a medium-sized single comb. The ear-lobes are red, while the color of the eye is reddish bay in most varieties.

Orpington hen, black

Porcelain Orpington cock

Porcelain Orpington hen

teen eighties by white and buff. An Orpington from that period was not of the same type as the representatives of the present breed: it reminded one far more of an Australorp. Breeders have concentrated on a type that is very characteristic. The modern Orpington can no longer be compared with any breed whatsoever.

APPEARANCE

The first thing that strikes one about the Orpington is that it is so big and heavy. With a little exaggeration, one might say that its body would fit neatly into a cube. The animals' build is not only large, it is extremely broad as well. This overall image is furthermore enhanced by a profuse and rather loose feathering. The breast line is deep and the back short. The back ends with a smooth sweep in the tail, which is short and is carried medium high. Due to the deep build and copious feathering, the Orpington's stand is very low, so that when looking at the Orpington's silhouette one can only just manage to discern a little bit of leg. However, it is important in this breed that one can still see something of the leg. Some ani-

do require a dry and clean roost, for their abdominal feathers easily get wet (also due to their short legs) and these should of course be able to dry well. The hens are good layers, annually producing on average two hundred eggs of a very light brown color. However, measured by the animals' size, the eggs are relatively small. Orpingtons easily go broody, in which case they prove to be reliable mothers who bring up their chicks without any problems. The cocks have a deep and full, relatively soft voice that is certainly not shrill.

PARTICULARS

One of the most frequently bred Orpington varieties is the color buff. This beautifully warm light yellow color has the disadvantage that it soon fades because of the sun and the rain. In that case, it is important to protect

Orpington cock, multiple penciled partridge

COLORS AND MARKING PATTERNS

In Great Britain, one sticks to the more or less original colors of black, buff, white and blue laced. In most other countries where Orpingtons are bred and exhibited, the breed is known in a far greater range of color variants. A few of these are birchen, buff black laced, silver black laced, barred, red, porcelain, black white mottled, white columbian, porcelain, and multiple penciled partridge ('triple laced').

QUALITIES

Worldwide, the Orpington has many enthusiasts and is therefore a familiar bird at almost every show. They are friendly chickens that are very soon 'trained to the hand' when taken good care of. The animals are very big, weighing between 3 and 4kg (6½–9 lbs, sometimes more) and even looking larger because of their full plumage. You can keep them in a run as well as letting them wander about freely. As they do not fly and have rather short legs, a low garden fence usually suffices to keep them within boundaries. However, the animals

this color against these influences. In spite of this, at the end of the year most birds, before starting to molt, no longer look anything like those that have just finished molting. If you want to be successful at exhibitions, you will

Orpington hen, multiple penciled partridge

have to take this discoloration into account when building a run or letting them run free. Provide lots of shade for the birds by planti-

White Orpington cock

ng trees and bushes in their area or by entirely roofing over your run. And keep them out of the rain.

Plymouth Rock

COUNTRY OF ORIGIN
The United States of America

ORIGIN
The breed takes its name from the American town of Plymouth. Dr Benneth created the breed out of Dominiques, Brahmas, Cochins and Javas, aiming to develop a good and vigorous layer breed. As early as 1874, the breed was already recognized in the United States under the name of Barred Plymouth Rock. 'Barred' refers to the markings the breed inherited from the Dominiques. Later on, also white and buff-colored Plymouth Rocks were recognized and the adjective 'barred' was dropped. Even previous to its official recognition, the breed found its way to other countries, including Great Britain.

Plymouth Rock rooster, multiple penciled silver partridge

APPEARANCE

The Plymouth Rock is a fairly large chicken: a cock weighs 4.5kg (10 lbs). Typical of the 'Rock' breed's shape is the even, almost hori-

Plymouth Rocks, multiple penciled partridge

zontal line of the back ending in the tail. In the cock, this is less clear than in the hen. The reason is that the cock has a more full-feathered tail, which due to this seems to be carried a bit higher. The tail is moderately spread. As the hallmark of good layers, laying hens have a deep, full abdomen. The breast is broad, rea-

Plymouth Rock chick

Plymouth Rock cock, black

sonably deep and well rounded. The legs are bright yellow. The skin of the face is red, the beak yellow and the ear-lobes red. On its head, the Plymouth Rock sports a single medium-sized comb. Furthermore, the chicken has lively reddish bay eyes.

COLORS AND MARKING PATTERNS

This breed is raised in many different varieties, barred, white and buff being the more or less classic ones. Besides this, there are also colors like multiple penciled ('triple laced') or penciled partridge, multiple penciled silver partridge, columbian, buff columbian and blue laced.

QUALITIES

Plymouth Rocks are friendly, rather placid birds that easily become tame. They do not need all that much space, even though they appreciate running free. Because their build is rather heavy, they are not really keen flyers, so when they are left to run free, the fencing around their area need not be very high. The animals remain true to their origin, laying a great number of cream-colored eggs of a nice size. Among themselves, the breed is tolerant. Several cocks in a spacious coop together with

160

Plymouth Rock hen, black

a large group of hens, or preferably with the possibility to wander about, usually does not afford any real problem.

PARTICULARS

- This is perhaps the most popular breed in the United States and it has many followers in all countries where there are chicken fanciers.
- In the barred variety, the black bars in the hens are broader than the white ones, while in the cocks bars of similar width are required. This is caused by the sex-linked heritability of the factor ruling the barred markings ('linkage'). True-breeding barred cocks have one more gene for barring than the hens have. The visible outcome is a black bar that is narrower than in the hen.

If there is a lot of inbreeding using the same strains, the barring factor quite often tends to result in anomalous feathering. Normally speaking, a chicken molts three times before reaching adulthood and a chick's primaries are considerably smaller, their tip being moreover a bit more pointed than in adult animals. During the last molt, these primaries are usually changed. In barred Plymouth Rocks, the outside 'chick flights' are often retained.

Rhode Island

COUNTRY OF ORIGIN

The United States of America

ORIGIN

The Rhode Island is a true utility breed, specially developed for the laying of eggs. As early as the second half of the nineteenth century, the breed was created in the United States, specifically in the State of Rhode Island. By crossing a hotchpotch of layers with Asiatic birds like Cochins and Malays, there arose, after a focused selection for good laying, a reasonably uniform breed. The red variety was a favorite with the local breeders, as the hens of this color were rumored to be the best layers. It took as long until 1904 for the breed to be recorded in the standard of perfection, at first only with a single comb. Two years later rose-combed birds were also recognized, as were the whites. Even previous to recognition in their country of origin, these animals were already exported to the mainland of Europe, where they became very popular as utility fowl. Until this very day, the Rhode Island's genetic material can be found in many commercial stocks used with a view to breeding egg hybrids.

APPEARANCE

The Rhode Island's shape is that of a long rectangle. It has a well-rounded breast and a tail that is rather short and is carried a little above

Rhode Island cock, red

the line of the back. When taking in a Rhode Island's side view, you will see that it is possible to place its shape in a rectangle. Naturally, leg and neck do not come within this rectangle. In poultry parlance, this is sometimes referred to as 'brick-shaped'. The Rhode

161

A study of the head of a Rhode Island cock

Island's leg color is yellow. It can have either a single or a rose comb. The breed has fairly large eyes of a reddish bay color. The ear-lobes are red, being a legacy of its Asiatic ancestors.

COLORS AND MARKING PATTERNS

The breed is found in two colors: red and white. The reds have either a single comb or a rose comb. The whites are, in the few countries where they are recognized, only considered right with a rose comb. The color red is far better known than white. It is even true that breeders and fanciers of these chickens usual-

Rhode Island chicks

ly refer to them as 'Rhode Islands Reds' or simply 'Reds', while this is merely a color variant and not the breed's true name.

QUALITIES

As befitting to a layer breed, Rhodes Islands are famed for their great egg-laying capacity. On average, hens can annually lay around 220

Rhode Island hens

light brown eggs, each weighing between 50 and 60g (1¾–2¼ oz), which compared with the body weight of the hens is not really a lot. The breed is very calm and friendly. Due to their rather heavy build, they are not really good flyers. They can certainly fly, but hardly ever take the trouble to do so. These are chickens that may very well be kept in a closed run and that are reasonably tolerant of one another. Occasionally, however, cocks do tend to fight. If you have the possibility to give them the free run, there should be no problem. In that case, you will soon notice that this wandering about, during which they eat all sorts of things, has a positive effect on the yolks' color and the eggs' flavor. Young Rhode Island chicks are normally fast growers and will start laying their first egg at the age of four or five months. The breed is hardy, and due to its friendly nature also suitable for beginning fanciers.

PARTICULARS

As mentioned, the breed is also known under the name of Rhode Island Red, in spite of the fact that white birds are recognized as well. However, the latter have never been able to reach the popularity of the red ones. In

America, whites and reds are regarded as two different breeds, having been introduced into the standard of perfection separately. In most other countries, poultry associations have restricted themselves to the Rhode Island Red.

Rheinlander

COUNTRY OF ORIGIN
Germany

ORIGIN
The Rheinlander was developed from an ancient, unimproved country fowl breed that had been around for centuries in the German Eiffel district. During more or less the same period, the Alsatian Fowl came about in the Alsace. The breeds are very similar and it is not clear which breed has the oldest rights. Due to being crossed with other old country fowl breeds, both breeds have developed into pro-

ductive, healthy and strong layers. At the beginning of the last century, they became recognized.

APPEARANCE

Black Rheinlander cock

The Rheinlander is a fairly heavy country fowl with a somewhat lower stand and a remarkably elongated build. Its breast is broad, deep and well rounded. The line of the back is practically horizontal, ending with a smooth, continuous sweep in the tail. The tail is long, its carriage being somewhat below the horizontal and well spread, and the cock has long, broad and nicely curved sickles. In most varieties, the shanks, which are certainly not 'stilty', are blue. In comparison to its body, the Rheinlander's head is rather small. Rheinlanders have white ear-lobes and dark eyes, the exact color of which depends on the variety. Thus, white Rheinlanders have reddish brown eyes, while black Rheinlanders have dark brown ones. The birds have a rose comb: a small comb covered

Black Rheinlander hens

Silver partridge Twente hen

with fine and tiny rounded points and with a short spike or leader.

COLORS AND MARKING PATTERNS
Apart from the original color black, there are blue laced, cuckoo, partridge, silver partridge,

A study of the head of a Rheinlander cock

Black Rheinlander hen

white, silver necked and golden necked Rheinlanders. In a number of countries, only the black variety is recognized.

APPEARANCE
The Rheinlander is a strong and active bird. The hens are excellent layers, even in winter. Broodiness is not common among them. The breed grows up fairly quickly, although it takes a little longer than in most other fast growing breeds before cocks acquire their full ornamental tail. The Rheinlander is a rather placid chicken and has a friendly nature. Although they are not incompetent as far as flying goes, they do not tend to do so often because of their quite heavy build. Due to this, it is fine to give them the free run in an area with a fencing that is not very high. The breed will also thrive in a closed run. Among themselves, these chickens are gentle creatures. Also young, growing cockerels tend to tolerate one another's company for a rather long time.

Twente Fowl

COUNTRY OF ORIGIN
The Netherlands and Germany

ORIGIN
The Twente Fowl arose in Twente, a region in the eastern part of the Netherlands, and in the neighboring German county of Bentheim. The breed was developed by crossing the country fowl from these districts with Malays and silver partridge Leghorns. The breed was pre-

Cuckoo-colored Rheinlander hen

Partridge Twente hens

sented to the Dutch general public for the first time during an exhibition in 1884.

APPEARANCE

Twentes are elegant, fairly large chickens of a type that has a streak of both the country fowl and the game breeds. From the former, they have inherited the elongated and graceful build with the richly feathered tail. From the latter, they have the erect, challenging posture and typical head. The breed has a short build. The ear-lobes are small and red; the beak is yellow and of a short, powerful structure. The reddish bay eyes show a fierce expression. The birds have a small comb in the shape of half a walnut, covered with tiny points and some

Twente cock, partridge

furrowing (walnut comb). The hen's comb is hardly developed. The wings are carried in a well-tucked fashion. The leg color is yellow.

Silver partridge Twente cock

COLORS AND MARKING PATTERNS

Partridge, silver partridge, blue partridge, silver blue partridge.

QUALITIES

The fact that the animals are descended from game cocks can clearly be seen from the Twente's type and its head. But they also have a fighting bird's streak in their character. The cocks can be really aggressive towards each other, so that you had better run just the one cock with a number of hens. The animals are vigorous and hardy. They thrive both when running free and when kept in a spacious coop. They are fairly good flyers, so a high fence or closed run is to be preferred. In spite of this, these chickens are rather easily tamed.

Twente cock

Twente Fowl chicks, silver partridge and partridge

The hens are not broody often, but they are good layers, having large eggs. Usually they also keep on laying in wintertime.

PARTICULARS
In the Dutch part of their homeland, these birds are also referred to by their old name, *Twentse Grijzen* ('Twente Grays'), referring to their original color, silver partridge.

Welsummer

COUNTRY OF ORIGIN
The Netherlands

ORIGIN
The Welsummer was created at the end of the nineteenth century from a mishmash of 'mongrel' poultry and standard breeds. Besides non-standard farmyard chickens, the Orpington, Malay and Brahma are mentioned. The breed was named after the village of its origin, Welsum on the river IJssel. In 1924, the breed was introduced into the Dutch breeding standard, a date that proved too early. It took at least

another five years before agreement was reached as to its type and color. Even at an early date, there was a lot of foreign interest in

Day-old Welsummer

this breed, while the eggs were also exported abroad.

APPEARANCE
The Welsummer's type is a bit similar to the familiar brown 'battery-cage chicken'. The carriage of the tail is fairly high and in the hen is more or less folded. A single, not really big comb adorns the head. The leg color is yellow, though this will in practice recede to pale yellow and even white in hens that lay a lot. A Welsummer hen must 'flaunt' the fact that

Welsummers

she is a good layer, so her behind should be full and deep. Welsummers have lively reddish bay eyes.

COLORS AND MARKING PATTERNS

In its country of origin, the breed is only found in the variety red partridge, which is considered to be the true, original coloring. In Germany, the Welsummer has been bred in a number of colors. Red partridge is typical of the breed here; actually this is a variant of the regular partridge color. Welsummer cocks always have some reddish brown mottling on their black breast.

QUALITIES

Welsummers are renowned for their beautiful, warm red partridge color and their dark brown

A Welsummer's eggs

eggs that are speckled. The eggs are relatively large; in this breed there are hens laying eggs of around 80g (2¾ oz). Broodiness does occur, but often a bit later in spring. In winter, the birds lay a great deal less. Welsummers can be kept in a closed run, but also thrive when wandering about your yard. The advantage of giving them the free run is that they will forage for themselves, gathering most of their food.

PARTICULARS

A breeder should really be stopped from only getting the eggs hatched that have the best color, for such eggs usually come from the worst laying hens; in good layers, the egg color tends to fade after a couple of weeks from dark to light brown. If the breeder selects the hatching eggs to be a nice dark color, he unwittingly also selects bad laying, that is to say a low egg production.

Wyandotte

COUNTRY OF ORIGIN
The United States of America

ORIGIN
It is not entirely clear what chicken breeds contributed towards the Wyandotte's cre-

Wyandottes, multiple penciled partridge

Wyandotte chick, multiple penciled partridge

ation, but in all probability Cochins were of great influence here. The first reports of Wyandotte-like chickens are from the 1860s. These chickens were known by various names, and 'American Sebrights' and 'Excelsiors' are two of them. One of the first Wyandotte breeders, Houdlette, finally named the breed after his father's ship, the *Wyandotte*. This was the name under which the breed was entered into the American standard of perfection, being officially recognized ten years later. The silver laced variant was the initial color. Later on many other varieties were added.

APPEARANCE

The Wyandotte is quite a large chicken, weighing around 3kg (6½ lbs). Its rounded shape is striking, while this image is enhanced by its full, profuse feathering. These chickens have broad bodies. Their back is of medium length,

Wyandotte cock, silver black laced

Black Wyandottes

A study of a head of a Wyandotte cock

QUALITIES

In recent years, the large Wyandotte's popularity has been surpassed by the breed's diminutive counterpart. These chickens are friendly and trusting creatures. Their placid nature also makes them very suitable for people who would like to have a couple of tame chickens. They are not really keen flyers and therefore can be very well kept running free in the yard or in an open run. These are strong and vigorous birds. The hens are easy and reliable 'broodies' and look after their offspring excellently. The eggs have different colors ranging from a light shade to brown. As the hens get broody rather often, you must take into account that they need a bit more personal care during these periods.

ending with a concave sweep in a tail of medium high carriage. The tail section itself is made up of short, firm tail feathers. When looking at a Wyandotte from the back, the tail has the shape of a V turned upside down. In the cock, the tail is entirely covered by short, well-curved main and lesser sickles. The hen's deep backside shows that she is a good layer, and the breast is deep and beautifully rounded. The breed's stand is not very high and even looks lower because of the full, fluffy feathering. The leg color is yellow. Wyandottes have a typical round and short head. The breed has a rose comb, the spike or leader of which follows the neck line. The comb itself has small rounded points, called 'comb work' in some countries. The ear-lobes are bright red and the color of the eye is a reddish bay.

PARTICULARS

- Animals of this breed look heavier than they actually are, due to a considerable amount of down feathers.
- It is strange that, according to historians, the silver black laced variety – considered this breed's original color – was created by way of Sebright Bantams. It does not seem very logical that this small decorative chicken was essential in creating such a large utility fowl. However, one has no idea what other progenitor might have contributed the silver black laced streak.

Wyandotte hen, silver black laced

COLORS AND MARKING PATTERNS

Wyandottes are bred in many different varieties, including white, black, blue laced, blue self, buff, red, barred, golden black laced, yellow black laced, silver black laced, golden blue laced, yellow white laced, columbian, buff columbian, buff columbian blue marked, columbian blue marked, cuckoo partridge, multiple penciled partridge ('triple laced'), multiple penciled blue partridge, multiple penciled silver partridge, barred and black white mottled.

Crèvecoeur cock, black

14 Table Breeds

Old and new breeds

To those who like animals and certainly to chicken fanciers, terms like 'table breeds' or 'meat breeds' sound rather unfriendly, to say the least. Still, one should never forget that the majority of chicken breeds was originally developed on behalf of some utility. This usefulness might be a good laying capacity of nice-looking or large eggs, and also – as these chickens are fast growers – a bit of inexpensive meat. When farming table breeds, chickens are selected as to how fast they grow and whether they put on meat well, together with a feed intake that is not all too expensive. Nowadays, this is done in a highly professional way, but in previous centuries local table breeds often came about by coincidence. Unintentionally mating up local chickens with standard breeds sometimes resulted in a striking size and weight. Breeding from these animals and selecting for fast growth, among other things, after a while led to a reasonably uniform group of birds. The name of a breed is often connected with the village or region where it arose. A couple of breeds created in the nineteenth century came about in a more intentional way. In the twentieth century, many table breeds were transformed into pure show birds. Commercially regarded, they were made obsolete by table hybrids surpassing the existing breeds in fast growth and moreover managing this on less feed. The chicken fanciers initially breeding these birds for exhibitions saw to it that they were preserved for posterity.

Qualities

Basically, the breeds within this category have in common that they are large and heavy, so in principle these are not chickens that can be lifted up easily by small children. On the other hand, these animals are placid by nature, for a bird does not put on meat by be-

Table fowl are bred for their ability to put on flesh fast.

having nervously and being active. Due to this, they are preeminently suited to active people or families with children. The problem afforded by their size and weight may however be circumvented by choosing a miniature form of these breeds. Such animals you are able to keep in smaller runs, though you will have to give extra attention to their feed. If the birds in this category get too much feed or feed that is too rich in calories, they will easily grow fat.

The Jersey Giant is an impressive table breed.

These breeds are not much given to flying, which is a great advantage for people who want to keep their birds behind a low fencing. Among themselves, these chickens are usually very tolerant. Because they have been selected with a view to meat production, they are less impressive layers than the real egg breeds. On the other hand, broodiness is a quality that is regularly found in this category, and that again is an advantage if you like the idea of having eggs hatched by your own chickens.

Standard breed descriptions

Crèvecoeur

COUNTRY OF ORIGIN
France

ORIGIN
In the book *Toutes les Poules*, published in 1924, the Crèvecoeur is said to be the oldest French breed. Not much more is in fact known about its origin than that these birds were already around in France in the sixteenth century. The region of their origin is the vicinity of the small town of Crèvecoeur in Normandy.

Crèvecoeur hens, blue

The breed falls into the category of crested and bearded fowl, of which it is assumed that they all stem from the Padua, a fairly common bearded and crested breed in the fifteenth and sixteenth century. Darwin also points out the Padua as a forebear of the Crèvecoeur. In France, the breed is kept as a 'producer' of large quantities of tasty meat. Because the original Crèvecoeur was not all that big, they were mated up in the nineteenth century with Dorkings. The present Crèvecoeur is the result of this crossing.

APPEARANCE
The Crèvecoeur's original purpose as a table fowl can be clearly seen from its heavy, massive build. The body is broad and rather long, with an almost horizontal back line, so that the trunk's shape is 'rectangular'. The wings are carried well tucked. The tail is reasonably spread and is characterized by a medium high carriage. The feathers are profuse and broad, which in the cock results in long, broad and well-curved sickles and many lesser sickles. The breed's legs are clean, not all that long and of a dark leaden blue. The head is this breed's hallmark. Apart from a full crest on a skull knob as well as a full three-clump beard, the birds also have a spectacular comb, placed in front of the crest. This comb, called a V-shaped or horn comb, stands up on either side of the head like two horns. These horns merge at the bottom, so that the comb is bulbous there. For practical reasons, French breeders have always been advocates of giving this utility breed a clear view. That is why the crests are not as long and droopy as for instance in the Dutch

Crèvecoeurs at the beginning of the twentieth century

Crested and Bearded Fowl, but crests were preferred to be as globular as possible, having a firm structure. Small wattles are required in this breed, largely disappearing within the beard, and this simply in order to maintain the crest. For if these wattles are systematically bred out, the result is that the crest becomes smaller and smaller and is even lost in the long run.

COLORS AND MARKING PATTERNS

The Crèvecoeur is recognized in merely a few varieties. There are black animals, white ones and self blue ones.

QUALITIES

Originally a utility fowl in the table breed category, the Crèvecoeur is a rather fast grower. To prevent animals losing too much energy due to being quick-tempered and active, they have always been selected for calmness and placidness. For the chicken fancier, this has the advantage that the breed can become really tame and trusting, provided it is treated calmly from 'chickhood' onwards. The presence of a full crest requires regular louse checks. It is important to treat lice straight away in order to prevent the formation of crusts, inflammations and a general loss of condition. Due to their placid nature, this breed can be kept well in a closed run. Still, in that case, you should see to it that the animals get sufficient exercise, as these meat producers will otherwise soon turn to fat. In principle, you need not worry that they will fly out of their run, though roofing it over is recommended to prevent the crests and beards from getting soiled. However, when the weather is fine and dry, these chickens love having the free range. Crèvecoeurs are reasonably good layers, producing big white eggs. Broodiness does occur in this breed, though usually only at the beginning of the summer.

PARTICULARS

- Outside of France, this breed is rather rare, but even in France it does not have many enthusiasts among fanciers.
- There is also a diminutive form of the breed not described in this encyclopedia. Apart

from the size, its qualities are the same as those of the original form described here.

Dorking

COUNTRY OF ORIGIN

The United Kingdom

ORIGIN

How the Dorking arose is hard to say. Still, it is certain that this is a very ancient English breed. As early as Roman times, there were descriptions of chickens closely resembling Dorkings. It is remarkable that despite all of the giant breeds originating in Asia, there is no real evidence that the Dorkings – which with their weight of 4 to 5kg (9–11 lbs) certainly fall into this category – have Asiatic blood. Being a giant among poultry, this breed was already recognized at the beginning of the nineteenth century, finding its way to other countries a couple of decades later. In the nineteenth century, the Dorking was the basis of many different table breeds. Nowadays, people are disinclined to keep these heavy animals.

A study of the head of a Dorking cock

APPEARANCE

The Dorking is a large, broad and heavy breed. The cocks can weigh 5kg (11 lbs); the hens usually send the scales up to around 4(9 lbs). The animals' build is elongated and their stand is low. The breast is broad and deep. The line of the back is practically horizontal, ending in a tail of medium high carriage. Due to the elongated, straight back and deep breast, the shape is somewhat 'rectangular'. The tail is fairly long and is carried well spread. The legs are short, and there are five instead of the usual four toes. The legs are pinkish white. The neck is quite short and full-feathered. The head is rather large and usually has a fairly big single comb, tending to lop at the back in laying hens. There are also rose-combed Dorkings, having a rather crude rose comb that is broad in front and tapers off into a spike or leader, projecting almost horizontally backwards. The Dorking has red ear-lobes and reddish bay eyes.

COLORS AND MARKING PATTERNS

The most favorite color in this breed is silver partridge, but there are also partridge-colored, white, red and cuckoo-colored Dorkings.

QUALITIES

The Dorking is a large, heavy chicken. These animals do not need very much room, but they do need sufficient exercise to prevent them from turning to fat. With a calm approach, they can become reasonably tame. The hens often only lay in season (spring and summer). It is a pity that this breed is frequently so sloppy-feathered. In such cases, the coverts do not link up nicely and the tail is often quite unkempt. Good housing, running free and a run that is not roofed over, so that the rain can drench the birds, help to keep the feathers in good condition. With this breed, there is no harm in a bit of extra animal protein in the form of mealworms. When building and fitting out the henhouse, you should keep in mind the body's size and length. If you for instance make the nest boxes too small for the hens, their feathers will soon get damaged.

PARTICULARS

- On each leg the Dorking has one toe more than other breeds have. This is a rare phenomenon, and most breeds with this feature

have Dorkings as distant ancestors. In origin, we only find this trait in the Dorking, the Silkie and the Sultan. How this 'useless' mutation came about in three so very different breeds is unknown. The heritability of the quality ruling the five toes is 'incompletely dominant'. This means that when mating up a four-toed breed with a five-toed one, all sorts of variants occur. A brood with five toes is a possibility, but the progeny might also have four toes or else either four or five.

• There is also a diminutive form of the breed, not described in this encyclopedia. Apart from the size and the fact that they are very rare, its qualities are the same as those of the original form described here.

Dorking cock, silver partridge

Faverolles

COUNTRY OF ORIGIN
France

ORIGIN
At the end of the eighteenth century and the beginning of the nineteenth, France saw a large and growing market for table fowl. There was hardly any question of standard breeds at that time, and local farmyard chickens were used for meat production. In order to give them a bit more bulk, this local poultry was mated up with mainly Brahmas and Dorkings. From this mishmash the Faverolles emerged. The cradle of this breed stood in the department Seine-et-Oise. The breeding center was the small village of Faverolles, from which the breed takes its name.

APPEARANCE
This breed comes in three different types: the original French Faverolles (*Faverolles claire*), the German Favorelles (*Faverolles foncé*) and the British type. A common feature is that, with their heavy, deep and elongated build, all three of them clearly show that they were

Faverolles hen

175

pinkish white legs that are feathered, as is also the outside toe. As a standard feature, the Faverolles has inherited a fifth toe from the Dorking.

COLORS AND MARKING PATTERNS

The original color of this breed is salmon – the only variety of the French type that is recognized in the Netherlands. In other countries, including France, the *Faverolles claire* is also bred in cuckoo. In Germany and England, one also breeds them in white, black, blue and columbian. In the Netherlands, the German type is also recognized in these varieties.

bred to be table birds. Depending upon the type, the carriage of the broad but fairly short tail is either almost horizontal (the German type) or medium high (the French and English type). The animals have a broad, round head with a rather small single comb. The beard is striking, large and full-feathered, clearly consisting of three clumps, in which the middle one is 'pendulant'. The color of the eye is reddish bay. The Faverolles stands low and has

QUALITIES

Faverolles are very friendly, placid and gentle chickens that, when taken good care of, soon become very affectionate towards their minder. The animals thrive in a run, which need not be all that big. Do take into account that they easily turn to fat. In a small run, one should provide an amount of feed that is finished two hours before the next feeding time.

Faverolles at the beginning of the twentieth century

Of course they also love wandering about, and then the garden fence need not be all that high, as these chickens usually keep their feet on terra firma. As per the breeding objective, they are very fast growers and also develop fast. Furthermore, the hens lay well, both in summer and in winter. The eggs weigh about 60g (2 oz) and have a tinted, light brown shell. Broodiness seldom occurs in these non-sitters.

PARTICULARS

Apart from a fifth toe, the Faverolles has the color salmon as its special feature. The difference in color and markings between the cock and the hen is so great that someone who is not an expert often finds it hard to believe that cock and hen belong to the same breed variant. All three of the breeding directions have interpreted the color in their own way, in which mainly the shade of the ground color varies. This ranges from a pink salmon to a reddish salmon. The hens have this salmon color in their neck, back and saddle as well as on their wing shoulders. The basic color is a delicate salmon shade, edged by almost white lacing. The hen's breast is white with a yellowish hue. The cock's breast and thighs are black and the neck is creamy. The saddle feathers are of the same color as the neck. The back is reddish brown and the shoulders are red with broad white lacing. Thus they appear to be 'mixed'. In the Faverolles of the French breeding direction, the cock's wing shoulders are practically silvery white.

Houdan

COUNTRY OF ORIGIN
France

ORIGIN
In the second half of the nineteenth century, the Houdan was created in the French department Seine-et-Oise. Originally, the breed was called 'Normandy Fowl'. This name clearly refers to one of its ancestors, the Crève-coeur, the Normandy breed *par excellence*. The Crèvecoeur was crossed with local breeds

A study of the head of a Houdan cock

in order to get a heavier and faster growing breed for ending up on the plates of Parisian customers. Many of these birds were taken to market at the district's center, the town of Houdan. Eventually, this became the breed's name. To make them even heavier, they were later on mated up with Dorkings.

APPEARANCE
The Houdan is a heavy, massive looking breed with a long, broad and deep trunk. Its back is fairly long and is carried horizontally, and the breast is broad and deep. The outcome of this is a profile (silhouette) in which one can clearly discern a rectangle known as the 'brick shape'. The wings are carried almost horizontally and well tucked against the body. The tail's carriage is medium high, and the tail itself should be reasonably expanded. Very conspicuous on the clean legs, mottled with black, is the fifth toe. Whether it was there previous to being crossed with the Dorking or whether the toe is a Dorking legacy is difficult to determine with certainty. From the Crèvecoeur, the Houdan has inherited a large, full crest, placed on a bulge on the

Houdans have an extra toe.

skull's crown called the crest knob. Below the head, there is a full and clearly three-clump beard. Its middle section is big and heavy. In the gaps between throat beard and muffs, one finds the cock's short wattles. The comb is unique. It is called a leaf comb, but is in fact a buttercup comb that is positioned almost vertically and has not grown together at the back. The two single combs are thus only connected at the base, bearing a resemblance to a dentated oak leaf.

COLORS AND MARKING PATTERNS

Houdans are only bred in a limited number of varieties. They are found in black mottled, white and lavender, but in practice we only encounter the first color.

QUALITIES

Like any heavy and massive table breed of which the cocks weigh about 3.5kg (7¾ lbs),

Houdan cock, black mottled

the Houdan has the quality of being calm and placid. Because of their nature and their particular features, to wit the crest and beard, these birds can really only be housed in dry and roofed-over coops. The Houdan has become a rare breed, which has not done the breed's original quality of a fast, vigorous grower any good. In origin, Houdans are fairly good layers of large eggs. They do tend to get broody, but the hens are in fact too heavy to be sitters, easily breaking eggs in the nest, so that other eggs are soiled and germ cells die. That is why it is better to hatch eggs by way of either a hen of some other breed or an incubator. Due to the breed's large crest and full beard a special drinker is needed, preventing the beard and crest from becoming wet and dirty. A water bowl with just a little bit of water in it is what this breed needs.

PARTICULARS

The markings of the black mottled Houdan are very characteristic of this breed. They are called black mottled because the markings are not as clear and sharply defined in shape as those of black white mottled fowl. The white

Houdan hen, black mottled

spots on the feather tips are rather more half-moon spangled or crescentic. Typical of this breed is also that the crest's posterior has a lot more white in it than black, the idea being that of a large white stain. After every molting, these spots return larger. Therefore, a Houdan that has lived for several years has more white than black here.

Jersey Giant

COUNTRY OF ORIGIN
The United States of America

ORIGIN
This black table breed arose in New Jersey, North America. Around the year 1880, it was bred from Javas, Brahmas and Croad Langshans. In the 1920s, the breed found its way to Europe, where it was popular for a long time as a table fowl.

APPEARANCE
As its name implies, the first thing that strikes one about the Jersey Giant is its enormous

A study of the head of a Jersey Giant cock

bulk, as the animal's build is so tremendously large, broad, deep and elongated. The back is long and practically horizontal. Its breast is deep and well rounded. Because of their long back and deep breast, the bird looks rectangular, that is to say 'brick-shaped'. The wings are carried well tucked. The tail is quite big, with a well-spread, medium high carriage. The cock's tail is profusely covered by main and lesser sickles. In comparison to the body, the head is rather small and on it we see a medium-sized single comb. The ear-lobes and face are of a lively red. In the dark varieties, the Jersey's eyes are dark brown. The leg color ranges from willow to black with a green luster.

Jersey Giant hen

COLORS AND MARKING PATTERNS
The original color in which this breed was bred is black. Halfway through the twentieth century, the whites came into being. Blue laced Jersey Giants are of a more recent date.

QUALITIES
The Jersey Giant is one of the largest breeds in existence. The cocks can weigh up to 6kg (13 lbs), but are on average about 5kg (11 lbs). In the olden days, there were caponized roosters of this breed weighing eight and even more than 9kg (20 lbs), which is exceptionally heavy. Thus, it is no surprise that the chicks grow very quickly, though for a long time. In order to acquire the desired volume, breeders usually make sure that the chicks are born during the winter months. Then they have enough time to attain their right weight for

Jersey Giant cock

Jersey Giant hen

sheen and the soles of their feet are yellow. Because white soles are dominant over black ones, the first generations of crosses are immediately betrayed upon scrutinizing the color of their soles.

next year's exhibition season. Due to their size, the animals need quite a bit of space. They are unable to fly and therefore it is no problem to let them run free in your garden. The hens of this breed are quite good layers. The color of the eggs is brown and usually they weigh between 58 and 63g (2–2¼ oz). By nature, these birds are calm and very tolerant among themselves. With the right approach, these heavyweights can become really tame. The breed is less suitable for small children, as the animals are difficult to handle due to their size.

PARTICULARS
In order to pass on its bulk, the breed has been mated up with related breeds. Their crossing with the Australorps is well known, and these indeed look a bit like Jersey Giants. The outcome was that the Australorp clearly became heftier. And, the other way round, such crosses have also been done to improve the vitality of this relatively rare breed. However, there is an essential difference between the two breeds: Australorps have practically black legs with white soles, while Jerseys have black legs with a green

Kraienkoppe or Breda Fowl

COUNTRY OF ORIGIN
The Netherlands

ORIGIN
The Kraienkoppe, better known as Breda Fowl, is an old Dutch breed, not taking its name from the vocal quality of the cock, but from its typical head shape that reminds one of a crow (Dutch: *kraai*). How precisely the Breda Fowl came about is unclear, although it is obvious that crested fowl have been of great influence here.

Breda Fowl or Kraienkoppe, chick

A study of the head of a Breda cock.

Breda hen, white

The breed is known as the giant among the Dutch breeds. This does not imply that it is an enormous fowl – the Kraienkoppe weighs around 3kg (6½ lbs) – but simply that the breed is heavier than other old Dutch country fowl. Formerly the cocks were often caponized (neutered), making them a lot heavier. There are stories about Breda cocks weighing 5kg (11 lbs).

APPEARANCE

Bredas have an upright carriage and should be sturdy but also slim. Their backs tend to slope somewhat. The chickens have a high stand, meaning that they are raised considerably on their legs. The breed has a number of typical features. For instance, the animals do not have a comb, though the skull does have a bulge where normally a comb is found. On this protuberance, there are hairlike feathers growing backwards. The wattles are short and round in shape. Also what are called the 'cavernous' or wide nostrils, the vulture hocks and the feathered feet are characteristic of this breed. The tail is carried rather above the horizontal and in the cock is richly adorned with ornamental feathers.

COLORS AND MARKING PATTERNS

The breed is found in several colors: black, white, blue laced and cuckoo. The Breda's black should not have a sheen, and the color has to be a deep black.

QUALITIES

Bredas are likeable, calm birds that can either be given the free run or kept in a limited space. Broodiness hardly ever occurs, and a breeder wanting chicks usually solves this by turning to a foster mother or an incubator. Although this is originally a table breed, it is a slow developer, not growing as fast as other meat producers. However, the hens are excellent layers, so that one can usually also look forward to eggs in winter. The shell of the eggs is white.

PARTICULARS

- In its country of origin, the breed is called *Kraaikop*, but elsewhere it is almost always known as the Breda (next to 'Kraienkoppe', we find 'Breda Fowl' in Great Britain, *Poule de Breda* in France, and *Breda Huhn* in Germany).

Cuckoo-colored Breda hen

removal requires precise anatomical knowledge. When the testicles are taken out, the influence of the male hormones is brought to a halt, so that the cocks grow considerably bigger and heavier. This is the sole reason why, in the eighteenth and nineteenth century, many cocks were caponized.

Niederrhein Fowl

COUNTRY OF ORIGIN
Germany

ORIGIN
Before the arrival of the present poussins (or spring chickens), which are hybrids, there was around 1940 a demand for a fast growing table chicken that would provide short-stringed white meat. For its basis, one turned to the Dutch North Holland Fowl, mated up with the Malines or Mechelen Cuckoo, the Orpington and the Plymouth Rock. The German commercial chicken farmer Jobs, who stood at the cradle of this new utility breed, took pleasure in creating lots of different col-

- As a producer of good meat, the cocks were reared, fattened up and caponized. The latter is a castration technique that is no longer used. In a cock, the testicles are found inside the body, at the side of the back, and their

Breda cock, cuckoo

Niederrheiners

Niederrheiner cock

ors, seeking the advice of the German geneticist Regenstein on behalf of this. This resulted in many extraordinary and often new variants, like yellow cuckoo and blue cuckoo.

APPEARANCE
The Niederrheiner is a fairly heavy chicken, the cock weighing 3.5 to 4kg (7³/₄–9 lbs). Its body is broad, full and deep. Its back is quite long, ending with a short concave sweep in the tail section. The tail is of medium length, not carried much above the horizontal and is somewhat spread. In the cocks, the main tail feathers are almost entirely covered by the ornamental feathers. The wings are carried almost horizontally against the body. As a legacy of both the North Holland and the Mechelen Fowl, the backside (stern) is full and deep. The legs are of normal length, clean and pinkish white. The head sports a single comb, which is erect in the cock as well as in the hen. The ear-lobes are red and the eyes preferably a reddish bay.

COLORS AND MARKING PATTERNS
This breed is recognized in many exceptional varieties. Thus, there are Niederrhein Fowl in yellow cuckoo, blue cuckoo, cuckoo partridge, birchen and blue.

QUALITIES
Befitting their original purpose, Niederrhein Fowl are fast growing chickens, soon reaching adulthood. The fact that the breed was developed as a meat producer by way of several heavy breeds has resulted in their being placid and calm. A person taking good care of them will therefore have little trouble in getting the chicks to grow up to be trusting and very tame chickens. They are certainly not great flyers, so that you can easily keep them within a fencing that need not be closed from above. As the breed easily turns to fat, it is recommended that they have a fairly large run in order to get enough exercise. Rake a little fine grain into the run's loose litter, so that the animals keep on moving about. Niederrheiners are renowned for being good layers. The hens lay around 175 large, light-colored eggs a year.

PARTICULARS
- Notably, the yellow cuckoo variety is unique to this breed. However, it is rather similar to the New Hampshire's chestnut red color, and both cock and hen have a few hackles streaked with black in the shaft. Thus the color is interrupted in bars due to the cuckoo factor. In this way, one

Niederrheiner cock

North Holland Fowl

COUNTRY OF ORIGIN
The Netherlands

ORIGIN
In the Zaan region of the Dutch province of North Holland, at the beginning of the twentieth century, next to egg-layers one also kept table fowl to be consumed as young meat chickens. There was a lot of demand for these three months old animals, notably in Amsterdam. In order to attain larger and faster growing birds, one imported Malines or Mechelen Fowl from Belgium. However, this was not a success, as the breed afforded many problems when reared, due to the Zaan region's colder and particularly wetter climate. The Malines Fowl was therefore crossed with the local non-standard chickens, which that were reasonably resistant to this climate. Later on, it was also mated up with the Plymouth Rock to upgrade the laying capacity.

APPEARANCE
North Hollands clearly show in their appearance that they were originally kept for their meat. These are large, broad and heavy chickens. The weight of the cocks can reach between 3.5 and 4kg (7¾–9 lbs). In spite of their bulk, they are not 'rectangular' creatures, but have a rounded body shape. The breast is deep and broad, with a well-rounded breast line. The back is fairly long and broad, ending with a continuous concave sweep in the tail. The North Holland's tail is conspicuous due to its high carriage, relatively short feathers

gets light and dark gray bars in the black feather parts. The golden brown feather parts alternately have light yellow and golden yellow barring.

- There is also a diminutive form of the breed, not described in this encyclopedia. Apart from the size, its qualities are the same as those of the original form described here.

Day-old Niederrheiner chick

North Hollands are also called North Holland Blues.

North Holland hen

North Holland cock

and moderate spread. Because of this, it looks rather small in comparison to the large body. The breed's head is big, having a medium-sized single comb and red ear-lobes. The color of the eye is a reddish bay. In a table bird, the color of the skin is important. It is true that consumers tend to value a light colored skin on a bit of chicken. That is why this breed is white-skinned and has pinkish white legs.

COLORS AND MARKING PATTERNS
Although originally the North Holland was also bred in the color white, nowadays only a single variety is recognized, to wit cuckoo.

QUALITIES
A table fowl's most important qualities are fast growth and a well-developed fleshy body. This is usually accompanied by a placid nature, as a lot of nervous moving about takes energy, which goes at the expense of growing and putting on meat. That is why, being a true meat producer, the North Holland Fowl is a placid breed that seldom or never flies.

When taken care of well and approached calmly, these animals very easily become tame. However, it is not a breed for small children, as the birds are too large. The breed's diminutive form is far more suitable for them. The animals can thrive is enclosed runs with limited space, though in that case one should take care not to give them too much feed, as they grow fat easily. Also, you can let them run free, because being so heavy they are not keen flyers. Among themselves, the birds are

North Holland chick, six weeks old (cockerel)

North Holland hen

A study of the head of a North Holland cock

tolerant and certainly not looking for a fight. The hens lay reasonably well in winter and have light brown eggs. In the past, egg counts have been recorded that were as high as 175. The eggs are big.

PARTICULARS
This chicken's color and markings formerly gave it the nickname 'North Holland Blue'. For, in this breed the cuckoo variety is not a distribution of black and white, but more of a dark gray bar alternated by a light gray one. In the hens, the dark bars are twice as broad as the light ones. When seen from a distance, this coloring gives the idea that the hens look bluish gray. As it is the only color in which the breed comes, breeders soon put 'blue' into the breed's name.

Sussex

COUNTRY OF ORIGIN
The United Kingdom

ORIGIN
The beginning of the nineteenth century saw the development of the Sussex in the South-East of England. In its creation, one made use of non-standard country fowl and large, heavy breeds like the Dorking and Brahma. It was exported abroad only a century later. Nowadays, the breed is within the 'middle bracket' in regards to its number of fanciers; it has never been excessively popular, nor was there ever a lack of interest in it.

Sussex Fowl, porcelain

APPEARANCE

The Sussex is a fairly heavy chicken of a medium-high stand and with a 'rectangular' body shape. The tail has a low carriage, hardly above the horizontal line. It is well spread and the main tail feathers are medium long. The cock has rather short main and lesser sickles that cover the tail well. The Sussex has a broad and deep breast. Its leg color is white, also called pinkish white, and its ear-lobes are bright red, as is its featherless facial skin. The head sports a medium-sized single comb. The color of the eyes is reddish bay.

COLORS AND MARKING PATTERNS

The breed is raised in red porcelain (speckled), columbian, buff columbian, red columbian, fawn, brown, white, cuckoo and grayish silver.

Sussex cock, porcelain

Sussex cock, columbian

that keep a close watch over their chicks. The chicks grow up fast, and are fairly precocious and sprightly. Flying is not their second nature, so that one can easily let them run free in the garden or keep them in a run without roofing.

QUALITIES

The Sussex is a very friendly and calm chicken with an agreeable temperament. If you would like to have a really tame chicken, then it is an obvious choice. Their calm behavior towards people is kept up within the flock. If you have sufficient space, it is even possible to keep several cocks together. The Sussex is a robust and strong chicken, which makes it a suitable breed for beginning fanciers. The hens are excellent layers, usually also producing eggs during winter with some regularity. Furthermore, they are often broody, and are known to be superb mothers

Sussex hens, columbian

15 Multi-Purpose Breeds

Development of dual-purpose breeds

As can be seen from the descriptions of the previous breed categories, breeds may be segmented on the basis of their original purpose into layer breeds and table breeds, among others. Apart from these two groups, there are a number of breeds in which one has attempted to combine, within a single breed, a good layer's qualities with a good drumstick, achieving commercial value for both hens and cocks. Breeds falling into this composite category are sometimes referred to as 'dual-purpose breeds', and most breeds in this group were developed during the last century. This is understandable when we look at the price developments in both eggs and chicken meat. When comparing the first quarter of the twentieth century with the last quarter, there appears to be very little change in the price of eggs and chicken meat, so, relatively seen, they only became slightly more expensive than they were at the century's outset. On the other hand, the cost price of an egg and of a kilo of chicken meat has increased manifold. Chicken owners at the beginning of the last century were already aware of this. They tried to reduce their costs by breeding chickens that served a double purpose, and the dual-purpose breeds are the result of this.

Amrock hen

Qualities

For you as a chicken fancier, these dual-purpose breeds have the advantage of being calmer and less 'fly-happy' than most true layer breeds. Also, they grow accustomed to their minder more easily, while some of these breeds can even get downright tame. Apart from this, these birds often have a very fetching appearance and lay a great number of eggs.

Breed descriptions

Amrock

COUNTRY OF ORIGIN
The United States of America

ORIGIN
The Amrock was bred from the same initial material as the Plymouth Rock. The two can therefore be considered as one and the same breed coming in two types: the Plymouth

Amrock hens

Rock, which should be regarded as a breed developed as a show bird at a very early date, and the Amrock, which, from its creation until as late as about forty years ago, was mainly bred for the sake of utility. In the Amrock, for a long time its appearance was completely subsidiary. Until the 1950s, the Amrock was highly popular as a utility fowl and was kept commercially in many countries. However, during that period, egg hybrids were also developed and as the industry made more money on these, the Amrock was left to the fanciers. They have improved its type and color, and nowadays the Amrock need no longer be surpassed in beauty by the Plymouth Rock

APPEARANCE

Amrocks are rather large chickens weighing around 3.5kg (7¾ lbs). The Amrock's type is sometimes referred to as being of a 'church-bell shape'. It is indeed true that the hen's back and tail line, combined with the neck, rather reminds one of the shape of an old-fashioned bronze bell, as one might find in church steeples. The back's line is medium long, ending with a continuous hollow sweep in the tail. The tail itself is broad at the base, has a medium high carriage and is almost en-

A study of the head of an Amrock cock

tirely spread. The breast line is deep and well rounded. The head is adorned by a single comb and there are red ear-lobes. The color of the eye is reddish bay. The Amrock's stand is medium high and it has clean yellow legs.

COLORS AND MARKING PATTERNS

This breed only comes in a single variety, namely barred.

QUALITIES

Amrocks are fairly quiet, friendly chickens, that can become very tame when approached in a calm way. The animals show little tendency to fly and can therefore be kept in a garden that does not have a very high fence. The hens are famed for being excellent layers of relatively large brown eggs. These birds are generally non-sitters– a phenomenon shared by most chickens in the layer category. The chicks grow up fast and are precocious. At the start of the laying season, the hens have deep yellow legs, but this color fades to almost white under the influence of prolific laying. After the laying and molting period is done, the yellow returns to the legs. This can be influenced by providing feed that contains more natural coloring agents, as are found in carrots, kale and La Plata corn.

PARTICULARS

The barred marking in which this breed is raised has a unique feature. The cocks have white and black bars of the same width, while the black bars in the hens are twice as broad

Six week old Amrock chicks

Bielefelder

COUNTRY OF ORIGIN
Germany

ORIGIN
This well-known breed was created by the poultry keeper G. Roth in the German town of Bielefeld, from which it takes its name. It was first exhibited under the breed name *Deutsches Kennhuhn*, and later on acquired the name *Bielefelder Kennhuhn*. The Bielefelder was recognized in Germany in the year 1980.

APPEARANCE
The Bielefelder's body shape is best described as 'rectangular'. In poultry parlance, this is also called 'brick-shaped'. The tail is carried well spread and in line with the back. The breed is single-combed, has yellow legs, and its feathering is moderate. The color of the eye is bay. The Bielefelder is in the larger poultry category, with adult cocks weighing around 4kg (9 lbs).

as the white ones. The reason is that the heritability of markings is sex-linked. Male animals always have the factor for barring twice, which is visible in the birds' appearance. Amrock chicks are autosexing, meaning that the sexes can be distinguished at a very early age, purely by their color and markings. The heads of the hen chicks are clearly more dusky than those of their brothers.

COLORS AND MARKING PATTERNS
The Bielefelder's original color is cuckoo red partridge (*kennfarbig*). This combination of

Bielefelder hen

Amrock hen

Bielefelder cock

chicks and the large white spot on their head. Because of this, one does not have to sex the chicks in order to tell the cocks from the hens with 100% certainty.

La Flèche

COUNTRY OF ORIGIN
France

ORIGIN
The breed takes its name from La Flèche, a small town in France. It is an ancient breed, being mentioned in French documents as early as the fifteenth century. It is akin to the crested fowl that were common in Western Europe in the seventeenth and eighteenth century. Outside of France, this breed is rarely seen, but also in France it does not have many fanciers.

APPEARANCE
The La Flèche is quite a large chicken, raised rather high on its legs. Its body is long and fairly broad. The tail section is big and its carriage is spread. The tail of the cock has well-developed ornamental feathering, consisting of broad and well-curved main and lesser sickles. In most varieties, the leg color is dark slate. The head, also called a 'devil's head', makes the La Flèche an exceptional breed. The resemblance to the devil is understandable if we look at the comb's shape, which consists of two little round horns placed upright on the head, parallel to each other. Just behind this comb are a few frizzy feathers. This last remnant of a crest shows that the breed is akin to the crested fowl. This also goes for the 'nose

A study of the head of a La Flèche hen

red partridge with cuckoo markings causes all black feather parts to change to cuckoo. In the hen, the breast is not meant to have any cuckoo markings, something that is difficult to achieve. A number of breeders is involved in creating a silver variant, called silver cuckoo.

QUALITIES
The breed has been developed as a 'layer-cum-table breed'. Apart from the fact that the chicks grow up smoothly and fast, the hens are famed for being good layers. As the breed has a bit of Asiatic blood in its veins, young hens tend to lay on in winter– a feature of many Asian breeds. The eggs are of a good size and have a light brown color. The breed's character is placid and affectionate, so that the birds become very tame. With some 'candy' in the form of mixed grain, you can soon get them to feed from your hand. It is fine to let Bielefelders enjoy wandering about freely, but they also feel at home within a closed run.

PARTICULARS
As both the cuckoo factor and the gold factor are sex-linked in chickens, true-breeding cocks are far lighter in color. This is seen in the lighter shade of the fluff in newly born cock

La Flèche hen

plugs' in the beak's upper region, which clearly protrude and are wide or 'cavernous'– a feature found only in crested fowl. The ear-lobes are white and the wattles are quite long.

COLORS AND MARKING PATTERNS
In its country of origin and in most other countries, the La Flèche breed comes in four colors, namely black, white, cuckoo and blue laced. In Scandinavia, only the black variety is recognized, which is also the breed's original color.

QUALITIES
This animals can be left to run free, as long as you provide them with sufficient space. For they are able to fly very high and will certain-

La Flèches at the beginning of the twentieth century

ly do so. By feeding the birds in their roost before it gets dark, you can teach them to spend the night there. Otherwise, there is a good chance that a La Flèche will choose some high spot in a tree to roost in. The animals are not aggressive, but very rarely become tame. They produce large white eggs, but were originally also bred for being fast growers, for their sturdy build and tasty meat.

PARTICULARS
- The exceptional V-shaped comb, also called 'horn comb', and the fact that their original color is black has provided this bird with the nicknames 'devil-headed chicken' and 'Satan's fowl'.
- In France, the breed is still raised for its original purpose. Thus, they are selected for body mass, so that these birds tend to look rather plump. German breeders have bred a more slender and elegant La Flèche.

Langshan

COUNTRY OF ORIGIN
Germany

ORIGIN
The Langshan is a German breeding product, developed at the beginning of the twentieth century from crossings of the original Croad Langshans with Minorcas and Plymouth Rocks. German breeders had a good layer in mind, which – contrary to the original Croad Langshan – would have clean legs. The Croad's stand was nevertheless retained, and was even bred in more extremely. For the Croad Langshan, hailing from China, this meant practically the end of its justification as a breed in Germany.

APPEARANCE
The 'German' Langshan is a large, heavy chicken, of which the cocks can weigh between 4 and 4.5kg (9–10 lbs). The animals have a striking back line that runs up sharply. Regardless of angle, this back line ends in a tail carried somewhat above the horizontal and more or less spread. In the cocks, the main tail feathers are totally covered by short, broad sickles. The

wings are well tucked against the body. The neck is fairly long and slightly arched. The head is small and rather narrow. On the head, there is a small single comb with five broad points. The ear-lobes are red, as is the featherless part of the face. The eyes of this breed are brownish black in the black variety and reddish brown in white birds. Langshans are required to have

a high stand. For this, it is necessary that the shanks and the thighs are of more than medium length. The latter feature is not easy to breed.

COLORS AND MARKING PATTERNS

The Langshan is only bred in a few colors: black, white and blue laced. An enterprising breeder has recently started to raise barred Langshans. Unfortunately, the Langshan of the German type discussed here is not found in Germany very much, and the breed is also rare in other countries.

QUALITIES

Langshans are strong, robust chickens that grow up rapidly and lay many cream-colored eggs of an impressive size. The animals thrive when running free. Due to their weight, they are certainly not good flyers, so that a fencing around their area need not be very high. The birds also feel at home in a run. In a flock, the animals are tolerant and seldom cause problems. By nature, they are fairly placid and with a little patience and attention can become tame soon. This is a necessary quality in the breed, as their high stature or carriage does need some training for exhibitions. For, in the run, these animals often show their erectness of carriage perfectly, but at a show, where they

La Flèche cock

Langshan cock, black

White Langshan hens

may be detracted by all sorts of new impressions, they often tend to stoop, letting their wings sag slightly. Experienced breeders circumvent this problem by often picking up their birds, getting them get used to the exhibition pen and by correcting the birds' carriage by hand. Even after a few trainings, the animals cotton on to this trick, so that at the slightest

A study of the head of a white Langshan cock

touch they jump into the position that is characteristic of the breed.

PARTICULARS

A diminutive form of the Langshan has also been bred. It is not described in this encyclopedia, but, apart from the size, its qualities are the same as those of the original form described here.

Sulmtaler

COUNTRY OF ORIGIN
Austria

Langshans

ORIGIN

In Austria, in the valley of the river Sulm to the south and south-west of the town of Graz, the climate is mild and the food range varied. Local small farms have made good use of this and have concentrated on poultry farming, alongside of winegrowing and arable farming. At one time, there was a great demand for large, heavy chickens. Initially, one attempted to breed these by selecting the largest and heaviest birds from the endemic Altsteirers. In that way, one succeeded in getting capons, fit for the slaughter, with a weight between 3.5 and 4.5kg (7¾ –10 lbs). Subsequently, the Altsteirers were mated up with Cochins, Brahmas and Langshans. The outcome of this was reduced laying but a bigger bird. A further cross with Houdans and Dorkings followed. Armin Arbeiter from Feldhof set to work with this hotchpotch and by way of selection managed to achieve a uniformity in size and type. He

195

called the newly acquired composite breed Sulmtaler. Unfortunately, it is very rare in many countries. Both in its country of origin and in Germany, its following is a bit larger. Since the turn of the century, the breed also became known in England, but as yet has not been standardized there, always being exhibited in the 'rare-breed' category.

APPEARANCE
Sulmtalers are quite big chickens with

Sulmtaler cock

a rather elongated build and a deep, broad body. The horizontal back is fairly long. The short tail section is well spread, its carriage being medium high. The neck is not very

Sulmtaler cock

Sulmtaler hen

long and rather densely feathered in cocks. A Sulmtaler sports a small tuft, following the line of the head. Right in front of this tuft there is a single comb of which the blade is quite short and the points ('spikes') are not deeply indented. In the hen, the front of the comb is folded in a double wave or twist. This is called an 'S-shaped comb'. The ear-lobes are white and the color of the eye is bay. As a typical table breed's feature, the Sulmtaler has white skin, which one can tell from its white or pinkish white legs.

COLORS AND MARKING PATTERNS
The breed is found in the colors white and wheaten.

QUALITIES
Sulmtalers are mainly calm creatures that are easily tamed. These animals are best kept in a closed run, for in spite of their voluminous appearance (cocks can weigh up to 4kg (9 lbs)), they are excellent flyers. The hens lay well, their eggs usually being of a light shade and weighing 55g (2 oz) on average. Sulmtalers very rarely get broody. These are birds that grow up quickly and without problem.

Wheaten Sulmtaler chicks are born yellow. After two and a half weeks, one can already tell the cocks from the hens by the sprouting pin feathers.

Vorwerk

COUNTRY OF ORIGIN
Germany

ORIGIN
This breed takes its name from its developer, the German O. Vorwerk. At the outset of the last century, he wanted to breed a good utility fowl with a belted marking (see 'Lakenvelder'), though not in combination with a white trunk, but with a buff one. These chickens would allegedly not look dirty as soon as white ones. At the breed's starting point are, among others, Lakenvelders, Orpingtons, Ramelslohers and Andalusians. In 1919, the Vorwerk was recognized in Germany. After the Second World War, the breed was all but lost and has been reconstructed with the aid of some remnants.

APPEARANCE
One's first impression of the breed is that of a Lakenvelder with a different ground color. On closer inspection however, there appear to be a number of marked differences. Although this breed – just like the Lakenvelder – falls into the country fowl category, the chickens have a somewhat heavier and fuller build and carry their tail a little lower. The tail is medium long and not entirely spread. Due to its lower carriage, the bird looks a bit longer than the Lakenvelder does. Its breast is broad and fairly deep. The legs are slate blue and of medium length. The head has a medium-sized single comb and white ear-lobes. The color of the eye is a yellowish bay.

COLORS AND MARKING PATTERNS
The breed is only found with black belted markings and a buff-colored body. This color pattern takes a lot of time to develop, and often the final color and markings are only in evidence after the third molt.

QUALITIES
Due to the unusual markings and color combination, this breed is unique among chickens. The Vorwerk is not fussy about its surroundings and may therefore be kept either wandering freely about the yard or else in a closed run. However, these birds are good flyers, so one should bear this in mind. The hens lay a considerable number of white eggs, usually also in winter. The animals are lively, active and not shy, and with a little tact become reasonably tame. If there is enough room, the cocks usually tolerate one another. Chicks of this breed are fast growers and are very vigorous.

Vorwerk hen

Vorwerk cock

16 Game Fowl Breeds

Backgrounds

The category of game fowl breeds stands out due to its diversity in color, shape and carriage, the latter sometimes being called 'station' in these birds. However, all of its members have one thing in common: they were originally selected for their 'gameness', their desire to engage in prolonged fights with one another. The basis of these breeds is ancient. From time immemorial, mankind has felt an urge to set animals upon one another; in the olden days probably due to lack of other amusement. In many domesticated species, this has resulted in the development of a number of specific fighting breeds, for instance game fish, pitbull terriers and fighting bulls. Putting these animals in the ring or pit with the intention ot letting

them fight to show which is the strongest, is generally regarded as cruel in Western countries. In most countries of the Western world such fights are therefore prohibited. In the United Kingdom, where animal fights were highly popular for a long time, they were banned as early as 1849. In many countries in Asia, however, it is still an accepted pastime, being part of a lifestyle, sometimes even of an ancient culture. For that matter, many of the breeds kept for exhibition purposes in the West are Asiatic in origin.

Every country and even every region has a preference for a particular style of fighting. It is not always a question of the death of one of the cocks deciding the game ('dead game'). Many a breed is entered into a fight until the moment there is a clear winner, whereupon

Cock fight in Indonesia at the end of the nineteenth century

Shamos are impressive birds.

A study of the head of a Shamo cock

that they can enter the pit in optimum condition.

General appearance

The various aspects of the general appearance of breeds within this category are: a challenging, often upright station (carriage); hard and highly developed muscles; high, wide shoulders and powerfully muscled wings; a tight, moderately developed feathering. The latter aspect is of great advantage to the birds during a fight, as their opponents then have less grip on them. Being hard-feathered is clearly in evidence in most breeds, and manifests itself in a featherless breastbone. Also, the ornamental feathers of neck and saddle are shorter than in country fowl, and as a rule, only part of the neck is covered by hackles. It was very important that the vulnerable parts were well protected. This is obvious from the head's highly developed skin folds, seeing to it that the eyes are well protected under the 'eyebrows'. In most breeds, the comb is very small and set well forward on the head. The wattles are also very small, thus reducing the chance that the opponent can get a grip on them. The beak, an important weapon in combat, is powerful and short.

the birds are separated. The various fighting styles have resulted in a great variety of breeds. Here, the colors of the animals are hardly important at all. Once in a while, there appears to be a preference for a certain color pattern, but the main criteria of selection are strength, fighting style and the will to fight, 'to be game'. Before the birds go into the ring to fight, they have to be completely developed and at least a year and a half old. The animals are perfectly taken care of and trained, so

Aseels at the beginning of the twentieth century

200

QUALITIES

In the show breeds character is still foremost, and color and markings are of only secondary importance. As a rule, it is the animals' provocative attitude and their often fierce, shrewd expression that makes them so attractive to fanciers. If you consider getting a breed from this category, you must certainly keep this in mind. For these are not birds that can be housed together with other breeds, and also amongst themselves they can cause problems. Both cocks and hens show the fighting spirit when it is a question of their rank in the pecking order. Thus taking a chicken out of the flock or putting new animals in should be avoided as far as possible. If you start breeding these varieties, you must remember that the brood of chicks to be reared should not be too large and will require quite a bit of space because of the possibilities of hiding and fleeing. Against these disadvantages there is the advantage that most game fowl are extremely tame and trusting towards the person taking care of them. This makes them very suitable for people who want calm birds they can bond with. As layers, all game fowl are disappointing. This will not surprise you if you take into account that this quality has been considered subsidiary from time immemorial. Laying usually remains limited to spring and part of the summer. Most Asian breeds tend to get broody. The hens are fierce, highly defensive and caring mothers.

Breed Descriptions

Aseel

COUNTRY OF ORIGIN
India

ORIGIN
The Aseel (or 'Asil' as it is also spelled) falls within the oldest category of game fowl breeds. This group stood in high esteem with the upper classes of India. These chickens were also familiar in the surrounding countries and there were many different varieties. From 1750 onwards, Europeans regularly brought back this type of fowl to Europe. The present show

Aseel cock, partridge mottled

Aseel has been bred from all sorts of varieties of these animals. In a number of countries, including the Netherlands and Germany, there are two breeding directions: the Madras Aseel, which is the largest of the two, and the 'regular' Aseel.

APPEARANCE
The Aseel is a broadly built bird with a low stand, high shoulders and a provocative carriage. Its short trunk is rather egg-shaped and is carried upright. Due to its tight, sparse feathering the breastbone is visible. The short wings are carried parallel to the incline of the body

Aseel hen, partridge mottled

(rather sloping). The small short head has both thick 'eyebrows' ('beetling brow') and a light pearl iris, giving the animal a distinctive appeal. The comb has three low lengthwise ridges. Wattles are either lacking or underdeveloped, and the throat's dewlap (a small skin fold) is practically featherless. The muscular thighs are quite visible. The leg is yellow, irrespective of color or feather markings.

COLORS AND MARKING PATTERNS

In game fowl, not as much importance is attached to color as it is in most other breeds. Of the Aseel, there are many different varieties recorded that are exhibited on the European continent, including white, partridge mottled, wheaten, fawn, black white mottled and silver necked blue. In Great Britain, these birds may in fact have any color whatsoever.

QUALITIES

Among themselves, Aseel cocks are aggressive. When rearing young cockerels, fierce fights regularly break out to determine precedence, so sufficient space and possibilities for escape

Aseel cock, partridge mottled

are necessary to raise these creatures successfully. Many breeders run an adult cock together with a flock of growing cockerels. He will be the boss for a long time and keep in hand the ranking fights. However, at a particular moment the tide turns and the cockerels start 'running rings around him'. From that moment on, it is wise to house all of the cocks separately. Also the hens can be disagreeable towards one another. However, this is not a general rule, but it depends on whether they have grown up together and on the amount of space they have. Aseels have strong wings with quite a bit of lift. Still, they are not really flighty, also because they are not shy and very curious indeed. Usually Aseels soon become trusting towards their owner. The breed is mostly monogamous, therefore it is better to keep the animals in pairs. The hens lay few eggs, but are good sitters and excellent, very fierce mothers.

PARTICULARS

Next to the regular Aseel, there is also a kind known as the Madras Aseel. This animal is not only larger, it also differs in type. At first sight, it looks like a more sturdily built game fowl, with a carriage that is less erect. The skin of the throat does not have a highly developed dewlap as in the regular Aseel. The Madras Aseel is only found in one color that is typical of the breed and closely resembles blue wheaten.

Indian Game Fowl or Cornish

COUNTRY OF ORIGIN
The United Kingdom

ORIGIN
At the end of the eighteenth century, the British merchant navy brought quite a number of game fowl from Asia, usually Aseels from different breeding directions. As fighting cocks, these Aseels were superior to the English game fowl, so that English breeders, notably in the counties Devon and Cornwall (hence 'Cornish'), mated them up with Old English Game, among others. The Aseels they

A study of the head of a Cornish cock

A study of the head of a Cornish hen

used were of the large, broad and heavy Madras type. The crosses acquired in this way were extraordinarily broad and had a fairly low stand. However, in fights they proved too clumsy and slow, which is the reason that the breed was never really used as a game fowl. The breeders soon realized this and, due to its enormous width, started to develop the breed into a table fowl. As such, the 'Indian fighter' stood at the cradle of the modern broad-breasted table hybrids.

APPEARANCE

The Indian Game or Cornish (as it is known in the United States) is sometimes called 'the bulldog among poultry breeds'. With its massive build and extremely 'straddle-legged' stand, the Cornish indeed looks a bit like a bulldog. The cocks of this large, heavy breed weigh between 4 and 4.5kg (9–10 lbs). The Cornish's build can be described as 'cube-shaped', meaning that the bird's trunk is almost as long as it is deep and broad. Its back tends to slope slightly and the shoulders are well developed, being held a little away from the body and somewhat prominently above the back's line. The thick tail is of average length. The head is fairly big and broad, while the broad skull forms the 'beetling eyebrows' above the rather deep-set eyes. On top of the

head, there is a comb with three low lengthwise ridges. The ear-lobes are red and the eyes, having a fierce expression, are pearl-colored. The short tail is carried closely folded (gamy or whipped). The thighs of the Cornish are medium in length, broad and muscular, while its shanks are short, stout and round. The legs are set widely apart, the shanks being clearly positioned on the outside of the body. The muscles of these chickens are very well – developed. The birds are also very tight and hard-feathered, the plumage being so hard that main tail feathers and flights tend to break easily.

Double laced Cornish hen

Double laced Cornish cock

COLORS AND MARKING PATTERNS

The breed is only recognized in a few varieties, to wit: double laced; red white double laced; and white and red white laced.

QUALITIES

Cornish are chickens for lovers of the extreme. These fighting cocks are not easy to breed and in rearing require extra care from their minder. In order to attain their enormously broad and deep build, they need more than the free run and a handful of grain. A large amount of carbohydrates boosts the development of the extremely broad breast muscles. However, you should beware of these animals growing too rapidly and becoming very heavy at an early age, for the skeleton must be able to carry the weight effortlessly. By nature, this breed is very calm and placid and can become really tame. Housing them in smaller runs is no problem for these chickens, though in that case you will have to watch out that they do not grow over-fat. Giving them free run on grassy land provides them with a little more diversion. The animals are very hardy and can stand all kinds of weather. They are absolutely unable to fly, as they are too heavy. Although they never

have been used as game fowl, they have inherited the fighting spirit from the Aseels and the Old English fighters. They are very friendly and tame towards people, but they are less tolerant of other animals. The cocks in this breed are quite monogamous. Thus it is best to make up a breeding flock of a cock and a hen, or two hens at the most. The hens lay very few eggs, only doing so in spring. However, this is more than enough for the breed's survival.

PARTICULARS

- Because of their extremely broad build and very low stand, breeding Cornish is hard, as fertilization is a problem with these giants. Experienced breeders are aware of this and in forming a breeding flock select a broad but not too low-standing cock, which is able to successfully fertilize the hens.
- The color red white double laced is sometimes called 'jubilee'. This name refers to the first time this variety was shown to the general public, in the year Queen Victoria celebrated her jubilee, being a reigning monarch for sixty years.

Malay

REGION OF ORIGIN

Asia

ORIGIN

The first imports of this purely Asiatic breed took place as early as 1830. It is impossible to determine this giant breed's origin. There are written descriptions of fighting cocks dating from long before our era. Some theories claim that the original Malay is a direct descendant of a giant fowl that is now extinct. The fact is that Malays have contributed to the creation of many large poultry breeds. After the first imports, the original Malay was developed by mainly English and German breeders into the exhibition birds we know today.

APPEARANCE

Malays are real giants among poultry. Not only are they huge, but they also have an extremely high stand and long necks. An adult Malay

Wheaten Malay cock

Malay hen, wheaten

Malay chicks

cock weighs about 4.5kg (10 lbs) and can easily measure 90cm (3 ft) from the ground to the crown of its head. It is a breed with typical game fowl features, such as being tight-feathered, and having hard muscles and a short head. On its head there is a small walnut comb. The skull is broad and the animal is very clearly 'beetle-browed'. Due to this, the eyes are set rather deep and are well-protected. The yellow beak is stout and powerful. The eyes have the typical 'pearl iris'. The Malay's shape is sometimes referred to as being 'triple arched'. The first arch is made up of the long neck, which is slightly bent. The second arch is formed by the wings, of which the pinions are carried on the saddle, as well as by its steeply sloping back. The third arch is due to the tail being carried folded and below the horizontal. The shoulders are wide and angular, standing out slightly from the body. The stand is extremely high. In order to achieve this, both thighs and shanks must be long. All this emanates power and toughness.

COLORS AND MARKING PATTERNS

The color in which Malays are usually bred is wheaten. Apart from this, there are also white, bloodwing white and red porcelain.

QUALITIES

Malays are truly 'shapely' birds, and that is the only aim with which they are bred. Originally they were not nearly so extreme in type. Their present type would have more disadvantages than advantages in a fight. By nature the breed is self-confident, meaning that these chickens can become extremely affectionate towards the person taking care of them and thus very tame. Among themselves, they are not so tolerant.

The cocks are very headstrong and do not avoid each other, but in fact seek confrontation. Hens that are not familiar with each other can really get into scrapes. Do not keep these animals in large groups for the outcome will be fighting. You can best house one cock with one or at the most two hens. Preferably separate the growing birds at an early age by sex. Small groups of around six pullets are usually satisfactory. Run young cockerels together with an old dominant cock and see to it that they have enough space. In that way, they can remain together a bit longer. As soon as they start quarreling, you will have to decide on individual housing. Malays are strong, hardy birds that can stay outside in all weather conditions. A dry and draft-free abode to spend the night in is in fact all they need. You will have to keep in mind the great height of these animals when putting down feeders and drinkers. Do not place these on the ground, but on a board about 45cm (1½ ft) above ground level. The hens do not lay many eggs, and the laying period is usually limited to a couple of months a year.

Modern English Game Fowl

COUNTRY OF ORIGIN
The United Kingdom

ORIGIN
The Modern English Game Fowl or Modern Game was developed after the British ban on cock fights in 1849. Due to this, people grew more interested in having the game breeds compete at exhibitions, where it was not a question of fighting spirit and stamina, but of good looks. Opinions about the 'ideal type' tend to vary. A number of breeders mated the Old English Game Fowl with Malays. More-

Partridge Modern English Game Fowl hen

over, one selected strictly for slenderness, aiming to breed an attractive, exhibitable game fowl that no longer resembled the rather cobby and broad-shaped Old English Game.

APPEARANCE

This breed stand outs because of its very long legs, giving it an extremely high station. Its image is reinforced by a long, thin neck, which is the result of being tight-feathered. The tail is very tightly folded (gamy) and carried almost horizontally. The head is delicate, narrow and long. The birds have a single comb. Their trunk is quite short and broader in front than at the saddle. The body's tapering is however not so marked as in the Old English Game Fowl. The back line slopes down towards the saddle. The wings are carried well tucked against the body. The shoulders are projected a little above the line of the back. Seen from the side, the front of the wing's arch runs almost parallel to the breast line. The thighs are long and the animals stretch themselves greatly, so that thighs and shanks almost form a straight line.

COLORS AND MARKING PATTERNS

The breed is found in several varieties, including birchen, golden birchen, partridge, silver partridge, bloodwing white, bloodwing silver partridge, black, blue and white. The leg color is yellow in the partridge varieties. The birchen, golden birchen and black birds have dusky legs.

QUALITIES

This breed can be trusting towards people. As these birds were originally bred for shows, they clearly have less fighting spirit than other game fowl. The advantage of this is that the animals can be more easily kept in a flock and that strange chickens accept one another sooner. As layers, the hens are not impressive, tending to produce for merely a few months. Although the hens become broody, their long legs and tight, hard feathers make them less suitable as sitters and mothers. In a number of countries, including the Netherlands, the breeding population is very small, so that unfortunately its vitality leaves much to be desired.

PARTICULARS

- For exhibitions, animals need to be trained as to their 'ideal' station, in which the legs should be stretched well. The easy-going nature of this breed is an asset when training it. After a few days, the animals figure out what is expected of them and they stand quietly. This makes the breed very attractive for people who like placid chickens, besides falling for extreme shapes.
- Formerly, the breed's comb used to be 'dubbed' (trimmed), but this is now prohibited in many countries. The original objective of 'dubbing' the animals was to protect them during fights, for comb and wattles are vulnerable and saturated with blood. In order to retain the typical expression of a dubbed bird's head, the ban on dubbing has stimulated one breeder to breed a Modern English Game Fowl in Germany with a comb that has a different shape, to wit a pea comb, which is naturally compact. Up to now, this variant has not been very popular.

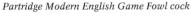

Partridge Modern English Game Fowl cock

Shamo

COUNTRY OF ORIGIN

Japan

ORIGIN

The name given to this breed in Western Europe is in fact not correct. In Japanese, 'Shamo' simply means 'fighter' and stands for an entire category of game fowl breeds, not just for a single variety. The Shamo, as we know it, corresponds with a breed that is called 'Ô Shamo' in Japan. The Japanese believe that this ancient breed originally hailed from China. Around 1880, Germans brought the first Shamos to Europe.

APPEARANCE

Even a layman can see right away that the Shamo falls into the game fowl category. Its upright and provocative carriage and its glaring expression leave no doubt about that. All of the advantages that birds may have as regards fighting are very much in evidence. The feathering is short and hard, offering the animal protection and preventing the adversary from getting a grip easily. Its station (carriage) is almost vertical; the breast is broad, hard and muscular. The shoulders are placed high and away from the body. The neck is long and somewhat arched. The hackles of the cocks are short, only covering the neck's top part. The head is broad and the protruding brow offers good protection to the eyes. On the front of its head, the bird has a small pea comb with three low, lengthwise ridges. In the cock, the wattles are very small, in the hens they are entirely absent. The birds have a featherless dewlap. The eyes are fierce and alert, their color being pearl. The tail is carried somewhat folded and below the horizontal. The tail's ornamental feathers are only mod-

White Shamo cock

A study of the head of a Shamo hen

208

erately developed. Shamos stand high and have long thighs and shanks. The legs are yellow or – in dark-colored animals – swarthy to black with yellow foot soles.

COLORS AND MARKING PATTERNS

In fact colors are not important and not well standardized in this game breed. In Europe, one has a problem at exhibitions with this fact. That is why a number of recognized colors have been laid down, with the restriction that, if anything, these are 'type birds', so that in judging them color and markings do not count for a great deal. The following colors are described: wheaten, red necked black, silver necked black, black, white, blue laced and red porcelain.

QUALITIES

The Shamo is a breed that comes into its own among lovers of an extreme shape and a headstrong nature. Although cock fights have been banned in Western Europe, the centuries of selecting as to fighting spirit have determined the qualities of these strong chickens. Towards their owner, they can be very tame and affectionate. Among themselves, it is a different story, for the cocks have one goal: becoming the strongest bird. If they get a chance to pick a fight, they will go on until there is one cock less. When their adversary is not a cock of a game breed, the outcome is soon decided to the Shamo's advantage. If both animals are Shamos, the fight will turn into a battle of attrition. This means that the animals need to be housed in well-enclosed coops. You can best keep them in pairs, as they are practically monogamous. If you want to keep several pairs, then put in partitions, so that the birds cannot see one another. This gives them the necessary peace and quiet. The hens do not lay very much. The eggs are enough for a good number of chicks, but no more than that. The housing for this hardy and robust breed can be fairly Spartan: It is enough that the birds remain dry and out of the wind.

Shamo cock, porcelain

Shamo hen, white

209

17 Ornamental Long-tailed Breeds

Backgrounds

The category of ornamental and long-tailed breeds in fact only has in common that these birds were originally not bred for some utility purpose like laying, meat production or fighting. Still, this category includes a number of breeds that are positively ancient. In Europe, and notably in the United Kingdom, it was fashionable in the eighteenth and nineteenth century to live on a country estate if one was wealthy. These estates had all sorts of luxuries to show that one was super-rich – in any case richer than the neighbors. To adorn the estate, many exotic trees and bushes were planted. In the gardens, one kept chickens that had but one purpose: to look exotic and beautiful. This we see in old paintings from which we can glean historical information about a number of breeds. Thus, in paintings from the eighteenth century, we encounter Dutch White Crested Chickens, Bearded and Crested Fowl and Japanese Bantams. In other cultures, for instance Japan, certain breeds were developed that were very time-consuming and had no utility purpose whatsoever. These animals were purely kept for the pleasure of taking care of chickens, having them around, and even keeping them in one's home. The latter aspect was literally the case as regards some chickens, of which the Japanese Long-tailed Fowl is an example. Onagadori and Phoenix cocks,

A Phoenix cock's extremely long tail feathers (illustration from the beginning of the 20th century)

for instance, have the feature that their sickles do not molt. They keep growing, becoming many meters long. In Japan, the best cocks are kept in special cages once their tails get so long that they drag along the ground at the age of about six months. Each cock has his own cage, somewhat resembling a grandfather clock. In the top, the cock sits on a perch, with sometimes part of a floor right under it. Whatever the case may be, its tail can hang down freely without getting soiled or damaged. In order to provide the cocks with the necessary exercise, they are taken out of their cages every day. A minder carries the cock's tail for the bird, to relieve him of the weight and of course to prevent it from getting either dirty or damaged. Of cocks held in this manner, certain specimens aged ten are recorded to have had tails 10m (30 ft) long and more. It goes without saying that such feather growth requires high-protein food. As a rule, Europeans do not have the facilities or indeed the patience for

Silkie hen, buff

this, and therefore have to be satisfied with cocks that have tails of a 'mere' 2 or 3m (6½–10 ft). However, it is clear that these creatures need a great deal of attention and care. This is something you will have to realize when you make a choice for one of the ornamental breeds. Depending upon the breed, these birds will require a lot more work than the ones in the other categories, while there will be no reward in eggs. Often they do lay enough eggs for good reproduction, but that is as far as it goes. For you, in this case, the pleasure is found in the chickens' nature, their appealing appearance and in taking care of them.

Qualities

In this group, you will find breeds with special hereditary features like feathered feet, crests, beards, extremely long tails, unique feathering and very short legs. Such qualities are quite often criticized by animal lovers who are not familiar with the poultry fancy. It is allegedly cruel to breed such features into animals. However, many of these characteristics have been found for ages in chicken breeds. The ancestors of our contemporary animals can be seen in old paintings, for these breeds have been living together with people for centuries. One can safely regard those birds as a histori-

cal heritage. It only becomes cruelty when the chickens do not get the care they need. Unfortunately, too many animals are purchased on impulse because of their attractive appearance, and people only stop to think afterwards. After reading this introduction, we hope you will not make that mistake. These chicken breeds often require adapted housing, and when necessary you will find details about this under the breed's description.

Breed Descriptions

Brabanter

COUNTRY OF ORIGIN
North of Europe

ORIGIN
The Brabanter is originally a breed of crested fowl that was probably found in the north of Europe, including the Netherlands, as early as the seventeenth century. The breed is often taken to be Dutch, but the Netherlands are not the only country where these birds are known

Brabanter cock, golden black half-moon spangled

Black Brabanter hen

'from way back when'. Around the year 1900, the breed was, in fact, practically extinct in the Netherlands, but could be recreated from German breeding material, among others. Brabanters are closely related to the Owl Beards. These were used frequently for the Brabanter's survival – and still are.

APPEARANCE

The Brabanter is a typical representative of the country fowl type. This chicken is of medium high stature, with a slightly upright alert carriage. Its back is fairly long and slightly sloping. The tail is carried rather above the horizontal line, and is long and well spread. The Brabanter cock has long, broad and well-curved main sickles in its tail, as well as abundant lesser sickles. In most varieties, the leg color is slate blue. The head is the breed's most striking standard feature. The birds have a full three-clump beard, with clear gaps between the throat's beard and the muffs. As the hallmark of crested fowl, also here the nostrils are somewhat 'cavernous' and 'flared'. The comb has two horns that are rather V-shaped (as horn combs usually are). The crest has a characteristic form, reminding one of the Appenzeller's pointed tuft. It consists of vertically growing feathers, standing up on the head in a compact bunch that is flattened sideways. A skull knob is not present in this breed. This typical crest is sometimes called a 'shaving-brush crest'.

COLORS AND MARKING PATTERNS

The breed is found in self black, white, blue laced, cuckoo, golden black half-moon spangled, silver black half-moon spangled, yellow white half-moon spangled, golden blue half-moon spangled and lavender.

Brabanter hen, golden black half-moon spangled

Brabanter chick, three weeks old

QUALITIES

Brabanters look striking, are found in a range of colors and have an agreeable nature. So it is strange that the breed is still relatively rare. The hens lay fair-sized eggs, though the number leaves something to be desired. Usually the hens lay their white eggs in spring and Summer, while in Fall and winter you can expect the odd egg only occasionally. As a rule, Brabanters are rather placid and do not need much room. You can keep them in a somewhat smaller run, as long as you take into account that they need a bit of exercise to keep them from growing too fat. As they have a small crest that does not get dirty as easily as those of the other crested breeds, they can be given free run. Of course they will always remain country fowl, meaning that they are friendly when you approach them in the right way, but are not easily tamed.

PARTICULARS

Breeders of this rather rare breed often are grateful to be able to use its kinship with the Owl Beard and frequently mate them. This is possible because the crest is dominantly inherited. Due to this, Brabanters are always the outcome of such crossings. That this happens a lot can be seen from the disappearance of the typical differences between these breeds. Thus, we like to see our Brabanter with a three-clump beard, while a full, round beard is required in the Owl Beard consisting of one continuous, unbroken development. Brabanters are bred in a number of half-moon spangled varieties, but in an Owl Beard half-moon spangles mean a disqualification as they normally should be spangled. The result of crosses is, alas, that often the Brabanter has neither the right markings nor the right beard shape.

Brahma

COUNTRY OF ORIGIN
India

ORIGIN
In 1852, this breed was first imported to Europe from North America. Initially, it was called 'Chittagong' or 'Shanghai', but later on its name was changed to Brahma. It is not clear whether the breed was an authentic importation, via the port of Luckipoor (on the river Brahmaputra) or whether it was developed in America from a crossing of Cochins and Malays. The chickens are well known as one of the largest breeds, which is one reason why it is sometimes called 'the King of Chicken Breeds'. The Brahma has contributed towards the creation of innumerable new breeds and of new colors within existing ones.

Brahma hen, multiple penciled silver partridge

Brahma cock, columbian

ending with a smooth, continuous sweep in a tail of low carriage. The tail section is short and well spread. Because of the breed's broad build, the tail, seen from behind, is more horse-shoe-shaped than V-shaped. The wings are carried well tucked. Brahmas have a rather short, full-feathered neck. The head is small in comparison to the bulky body. The skull is very broad, so that the Brahma's 'eyebrows' project a little over its eyes. The bird has a small pea comb with three low lengthwise ridges. Brahmas have short wattles, among which one can also find the feathered skin fold, the dewlap. This breed's yellow legs are fully feathered and its toes have feathers on them, resulting in big, 'floppy' feet.

COLORS AND MARKING PATTERNS
The breed is rather popular and is found in different varieties, including multiple penciled partridge ('triple laced'), multiple penciled silver partridge, multiple penciled blue partridge, columbian, buff columbian, columbian blue marked, buff columbian blue marked, cuckoo, birchen, white, black, buff and self blue. These colors are, however, not accepted in all countries. The most common and popular variants

APPEARANCE
Striking in this breed is its large and heavy build, which is even further enhanced by its full feathering. The posture of this chicken is upright with a fairly low stand. The body is broad, full and deep. The back is quite short,

Brahma chick, silver partridge

Brahma hen, columbian

are the multiple penciled partridge and the columbian markings in different colors.

QUALITIES
Brahmas are very placid, trusting animals that, when well taken care of, can soon become very tame. If you want to keep a number of Brahmas, you will have to take into account that these birds need quite a bit of space, as they are big and heavy. The cocks can weigh up to 5kg (11 lbs). Also because of their size, Brahmas are not very suitable for children. Because they do not fly, the run need not be roofed in. If you want, you can also let them roam about the garden– a fence of 50cm (1³⁄₄ ft) high being sufficient. Young Brahmas are not fast growers, taking a long time to develop. A cock is in fact not fully grown until it is about a year and a half old. Hens do not reach adulthood fast. They only lay their first eggs when they are six or seven months old. As is often seen in larger chickens, their eggs are relatively small, sometimes no bigger than those of the larger miniature breeds. The animals go on laying their cream-colored eggs in winter. The hens usually have no difficulty getting broody and are reliable in this respect. Brahmas are tolerant chickens, so you need not expect problems when keeping them together with other breeds. Even cocks tolerate one another. If you want to breed these giant chickens, you should not make the harems too big for the cocks, as two or three hens are enough for these heavyweights. In spite of their bulk, Brahmas are moderate. Even when crowing they know how to behave: They make relatively little noise and are not fanatic crowers. All this contributes to their popularity among fanciers.

Cochin

COUNTRY OF ORIGIN
China

ORIGIN
Little is known about the Chochin's origin. The breed arrived in England in the nineteenth century, but was later also exported from Shanghai to other countries. The original Cochin bore little resemblance to the present type. European and American breeders have developed the present Cochin by way of selection.

Brahma hen, columbian

Cochin, cock, buff

The Cochins' henhouse must be dry and clean.

The Cochins' henhouse must be dry and clean.

Cochin hen, white

APPEARANCE

The Cochin is one of the largest and heaviest breeds in existence, cocks easily weighing 5.5kg (12 lbs). The animals are not only big, they are also exceptionally broad. This overall image is enhanced by the enormous number of feathers these chickens have. The Chochin's stand is low. Due to this and also due to its deep build, full feathering and richly feathered feet, the yellow legs cannot be seen. The breast is deep and well rounded. The neck is short and fully feathered. In comparison to the body, the head is rather small, sporting a single comb. The ear-lobes are red and the eyes are a reddish bay. The animals have a friendly attitude. The feathers are short and broad, and their texture is soft.

COLORS AND MARKING PATTERNS

The Cochin is bred in black, blue, white, buff, black mottled, cuckoo and multiple penciled partridge ('triple laced').

QUALITIES

Cochins are large, but also very placid, needing relatively little room. Because they do not fly, you can let them run free in a yard where the fence is not high. A 60cm (2 ft) fence is sufficient to keep the animals on your premises. In connection with their feathered legs and feet, show birds (exhibits) should always be kept on a clean, dry surface, i.e. within a roofed run. Cochins are not shy and can easily be tamed. The hens are good layers of light brown eggs. Moreover, they are regularly and reliably broody. As they are absolute non-fly-

A study of the head of a buff-colored Cochin hen

Cochin cock, white

Dutch Crested Fowl hen, white

ers and not a light breed to boot, you should not place the perches too high in the roost.

PARTICULARS

In many countries, this giant breed is seldom seen. They are rather slow in growing and continue to do so for a long time. Only when it is a year and a half old is a Cochin fully developed. Buff is the color that is bred most frequently, and this is very susceptible to the influence of sunlight. Feather discoloration is the result of letting them out into the full sun, and rain speeds up the process. A henhouse in the shade is thus ideal for this delicate color.

Dutch Crested Fowl

COUNTRY OF ORIGIN

The Netherlands

ORIGIN

This breed has a long history and was probably already found in the Netherlands in the fifteenth century, although not in the standardized form we know today. In the seventeenth

century, old Dutch masters immortalized various precursors of the Dutch Crested Fowl, often shown with a black body and a white crest. One presumes that all old Dutch breeds with a crest and/or a beard have developed from the Pavlova Fowl. This breed of Russian origin came to Western Europe as early as the Middle Ages.

APPEARANCE

The Dutch Crest is a slender and elegant country fowl, with a more or less erect carriage. The line of the back is slightly sloping and ends in

White Black Crest from round about 1900

a tail held rather above the horizontal. The tail itself is quite long and is kept well spread. The cocks have a well-developed ornamental feathering, which can be seen in their profuse sickles. The wings are held close to the body and are more or less carried at a slant. The leg color is slate blue in most varieties. This breed's trademark is its large, full and globular crest. This crest grows upon a lump on the skull's crown, called the crest knob. In the hens, the crest is preferably large and round, but also firm and closed. In the cocks, its structure is a bit looser and has a less rounded shape. This is because the cock's crest feathers are longer and narrower. The size of the crest should be in proportion to the body. A too large crest means a disqualification, as the chickens then cannot see enough. The eye color is bay. In the eighteenth and nineteenth century, there were also frizzled Crested Fowl. This variant has been bred back again in the Netherlands, but is as yet quite rare.

COLORS AND MARKING PATTERNS

There are three varieties of Dutch Crests: animals with a crest the same color as their body, birds with a white crest and those with a black

Dutch Crested hen, blue

one. The first two varieties are bred in black, white, blue laced, yellow white laced, cuckoo and black mottled, among other colors. Animals with a black crest are nowadays bred only in white, i.e. the White Black Crests.

QUALITIES

Dutch Crests are friendly, genial creatures, though they are sometimes a little 'jumpy' due

Dutch Crested cock, black mottled

Dutch Crested hen, black

to their limited vision, as the crest sees to it that the birds can only look sideways and downwards. These chickens are startled by unexpected approaches from above. This can be prevented by talking to the birds and approaching them with your hands at their eye level. It is not sensible to give them the free run of your garden, as their crests will get wet and dirty. A roofed-in, clean run is a better place for them, and it need not be very spacious. As there is still a risk of their getting soiled and wet, you had better buy feeders and drinkers especially designed for crested fowl. The full, warm crests are an ideal breeding place for lice. You can prevent problems by regularly doing a louse check and treating these pests with a good spray or powder. The hens lay a considerable number of white eggs. They do not get broody often. If you want chicks, you will have to revert either to a broody chicken of some other breed or to an incubator. The chicks of White Crests are droll little creatures. With their crest knobs, which have a different color than the down on their bodies, they look as if they have donned tiny bowler hats.

PARTICULARS

The white variety with the Black Crest is a couple of centuries old, but was at one time extinct. At the outset of the twentieth century, the Dutch geneticist Dr. Vriesendorp designed

Dutch Crested cock, white

a breeding program to get back the White Black Crest. In this, Lakenvelders and moor's headed Owl Beards were used. Now, 75 years later, the White Black Crest is still a very rare phenomenon, while the problem that not only its crest is black, but also the upper part of its neck (like in the moor's head or *moorkop*), has still not been solved.

Naked Neck

COUNTRY OF ORIGIN
Austria/Hungary

ORIGIN
The factor ruling the lack of feathers on a chicken's neck has arisen in different places in the world as a spontaneous mutation. Thus, we see Naked Necked Game Fowl in the Caribbean, and there are Necked Necks in France with a 'jabot' or bib at the neck, while the Naked Necks from Eastern Europe have been upgraded into the show birds we are familiar with today.

APPEARANCE
Naked Necks are fair-sized country fowl, an adult cock weighing around 2.5kg (5½ lbs) and a hen about 500g (1 lb) less. The body is elongated and is carried slightly upright. Its back is of medium length with a somewhat sloping back line. The tail is slightly spread and of medium high carriage. The cocks have well-curved, rather broad main and lesser sickles. The legs are clean and of a slate blue

Naked Neck hen, black

Naked Neck hen, black mottled

color in black animals. However, the preeminent hallmark of these chickens is their naked, featherless neck. In the cocks this is bright red, while the neck of the hens is of a pinkish white. The featherless skin continues more or less to the crop. The skull has feathers on it, and – due to the contrast with the naked neck – looks as if it has a little tuft. However, this is not the case. The ear-lobes are red. The Naked Neck's eyes are required to be a reddish bay. The comb is usually single, but birds with a rose comb are also recognized.

COLORS AND MARKING PATTERNS
Naked Necks are recognized in a number of different colors, like black, white, cuckoo, blue laced, black mottled, buff, red and partridge.

QUALITIES
Due to their naked, featherless neck, these chickens give the impression of being vulnerable. However, this is absolutely not the case. Of old, they survived the severe winters in Eastern Europe without problem. So, you need not fit your henhouse with extra facilities if

Black Naked Neck hen

Black Naked Neck cock

you want to keep these birds. They are hardy and vigorous and can be kept free-range, though they will also thrive in an enclosed area. As these are rather heavier country fowl, the breed is somewhat less inclined to fly. Also, they are calmer than other country fowl and therefore can be tamed. The hens are reasonable layers and tend to get more or less broody. As on the whole they are fairly tight-feathered, they are unable to keep as many eggs warm as broodies of other breeds. If you take this into account, you can safely entrust them with hatching their own eggs.

PARTICULARS
Many people find Naked Necks revolting and compare them to vultures. Of course, these birds have their naked necks in common, but their characters are entirely different, for Naked Necks are pleasant company. With a Naked Neck, you moreover have something really special in your chicken coop. Naked Neck chicks are hatched already having their naked necks. This is contrary to, for instance, naked neck pigeons, in which the naked neck only appears after the first molting. They are droll chicks that stand out among the chicks of other breeds.

Owl Beard

COUNTRY OF ORIGIN
The Netherlands

ORIGIN
This remarkable breed, sometimes also referred to as *Uilebaard* in the United States, has a long history. It developed from country fowl, being more or less a standard breed in the Netherlands as early as the seventeenth century. Various old Dutch paintings from that period depict Owl Beards in all shapes and colors. The breed was first mentioned in a book in 1882. However, at the end of the nineteenth century, the Owl Beards were almost extinct. With the aid of a couple of nonstandard chickens that showed some Owl-Beard features, new life was breathed into the breed. There were also crosses with Thuringen Owl Beards and La Flèches. At this point in time, the Owl Beard is still very rare, but has a number of inspired adepts among its breeders.

APPEARANCE
As to type, the Owl Beards remind one of the Dutch Crested Fowl. This is a breed of the country fowl type, having a tail carried well

Owl Beard hen, yellow white spangled

above the horizontal. Its trunk is long and rather broad in front. The wings are held tucked against the body at a downward slant. The eye color is bay. The legs vary from grayish blue to white, depending on the chicken's color. The head is the breed's most characteristic feature. The breed takes its name from its full round beard, which preferably should consist of one continuous, unbroken development. The animals have a V-shaped or horn comb, with a few frizzy feathers right behind it. This is a rudimentary crest, making their kinship with Dutch Crested Fowls obvious. The nostrils, situated at the top of the upper mandible, are 'cavernous' and rather wide. This is a typical standard feature of crested fowl and other kindred breeds.

COLORS AND MARKING PATTERNS

The best known varieties are black, blue, white and cuckoo. Next to these colors, there are also golden black spangled, silver black spangled and yellow white spangled Owl Beards.

Also golden and silver penciled markings are recognized, but are in fact no longer found. The most typical Owl Beard variety is the 'moor's head' or *moorkop*, which is hard to breed and extremely rare.

QUALITIES

Unfortunately, the Owl Beard is seldom encountered. It is a mystery why this is so, for the breed has a lot to offer. These are strong birds with special looks. They thrive when roaming about freely as well as in the run. Most Owl Beards are a bit stand-offish. Still,

Owl Beard hens, white moor's head

a relaxed minder treating these chickens with tact is able to get an Owl Beard reasonably tame. However, a hasty person with not enough time will have the opposite effect on the animals. The hens are excellent layers and, when taken care of well, tend to go on laying throughout the winter. The eggs are white, weighing between 50 and 60g (1¾–2 oz).

Owl Beard hen, silver black spangled

Owl Beard cock, white moor's head

Black Owl Beard cock

Owl Beard hen, golden moor's head

PARTICULARS

The moor's headed marking is very specific for the Owl Beard and found in no other breed. The name of this variety gives away its appearance immediately: its body is self-colored, either white or golden brown, while its head, including the top part of the neck, is black. This marking only becomes visible when the chicks have their definitive set of feathers after the third molt, for their chick feathers are mainly black. It is difficult to concentrate this black in the neck's upper part and in the head, for, when doing so, the black either tends to increase or to disappear entirely. Cocks of this color are prone to hen-featheredness, mean-

ing that they may lack a cock's ornamental tail feathers. This is convenient for breeders, because with regards to markings the cock is a lot more like the hen, so that it is easier to estimate his breeding qualities.

Black Owl Beard chick, three weeks old.

Owl Beard cock, golden black spangled

Sultan

COUNTRY OF ORIGIN
Turkey

ORIGIN
These fowl originally hail from Turkey, where, according to tradition, they used to live in the sultan's castle gardens in what was then called Constantinople. In the year 1854, a couple of white birds were exported to England. Apart from this reading of the breed's origin, there are references to Siberian Crested Fowl as these are allegedly five-toed, a quality that our contemporary Sultan has as well.

There is a drawing from 1881 that is remarkable, for it shows the Sultan with yellow legs, whereas its present-day leg color is blue. Due to the world wars in Europe, the animal was already more or less extinct, with the exception of the British stocks. Later on it was reconstructed from various breeds, so, sadly, most strains of the current Sultans on the continent no longer descend from the sultan's original chickens.

APPEARANCE
Sultans are quite small chickens, the birds having a rather cobby build together with a fairly low stature. The weight of an adult cock is about 2kg (4½ lbs). The animals are full-feathered, and the neck has a very profuse plumage, so that the back looks shorter than it actually is. The head is adorned by a full, globular and large crest. In front of the

Sultans at the beginning of the twentieth century

crest is a V-shaped comb (horn comb) which in the hen is almost buried within the crest. A full, three-clump beard replaces the wattles. A well-spread tail is carried medium high. The slaty blue legs are full-feathered, and there are well-developed vulture hocks. Finally, the birds have five instead of four toes.

COLORS AND MARKING PATTERNS
The breed is only recognized in pure white. These animals have slaty gray shanks, bright red ears (not visible due to the feathering) and reddish bay eyes. A few breeders have been working on other color varieties. Thus, in the past we have seen blue and black Sultans.

QUALITIES
The breed is not encountered often, but in most countries where chickens are bred and exhibited, one can find a small, dedicated group of fanciers. Sultans are calm, friendly birds. The hens lay reasonably well and the eggs have a light brown shell. In connection with the head's profuse feathering, you should provide the birds with a special drinker: a jar waterer (little 'water tower') is fine. In this

way, you prevent the beard from getting wet. Otherwise, the birds soon start looking rather unattractive. Because Sultans moreover have a great deal of foot feathering and the white feathers easily get soiled, you can best keep them in roofed-in, clean runs. Perches should not be fixed too high in the roost. There are not many breeders of these vigorous chickens even though they have such a pleasant, placid nature.

PARTICULARS

If you do not merely want to keep these 'pearls among fowl', but also want to breed them, then you will have to abide by a couple of rules. Breeding five-toed chickens is hard, as the fifth toe is not consistently heritable. Apart from this, in breeds with large, full crests, one should make a focused selection as to structuring these crests firmly. This way, breeders in a natural manner see to it that their birds retain sufficient vision. This can only be achieved if you have extensive breeding experience or get intensive supervision.

Sumatra

COUNTRY OF ORIGIN
Indonesia (Sumatra)

ORIGIN
The Sumatra is an old breed that cannot be compared with any other kind of poultry. Ancient manuscripts have it that the Sumatra was possibly developed from feral *kampong* chickens and a species of wild fowl that is now extinct. The Sumatra belongs within the Aseel category and is regarded as a long-tailed game fowl. Halfway through the nineteenth century, Americans took a few animals to the United States. A decade later, these elegant creatures found their way to countries in Europe, including Great Britain and Germany.

APPEARANCE
The Sumatra is a graceful, slender and profusely feathered chicken. The strong green sheen on its feathers is striking. The tail is long and its carriage is almost horizontal. The tail's feathering is profuse, with long sickles that are also broad and have a strong structure, preventing them from curving too soon

Sultan hen

Sumatra cock

and thus dragging along the ground. The comb has three low lengthwise ridges; the wattles are minute. A hallmark that really catches the eye is the dark purplish color of comb, face and wattles, a coloring referred to as 'gypsy'. The legs are a dark willow with an olive-green luster, and the soles of the feet are yellow. The characteristic feature distinguishing the Sumatra from other breeds is the tendency to grow several spurs. Most cocks of the standard breeds have only a single spur, while the Sumatra often has two or more. This phenomenon is considered to be a typical standard feature of this breed.

COLORS AND MARKING PATTERNS

In origin, the breed was only found in black with a vivid green luster. Later on, white specimens were developed in Germany through crosses with Yokohamas, and nowadays we also have a black-red variety. Up to now, these two divergent colors have not been generally recognized. Blue Sumatras have also been bred on occasion. However, for all of these variants it is true that they lack the breed's typical standard feature, its rich beetle-green sheen.

Sumatra cock

Sumatra cock

QUALITIES

The Sumatra is a strong breed that is still close to nature. Due to their long, profusely feathered tails and their busy, active characters, the animals need a large outside run. If they are allowed to wander about freely, they prefer roosting outside, even during sharp frosts. Giving them the free run is also a way of preventing fights between growing cocks. They are not shy, and if you approach them calmly, they will reward you by reacting rather affectionately towards you. If you let them spend the night in their roost, the perches should be placed fairly high– at least 1m (3 1/2 ft) above the ground– in order to prevent their tails from soiling and damage. Sumatras are not fast growers and are sexually mature later than country fowl. In order to form the abundance of broad feathers, they need feed containing more protein than regular chicken feed has. Sumatras lay white eggs, which is remarkable, because brown or tinted eggs are characteristic of Asiatic breeds. As they have remained close to nature and have escaped being 'improved' on, the breed does not produce many eggs. A Sumatra hen only lays for a couple months, which is more than enough for their reproduction.

PARTICULARS

* The vivid beetle-green sheen makes the Sumatra an attractive breed. This color combined with its abundant feathering and low tail carriage, makes people who are unfamiliar with the breed wonder whether it is a chicken or a pheasant. It is difficult, particularly in the cocks, to achieve the highly

desired gypsy-colored head piece. In the cocks, it is usually of a purplish red, which is accepted at exhibitions, as long as it is not bright red.

- If you rear young cockerels in a closed run, they will certainly start fighting to determine their ranking order. A good means of keeping this battle in check is to add an adult cock to the group. The 'old man' will interfere with the combats, exercising his authority. Do remember that as the cockerels grow older and stronger, they will certainly pounce on the old cock the moment he is out of shape, for instance due to molting. Therefore you should separate the animals in good time.
- There is also a diminutive form of the breed, not described in this encyclopedia. Apart from the size, its qualities are the same as those of the original form described here.

Yokohama

COUNTRY OF ORIGIN
Japan

ORIGIN
The Yokohama is one of the most graceful breeds in existence. It was initially imported in Europe in 1864 by a missionary called Girad. It is likely that there were some problems of communication between this French importer and the Japanese breeders, for in Japan there was never a breed called Yoko-

hama. Of course there is the Japanese port of that name, and this was precisely whence the animals were shipped to France. So, we will probably never know the history of the breed's origins, except that the Yokohama's progenitors came from Japan.

APPEARANCE
The Yokohama falls into the category of long-tailed fowl and is a graceful bird of elongated build. Its most outstanding feature is its very abundantly feathered tail, with an almost horizontal carriage. The cock's sickles are long and narrow, though their structure is strong. Due to this strength, one gets the image of sickles slowly bending downwards. The cock's

White Yokohamas round about 1900

saddle is very densely feathered, with long, narrow feathers that almost touch the ground. Also the hens have a long tail, of which the top feathers are a bit longer and curved. The comb is of a small walnut or cushion shape and is set well forward on the head. The breed has small wattles and a small dewlap. Its most common, characteristic coloration is a striking red on the shoulders. The Yokohama has yellow legs.

COLORS AND MARKING PATTERNS
The breed is most common in red shouldered and white. In Great Britain a number of other varieties are recognized. In the past, red shouldered birds were entered in shows under the indication 'red saddled white'. But as the saddle is white in this variety, the name was changed. A striking feature of this color is the

Yokohama hen

white mottling at the tip of the breast feathers, which are furthermore of a brownish red color.

QUALITIES

Yokohamas are lively and full of character, needing lots of room. This is not a breed for those wanting 'good layers'. The long tail creates many requirements on their housing. Cocks can be slightly aggressive towards people, and very aggressive towards their own kind.

As the cocks have very long tail feathers that get easily soiled, damaged or broken, you had better place the perches reasonably high: at least a meter (3½ ft) from the ground. For the same reason, you should keep these birds on clean, dry litter, which means housing them in a roofed-over run and cleaning this very frequently. Due to the tail and the mutual pecking behavior, it is better to house handsome ornamental cocks separately. If you do not do so, it will be difficult to keep the animals in good condition. Within a breeding flock, the

Yokohama cock

beautiful ornamental tail is soon damaged and soiled. The hens are not really good layers, nor are their eggs very big. However, they easily go broody and in that case can cope very well.

PARTICULARS

This breed is also raised in a diminutive form not found in this encyclopedia. Apart from the size, its qualities are the same as those of the original form described here.

Silkie

COUNTRY OF ORIGIN
China

ORIGIN

The Silkie has a very long history. This breed was already found a thousand years ago in China, or in any case its precursors, with a similar, typical 'semi-plume' feather structure were. Silkies arrived in Europe a couple of centuries ago, where sly merchants sometimes offered them for sale as crosses between rabbits and chickens. It is now hard to imagine the chicken fancy

White Silkie cock with beard

without Silkies as a popular and very well known breed.

APPEARANCE

Silkies are relatively small 'large chickens'. There is quite a bit of variety in their weight, depending on the country where they are bred. They can weigh between a 1000 and 1600g (2–3½ lbs), so that the lighter birds are as heavy as the average diminutive breed. The Silkie takes its name from the divergent structure of its feathers, which look like hairs. Silkies should have a rounded body shape and a low stand. In the cocks, the short tail is covered by silk-feathered sickles. Apart from its special feather structure, the Silkie still has a number of outstanding features, like a purplish blue skin color (also seen in the color of the beak, legs and head furnishings) and a fifth toe. Silkies have what is called a mulberry comb with small furrows (in fact a walnut comb, and genetically regarded as a rose

Silkie cock, multiple penciled silver partridge

Silkie hen with beard, buff

comb). Alongside the regular form, there is also a bearded Silkie.

COLORS AND MARKING PATTERNS

Silkies are bred in several varieties, including white, black, multiple penciled partridge ('triple laced'), multiple penciled silver partridge, gray, cuckoo, red, buff and self blue. However, not all colors are recognized in all countries.

QUALITIES

Animals of this breed are famed for their calm, very friendly and trusting nature. It is fairly simple to train Silkies 'to the hand', which makes this breed very suitable for children and people who like to bond with their pets. They do not fly, so you can let them run free in your yard; a low fence will keep them within bounds. Silkies do not need much room and can be kept in smaller runs.

The hens of this breed are not known for their large egg production and you may only expect about a hundred a year, notably in winter and in Spring. A very well-known quality of this breed is the stubborn and frequent broodiness of the hens. If you don't want the eggs hatched, you will have to keep in mind that they regularly need a bit of extra care to prevent them from exhausting themselves unduly. Because of their reliable broodiness, Silkies are often used as foster mothers.

Perhaps their rather 'unnatural', fluffy appearance gives a different impression, but this breed is very strong, robust and impervious to cold and the like.

PARTICULARS

- Typical of this breed is the clearly visible blue-black color of the skin and the head furnishings. Less well known is the fact that their meat – and even their skeleton – is highly pigmented. The Chinese attribute healing properties to this pigmentation, and

White Silkie hen with beard

Multiple penciled partridge Silkie hen with beard

Multiple penciled silver partridge Silkie hen with beard

Buff-colored Silkie cock

parts of the Silkie were used for all kinds of medicinal purposes– and in fact still are. In spite of the divergent color of the meat, its flavor and texture are no different than that of ordinary chicken meat. Next to these highly melanistic Silkies, there is also a fair-skinned variant.

- The typical structure of the feathers is due to their lack of barbicels. This is a recessive quality, meaning that when a Silkie is crossed with a normally feathered fowl, the outcome is always animals with normal feathering.

The stubborn feature of always going broody is often considered a nuisance, but is the reason that this breed has survived. In previous ages and far into the last century, incubators did not exist. That is why the breed was kept as a natural incubator by breeders of chickens, pheasants, partridges and ducks. For there is always a broody Silkie around somewhere when a couple of eggs of a poor sitter need to be hatched.

Part Three:
True Bantams and Diminutive Chickens

Introduction

In 'chicken land', one distinguishes between true bantams on the one hand and diminutive, miniature or dwarf fowl on the other. True bantams are essentially very small chicken breeds, of which there is no large variety. Often these breeds are very old, for instance the Japanese, Sebrights and Java Bantams. The name of the latter might cause some confusion, as there is also a large Java in the United States. However, this has nothing to do with the Java Bantam.

Apart from these true bantam breeds, innumerable smaller forms of the large breeds were developed, mainly at the end of the nineteenth century and the outset of the twentieth. The latter category we usually call 'diminutive fowl'. However, the breeds in this category are in fact also referred to as 'bantams': The diminutive or dwarf form of the Frisian is for instance called the Frisian Bantam.

It is a fact that both bantams and diminutive fowl are very well adapted to our day and age, as we have less living space at our disposal. Those who do not have the space for a few large chickens, usually have enough room for a tiny henhouse with a couple of bantams. For children, bantams and dwarf chickens are moreover a better choice than large poultry, as they are far easier to manage because of their smaller size. As miniature forms have been bred of most large fowl, you can almost always get a smaller version of the breed that appeals to you. Usually the large breed's qualities are very similar to those of the dwarfs, due to the fact that, to arrive at the smaller form, one has almost always made use of crosses between the original, larger breed and bantams.

18 Layer Breeds

Breed Descriptions

Ancona Bantam

COUNTRY OF ORIGIN
The United Kingdom

ORIGIN
The Ancona Bantam was originally developed around 1910 in England by mating the Ancona with miniature breeds. From 1930 onwards, the Ancona Bantam was exported to various countries. The quality of this young breed was however such that in most countries one started to cross them again with Anconas and true bantams, so the present Ancona Bantams usually do not have a pedigree that goes back so much as a century.

APPEARANCE
The Ancona Bantam's type bears close resem-

Rose-combed Ancona Bantam cock, black white mottled

Rose-combed Ancona Bantam hen, black white mottled

Single-combed Ancona Bantam hen, black white mottled

blance to that of the Leghorn Bantams of the German kind. It is the elongated country fowl type, with a tail that is carried rather above the horizontal and is well spread. The feathers are broad and rounded at the tip. The cock's ornamental plumage is quite abundant, with a fully feathered tail. In these bantams, the wings sometimes tend to be rather long, projecting beyond the backside, which is not how it should be.

Ancona Bantams are found with either a serrated single comb or with a rose comb that has a backwards pointing spike or leader. The earlobes are of average size, being of a broadened almond shape and enamel white. The eye is a reddish bay to reddish brown. The shanks are yellow with regularly distributed dark dots, though they can also be entirely yellow.

COLORS AND MARKING PATTERNS
The breed is found in the original color black white mottled and in the later developed blue white mottled.

QUALITIES
Ancona Bantams are active animals. In the coop, they spend a lot of time browsing through the litter for anything edible, and when given free range, they start all sorts of

digging activities among plants and bushes. It is not wise to let these birds run free in a nicely tended garden, if you want to keep it that way. See to it that these chickens get enough diversion by for instance raking some grain into the litter. Ancona Bantams are good flyers, so the run needs to be roofed-in. In smaller henhouses and runs, the birds can become reasonably tame towards their owner. Ancona Bantams usually have a good laying capacity. The eggs are white. These non-sitters almost never go broody.

PARTICULARS
- The breed's two comb shapes are quite frequently interbred. As the rose comb is dominant, all of the chicks tend to have it. However, usually the comb's shape is not good, as it is often too smooth, lacking the little rounded points, and being rather high. Breeding comb type to comb type is therefore better than mixing them.
- The typical Ancona markings with the small white, pearl-shaped mottling at the tip of a black or blue feather is very much influenced by the chicken's age. After every molt, the white spots return larger. This is why an older bird is whiter than a youngster.

Ardenner Bantam

COUNTRY OF ORIGIN
Belgium

White Ardenner Bantams

Silver necked Ardenner Bantam cock

ORIGIN
In its country of origin, there is a difference of opinion as to where this typical breed comes from. The view of the Agricultural Association (*Landsbond*) is that these bantams are a diminutive form of the large Ardenner. But contrary to this, a group of Belgian poultry devotees maintain that the breed is a true bantam. The most common opinion as to the breed's roots is that it is a cross, which took place at the beginning of the last century, between Bassettes, Old English Game Bantams and Ardenners.

Golden necked Ardenner Bantam cock

Golden necked Ardenner Bantams hens

Silver necked Ardenner Bantam hen

APPEARANCE

The tiny Ardenner Bantam is one of the country fowl. The animals have a rather erect carriage and are fairly slim and small; the cocks of this breed only weigh about 650g (1½ lb). Their back is of an average length and slightly sloping from neck to tail. The tail itself is medium high and is carried somewhat folded. The tail feathers are long. The cocks have broad, long and rather pointed sickles. The wings are carried more or less at a downward slant. The breed's stand is medium high. Ardenner Bantams have a delicate, small head, sporting a not so very large single comb. The color of the comb, ears and featherless facial skin is striking. In the hens, it is a bluish red. Belgians refer to the color as that of a ripe blackberry–an apt simile. The cocks have a little more red in it, but compared to other breeds they are nevertheless very melanistic. As a logical result of this swarthy pigmentation, the eyes are

a very dark brown having black eyelids, while the clean shanks are practically black. In Belgium, there is also a tailless variety of the Ardenner Bantam. Except for lacking a tail, the Ardenner Rumpless Bantam is completely similar to the Ardenner Bantam.

COLORS AND MARKING PATTERNS

Ardenner Bantams are recognized in golden necked black, silver necked black, black, white, salmon, partridge and silver partridge. Of those mentioned, we usually find only the golden and silver necked ones in practice.

QUALITIES

Although they are small birds, they nevertheless need a lot of space. This is due to their active nature, always being on the move. Having a free run in which they can dig and grub about to their heart's content is ideal for this breed. But you can also very easily keep them in a closed run, provided you see to enough exercise and diversion. For this, one can rake some chick crumbs or chick starter feed into the litter and hang up some greens. Housing them in a closed run has the advantage that the animals will come to you more often. When wandering about freely, they tend to show their natural, rather shy character more. With this breed, the minder's influence is considerable. If you yourself have a rather bustling personality, your bantams are only going to admire you from a distance. The hens of this breed are quite good layers, their eggs weighing about 38g (1.3 oz). When given the opportunity, they will lay their eggs in well-hidden spots and subsequently hatch them. As mothers, they are fierce and defensive. The chicks grow up fast and easily.

Ardenner Bantams chicks

Australorp Bantam

COUNTRY OF ORIGIN
The United Kingdom

ORIGIN
The Australorp Bantam is what we call a 'dwarf form' of the large Australorp, bred by British fanciers. However, German breeders have developed its present high quality. The breed was created by way of large Australorps that had remained too small, and of various bantam breeds, including Langshan and Wyandotte Bantams. The Australorp Bantam has been recognized since 1960.

APPEARANCE
The Australorp Bantam is a lively chicken with a fairly short build. It has a medium-sized single comb with either four or five points. The ear-lobes are red, while the feath-

Australorp Bantam hen

erless skin of the head is also of a lively red color. The eyes are brownish black. Its back line ends with a smooth, continuous sweep in a tail of medium high carriage. The tails of the cocks and the hens are well spread; in the cock it has an abundance of ornamental plumage, so that the main tail feathers are hardly visible. The legs are black, the soles of the feet white.

COLORS AND MARKING PATTERNS
The breed is found in black, white and blue laced. The first color is very popular.

QUALITIES
Australorp Bantams are lively but nevertheless trusting birds that are not inclined to fly. A fencing of around 120cm (4 ft) high usually suffices to keep them 'within bounds'. The hens are good layers, their eggs having an average weight of about 40g (1½ oz). They are good sitters and rearing chicks is usually no problem, as these grow fast and vigorously. Among themselves, the birds are quite tolerant, so that it is possible to rear cocks together. There is some difference in character between the various blood strains: thus, German Australorp Bantams are often a bit fiercer, which can be seen from the young, growing cockerels' intolerance towards one another.

Australorp Bantam cock

Barnevelder Bantam

COUNTRY OF ORIGIN
Germany/The United Kingdom

ORIGIN
The roots of this breed lie in both Germany
and the UK. The English breeders beat the
Germans at it, but the Barnevelder Bantam
they bred was soon lost. The Germans created
the breed by way of red Rhode Island Bantams,
Wyandotte Bantams, Langshan Bantams and
non-standard bantams. The animals bred in
this way were highly satisfactory as to type, but
lacked the specific double laced Barnevelder
marking. By way of Cornish Game Bantams
one finally succeeded. At a later date, the
Netherlands introduced their own line in
Barnevelder Bantams by mating Cornish Bantams with Barnevelders that had remained

Barnevelder Bantam cock, double laced

Barnevelder Bantam cock, double laced

small. Notably in the Netherlands, Barnevelder Bantams are among the most popular
breeds.

APPEARANCE
In everything, the Barnevelder Bantam should
be a miniature of the Barnevelder. It is a medium-sized bantam breed of which the hens are
clearly good layers, as one can tell from their
deep and full backsides. This bantam's back is
medium long, ending in a tail with a continuous concave sweep. In the cock, the tail is
well covered by broad main and lesser sickles.
Both sexes spread their tail well. The comb and
wattles are medium-sized. The breed has a single comb. The ear-lobes are red and the eyes

Barnevelder Bantam hen, double laced

Barnevelder Bantam hen, double laced

a reddish bay. The Barnevelder Bantam has legs of a warm yellow, which have a reddish brown touch on the front of the shanks in the hens.

COLORS AND MARKING PATTERNS
The breed is found in black, white, double laced and double laced blue. The most popular and typical color is the double laced variant with black or bluish lacing.

QUALITIES
One of the breed's standard features is that the Barnevelder Bantam – like its large counterpart – lays very dark brown eggs. As they are real layers, the hens seldom go broody. Therefore the eggs are often hatched by other breeds or else this is done artificially. But once a hen does get broody, she remains neatly on the eggs and often takes good care of her chicks. Barnevelder Bantams, including the cocks, are calm and affectionate birds. They are also very suitable for starting fanciers because of their laying capacities and robustness. Both in a run and wandering about freely, the animals thrive. A fence of around 1.2m (4 ft) is often enough to keep them within their own realm. They have little inclination to fly.

Bassette

COUNTRY OF ORIGIN
Belgium

ORIGIN
In Belgium, this breed is sometimes called the 'Liège Bassette'. This name is a direct reference to its region of origin, to wit the southern part of the Belgian province of Limburg, in the vicinity of Liège. At its origin are the local, very small farmyard chickens, possibly interbred with bantams. At the beginning of the twentieth century, the breed was used a lot as a natural incubator for raising pheasants and partridges.

APPEARANCE
The Bassette is occasionally referred to as a 'semi-bantam'. This is because the breed is hardly any smaller than a lightly built normal chicken. The Bassette has a long body, and the hen furthermore has a deep and full backside (stern)– the hallmark of a good layer. The carriage of the tail is fairly high and should be well spread. The cock's tail has full, broad ornamental feathering. The main and lesser sickles are long, broad and well curved. The wings

Bassette cock, quail-colored

Bassette cock, quail-colored

Bassette hen, quail-colored

Bassette hen, quail-colored

are not really tucked, but are carried at a downward slant. The head is rather big and has a medium-sized single comb. In laying hens, it should preferably lop at the back. The ear-lobes are white and the eyes dark brown.

COLORS AND MARKING PATTERNS
The Bassette is recognized in a number of colors: quail, silver quail, blue quail, lavender silver quail, white, black and buff columbian. The latter variety is recognized, but in fact not bred. In Belgium, we occasionally encounter it in other breeds and then it is called 'dun' (*vaal*). This is an uncultivated form of buff columbian. Probably it was recorded in the various standards, as such 'dun' Bassettes occasionally tended to crop up in Belgium. In the mother country, fawn-colored Bassettes are also recognized. In Germany the breed is reared as well, but mainly in quail and silver quail.

QUALITIES
The Bassette is an excellent choice for someone who has little space, but would like to gather lots of eggs. In fact, it is the only true bantam selected for its utility features. The birds lay a considerable number of good-sized eggs. These bantams can be kept in a run that is not all that big, but thrive better when running free on a reasonable patch of land. They are active, strong and vigorous. As birds to breed from, they are renowned for their fertility. It is clear from their fame as foster mothers for pheasants and partridges that Bassettes are sitters and are subsequently good, tender

mothers. The tendency towards broodiness is however not very strong and only arises in late spring. Due to their placid nature, the animals can be made reasonably tame.

PARTICULARS
The variety lavender silver quail is an exceptional color only found in this breed. The birds are in fact silver quail, in which the black is substituted by lavender ('pearl gray'). Due to this, a beautiful pastel shade arises. A disadvantage of this lavender color is that its gene interferes with the feather's structure. This is seen in the cock's narrow main and lesser sickles, which are sometimes a bit frayed.

Brakel Bantam

COUNTRY OF ORIGIN
The Netherlands and Germany

ORIGIN
Around 1935, first mention was made at a Dutch exhibit of the Brakel Bantam, which allegedly had come about through a cross between the Brakel and the Sebright Bantam. However, this new creation was soon lost, so that another attempt was made in the German federal state of Westphalia around 1950. The German breeder Werthmann mated up large Brakels with black German Bantams. It soon appeared that it was not easy to breed back the Brakel's desired barred penciling into this cross. It took the persistent breeder five generations before the required markings were achieved.

Brakel Bantam cock, silver

Brakel Bantams, gold

Brakel Bantam hens, silver

APPEARANCE

Brakel Bantams are the midget form of the large Brakel and do not have a very high stand, but are elongated like most country fowl types. The tail's carriage is rather high and the tail is well spread. The cocks of this small breed have fairly long, well-curved main sickles. The wings are tightly tucked and carried at a downward slant. The breast is rounded and prominent, while the neck is gracefully arched. The animals have abundant hackles. The head has a single comb, lopped sideways at the back in laying hens. The head is highly pigmented, as one can tell from the deep black eyes, the dark eye rims and some bluish pigmentation in the base of the hen's comb. The Brakel Bantam's ear-lobes are white.

COLORS AND MARKING PATTERNS

Brakel Bantams are recognized in the colors silver and gold. Both are in fact penciled marking varieties, in which the pencilings on the feathers of the hen's back, wing shoulder and breast are connected across the feather's shaft. In this way, one gets stripes across the feather, which is sometimes called barred penciling.

QUALITIES

The Brakel Bantam is a good copy of the large breed. Not only do they look the same, the utility features are also comparable. The breed is hardy and vigorous. The animals grow up quickly and are precocious. The hens lay quite a number of eggs annually, weighing around 35g (1¼ oz). However, these chickens are non-sitters, so in order to breed them you will have to use an incubator. The animals are highly active and rather restless. They are difficult to tame and seldom allow themselves to be touched. Due to their active nature, Brakel Bantams require a lot of room: For instance a rather large run in which you will have to provide some diversion for them. Letting them run free in a yard or a meadow is ideal, but as Brakel Bantams are excellent flyers it is not a good idea to let them wander about a garden in a residential area. If it is up to them, they prefer sleeping in a tree. You can prevent this by feeding them in their roost late in the evening and then keeping them in.

PARTICULARS

The barred variety cuts a dashing figure in the world of chickens. Typically the hens that have this barred penciling over most of their body, except for the neck. The neck is required to be without markings, and thus contrasts greatly with the body.

Drenthe Bantam

COUNTRY OF ORIGIN
The Netherlands

ORIGIN
As to the history of the Drenthe's diminutive form not much is known. Around 1960, an initial attempt was made to breed Drenthe Bantams by mating up a Rumpless Drenthe with a Holland Bantam. In later years, one used Frisian Bantams and again Holland Bantams to arrive at several varieties. At this moment, there is a stable circle of persistent breeders.

APPEARANCE
There are two variants of the Drenthe's minia-

Rumpless Drenthe Bantam cock

QUALITIES

Drenthe Bantams are active animals that do not necessarily need a lot of room, but must have enough to do. These birds are strong and vigorous. The hens lay relatively large white eggs, weighing about 40g (1½ oz). They are broody regularly and take good care of their offspring. Compared to most country fowl breeds, these animals are rather easily tamed, though it is not possible to really 'train them to the hand'. They should be kept in a closed run, as the birds otherwise will be found all over the neighborhood.

PARTICULARS

* The breed is quite popular in the Netherlands, Germany and Belgium, but the Drenthe is seldom or never seen in other countries.
* The laced partridge is a unique color, found of old exclusively in the Drenthe Fowl, both in the large chickens and in the miniature ones discussed here. In the 'regular' par-

Rumpless Drenthe Bantam hen, yellow partridge

ture form. Alongside of the normal form there is the tailless one, the Rumpless Drenthe Bantam. Drenthe dwarfs have an elongated shape and are of a slight build. Their breast is well rounded. The wings are carried at a somewhat downward slant. The tail is raised rather above the horizontal, is well spread and in the cock has beautifully curved main and lesser sickles. The breed's stand is medium high. Drenthe Bantams have light bluish gray legs. Furthermore, the chickens, sporting a single comb, have white ear-lobes and reddish bay eyes.

COLORS AND MARKING PATTERNS

The breed is found in the following varieties: partridge, silver partridge, blue partridge, yellow partridge, laced partridge, laced silver partridge, laced blue partridge, laced silver blue partridge, laced yellow partridge, golden necked black, silver necked black, golden necked blue, silver necked blue, cuckoo partridge, bloodwing white and bloodwing silver partridge. Next to these, the rumpless variety is recognized in cuckoo, various penciled colors as well as in black, white and self blue.

Drenthe Bantam hen, partridge

Drenthe Bantam cock

Frisian Bantam chick

tridge color, the feathers on the hen's back are a brownish gray, having little, evenly grayish black dots ('peppering'). This peppering is lacking in the laced partridge-colored Drenthes. Instead of this, they have dull black serrated lines in these places, running along with the shape of the feather. The hen has the same markings on her breast, while in hens with regular partridge markings the breast is an unpatterned salmon.

• The Rumpless Drenthe Bantam is a nice variant within the breed. The factor ruling taillessness is incompletely dominant, meaning that a cross between a chicken with a tail and a rumpless one results in birds being born either with or without a tail.

Frisian Bantam

COUNTRY OF ORIGIN
The Netherlands

ORIGIN
The first reports about Frisian Bantams are from 1930. These animals were allegedly bred from crosses of Frisian Fowl with Sebright Bantams. Later attempts to breed Frisian Bantams from such crosses failed. Crosses of Frisians with Holland Bantams were however successful.

APPEARANCE
Frisian Bantams are clearly representatives of the country fowl type. They are rather small birds, weighing about 600g (1.3 lb). The animals are of slender build and have a slightly upright carriage and a tail that is held fairly high. The tail is spread well and in the cocks has abundant ornamental feathering, with long, nicely curved sickles. The wings are held at a downward slant, but closely fitted to the body. The breast is rather prominent and well-rounded. Frisian Bantams have a single comb and white ear-lobes. Their legs are clean and of a slate blue color.

COLORS AND MARKING PATTERNS
Frisian Bantams are recognized in the varieties golden penciled, silver penciled, lemon penciled, yellow white penciled, red penciled, black, white, self blue, cuckoo and black mottled. Most interest is shown in the penciled colorings. Penciled Frisian Bantams have tiny, very fine penciling. On the hen's feathers in breast, back and wing shoulders there are three to four penciled markings of a rather oval

Frisian Bantam hen, lemon penciled

Frisian Bantam hen, lemon penciled

Frisian Bantam hen, lemon penciled

Frisian Bantam cock, lemon penciled

Frisian Bantam cock, lemon penciled

shape. Breeders compare this shape to a grain of wheat.

Frisian Bantam cock, lemon penciled

QUALITIES

Frisian Bantams have a lively nature. They prefer to keep some distance between themselves and their owner and thus do not easily become tame. A calm minder having these birds in a closed run may, however, get the hens to feed from his hand. Due to their light weight, the wings of Frisian Bantams have an excellent lift. Thus, they are neither impressed by a fence nor by even higher obstacles. One should preferably keep them in a run that is closed on all sides. It is a strong and vigorous breed, which manages well when running free, so it is fine to let them wander around a yard or meadow. Among themselves, they can be a nuisance occasionally, but if you offer them enough diversion in their coop, you need not expect problems. Hang up some greens high above the bantams and mix in some fine grain with the litter; so that they have enough to do. The hens lay eggs with a white shell. Broodiness is not often encountered. If you want to breed your birds, you will usually have to turn to an incubator or a broody hen of some other breed.

Frisian Bantam cock, lemon penciled

Holland Bantam

COUNTRY OF ORIGIN
The United Kingdom

ORIGIN
Both in the Netherlands and in the United Kingdom, various breeders attempted, soon after the development of the Holland Fowl (also called Hamburger), to breed a miniature form of it. The English were the first to exhibit their birds at a show, at the end of the nineteenth century. These animals were breeding products of the Englishman Farnsworth. He achieved his aim with the help of large silver black spangled Hollands, Sebrights and

Holland Bantam hen, silver black spangled

Holland Bantam cocks (around 1900)

Java Bantams. Before the First World War the breed was also seen in the Netherlands, and subsequently found its way to fanciers in other countries.

Holland Bantam cock, silver black spangled

APPEARANCE
The Holland Bantam is a small, slender and elegant dwarf breed. The animals weigh about 700g (1½ lb). The body looks rather elongated, which is emphasized by its long tail. This tail is carried well spread and medium high. The cocks have long, broad sickles ending in a rounded tip. A fully feathered saddle and a great number of lesser sickles complete this handsome image. The wings are quite long and are carried at a slight downward slant. The leg color is slate blue. As to their head, Holland Bantams somewhat resemble Java Bantams. On the delicate, rather small head, there is a rose comb, the leader or spike of which is round and projects straight backwards. The comb is covered by tiny rounded points. The wattles are oval and rather short.

The ear-lobes are reasonably big and round, and their color is white.

COLORS AND MARKING PATTERNS
The breed is found in golden black spangled, silver black spangled, golden penciled, silver penciled, lemon penciled, yellow white penciled, golden blue penciled, black, white, self blue and cuckoo.

QUALITIES
Holland Bantams, notably the cocks, cut very graceful figures. They can be given free range, as they love being up and about. You can also keep these birds in a run, as long as they have sufficient room and diversion. Even though they are small, they are as a rule not suited to small runs. It is a pity that these animals, in spite of good care and a calm approach, very rarely become tame, although several rather placid strains are known. They are more animals for 'looking at', and in that respect have quite a bit to offer. The hens lay white eggs. Broodiness is rare in this breed, so the eggs are usually hatched by some foster mother or in an incubator. The chickens

Holland Bantam cock, silver black spangled

grow up fast and reach adulthood fairly soon.

PARTICULARS
At first sight, the silver black spangled and golden black spangled Holland Bantams only differ in their basic color. However, next to that there is another difference. The silver black birds have a white tail with a big, round black marking, the 'spangle' at the end of each feather. The golden black spangled animals on the other hand have a totally black tail. For several years now, attempts have been made to breed golden black spangled bantams that have a golden brown tail with a black spangle at the tip. Achieving these markings is as such not so very difficult, but unfortunately it is attended by a fading of the ground color. Due to this, the animals are more of a yellowish brown than a golden brown. One assumes that the ground color loses its intensity because the black feather parts are bred out.

Lakenverder Bantam

COUNTRY OF ORIGIN
The Netherlands/Germany

ORIGIN
The Lakenvelder's miniature form was developed in different countries at different points in time. The first bantams of the large original were exhibited by Mr. Scheper, a Dutch breeder, in the 1930s. These stocks have however become largely extinct. Most of today's Lakenvelder Bantams are descended from birds bred more recently in Germany. A Hamburg breeder was the first to exhibit the German miniature form of the Lakenvelder in 1972.

APPEARANCE
The Lakenvelder Bantam is a slender-built bantam of the country fowl type. Its build is elongated and its tail is carried rather above the horizontal. The tail itself is well spread and richly feathered in the cocks, with broad, long and nicely curved main and lesser sick-

les. The wings are carried at a downward slant and are well tucked against the body. The Lakenvelder Bantam has a medium-sized, regularly serrated single comb. The ear-lobes are white and the eyes bay or reddish brown. The breast is well rounded. And, finally, the legs are of a slate blue color.

COLORS AND MARKING PATTERNS

Originally, the Lakenvelder Bantam was only found in the color black. Many decades later, the blue marked variety was developed. In this variety, the black has faded to a bluish gray shade.

QUALITIES

Lakenvelder Bantams are active, bustling creatures that are best left to enjoy the free

Lakenvelder Bantam cock

run. However, these birds are best not kept in residential areas, for they need a lot of space, can fly high and will seldom remain in their own yard. Housing them in a closed run might of course be a solution, but these chickens easily grow bored. In a small run, their excess energy soon finds an outlet towards their 'house mates'. Nasty habits like feather-pecking are the result. Therefore the animals need something to do in such cases. In spite of a good, calm approach, the breed as a rule will remain rather shy. The eggs usually are white or lightly tinted. Lakenvelder Bantams are mostly non-sitters.

PARTICULARS

The color blue in the Lakenvelder Bantam is a light bluish gray. This color does not breed true and is inherited intermediary, meaning that, in a brood with blue markings, you may expect about half blue marked chicks, while the rest is black marked or for the most part white. The latter is called 'splashed', as the white contains a few black spots. The blue color is susceptible to discoloration by sunlight. If you intend to exhibit them, it is therefore necessary to keep such animals in a shady run.

Leghorn Bantam

COUNTRY OF ORIGIN

There are several breeding directions as regards this breed, developed independently in various countries. Breeders in England, the United States and Germany have made contributions here. The Leghorn's precursor comes from Italy.

ORIGIN

The different breeding directions have resulted in various distinct types of Leghorn Bantams: the English, German (ibid. Dutch) and American kinds. The German type was initially bred by Herr Schumann and exhibited to the general public at a show in Germany in 1919. The American kind was developed in the United States and recognized there in 1940. In Great Britain, the breed was developed by way of Minorca Bantams, among others, and was recognized quite early on in the last century.

White Leghorn Bantam cock, American type

White Leghorn Bantam hen, American type

APPEARANCE

The three types are very different, though they also have features in common. Thus, all miniature Leghorns have intensely yellow legs. The ear-lobes are always white with a somewhat yellowish sheen; the eyes are a reddish bay. The build is fairly light and long. The various differences are mainly found in the tail and the comb. The Dutch-German type has a slightly folded tail that is carried rather below the horizontal. In the cock, this tail has an abundance of broad, well-rounded main and lesser sickles. Usually, the comb is single, although there is also a rose-combed variant. In laying hens, the comb mostly lops at the back. The American type carries its tail more spread and in the cock it has a great deal of lesser sickles. Also the saddle feathers are longer and more profuse than in the Dutch-German variant. The main and lesser sickles are narrower than in the German Leghorn Bantam. The comb of the Americans is smaller and of a finer texture. Also here, the back part of the comb lops over in laying hens. The comb's blade almost runs horizontally backwards, while in the bantams of the German direction, it follows the neck line. The English breeding direction has a very closely folded tail. Compared to the two other breeding directions, the cock of this direction has the least ornamental feathering in its tail. Furthermore, the birds in this breeding direction stand higher and are more like the Minorca type. Striking in the English animals is the extremely large comb, which lops over entirely in the laying hen. Also the size may vary; thus the American Leghorn Bantams weigh about 700g (1½ lb), the English around 950g (2 lbs) and the German ones 800g (1¾ lb).

COLORS AND MARKING PATTERNS

Which varieties are accepted differs per type and per country. The white color however is recognized everywhere. Apart from that, depending on type, there are many other colors, including buff, black, barred, silver partridge, yellow partridge, blue partridge, partridge, blue and red. The Dutch and the English type also has a black mottled or stippled variety, called 'exchequer'.

QUALITIES

The breed is famed for its enormous laying capacity. Irrespective of their color variety, the hens lay white eggs. The fact that the hens are mostly non-sitters is inherent in a layer breed's utility. Often the eggs are hatched by another breed or in an incubator. These are lively animals that should be approached calmly. They seldom become so tame that one can pick them up. The American breeding direction is in this respect a positive exception, as these animals are often rather more placid. Because of their richly feathered tail, they do need a bit more care. Leghorn Bantams can fly quite high, so that it is best to have a roofed-in run. However, they thrive when running free.

PARTICULARS

The black mottled or exchequer color is unique for this breed. Originally, this coloring was often found in commercial Leghorn stocks. One can still tell this from the less cultivated type. This color is only found in the Leghorn. The main part of the feathers should be as completely white as possible. Less than half of the feathers has an irregularly shaped black blotch at the tip. The tail's carriage is usually fairly above the horizontal and very closely folded. This is less the case in the bantams, but to a certain extent it is still true.

Marans Bantam

COUNTRY OF ORIGIN
The United Kingdom

ORIGIN

Most Marans Bantams today are descendants of birds bred in the United Kingdom. They were developed from the large Maranses during the twenties and thirties of the last century. In 1948, they were recognized in England. Later on breeders in other countries independently also developed a miniature version of the Marans.

Marans Bantam hen, brassy black

APPEARANCE

As a dwarfed version of the Marans, the Marans Bantam is a rather big bantam. Its build is somewhat elongated, indicating a good layer. The stand is medium high and the animals have a close-fitting and broad plumage. The comb is single and the color of the eye is reddish bay. As they produce brown eggs, the ear-lobes are red. There are various breeding directions of these birds. The most striking difference is in the leg feathering, which is lacking in the English and Ameri-

Marans Bantam cock, brassy black

Young Marans Bantam hen, brassy black

Marans Bantam hen, cuckoo

Marans Bantams are renowned for their relatively large, dark brown eggs. Yet most bantams are unable to meet the egg-color standards of the large Marans. As such, this is logical for a variety of reasons. In comparison with the large fowl, the bantam lays a bigger and heavier egg. The egg's shell surface is comparatively bigger than that of a large Marans' egg, and also bigger compared with the pigment gland coloring the shell brown. The result is that the egg has a less deep color. What is more, a Marans Bantam has been developed by way of crossings with other breeds, including the Cochin Bantam. And, finally the dwarf form is only selected as regards its physical appearance, contrary to the large Marans. Many Marans Bantams are therefore very beautiful, but the egg they lay is a mere light brown. The Marans Bantam is of a rather friendly nature, but does not tame easily. As they have been mated with other breeds, they have a stronger tendency towards broodiness than the large Maranses.

Minorca Bantam

COUNTRY OF ORIGIN
Germany and the United Kingdom

ORIGIN
In England and Germany, breeders independently created a miniature version of the Minorca. Thus the English poultry fancier Mc-Farlane, as early as 1910, exhibited black as well as white diminutive Minorcas at a show, while this breed was seen a couple of years later at German exhibitions. Over the years, the white birds became less popular and even were lost for a couple of decades, until they were bred back in the seventies of the last century. Much later, a few other colors arose.

APPEARANCE
The Minorca Bantam has a fairly high stand and a slender build, with a somewhat erect carriage. In comparison to the body, the head furnishings are strikingly large. Usually we encounter this breed with a single comb, though

can-bred Marans Bantams, while in France one has only Maranses with feathered legs. Some countries, including the Netherlands, have decided to follow the country of origin in this respect.

COLORS AND MARKING PATTERNS
Among other colors, the breed is found in brassy black, cuckoo and golden cuckoo. In the Netherlands, exclusively the brassy black is recognized. By now, one is also breeding *fauve*-colored birds. This color can be best described as wheaten, but with a rather reddish basic color.

the rose comb is also recognized. However, in England the Minorca's miniature form is not accepted with a rose comb. The single comb is large and, in the hen, lops at the back. The ear-lobes are large as well and are almond-shaped (oval), while being thick and smooth in texture, with a white color. Minorca Bantams of the darker colors have dark brown eyes. Their slender type is of an elongated build with a rather long back. The tail's carriage is medium high. The tail feathers are folded, resulting in a narrow shape. In the darker varieties, the breed's leg color is dark slate (bluish gray).

COLORS AND MARKING PATTERNS
Worldwide, black is without a shadow of a doubt the most common color. Apart from this, white, self blue, buff, barred and lavender Minoracas have been bred. The latter were developed in the Netherlands.

QUALITIES
Minorca Bantams are popular because of their graceful, elegant appearance. Unfortunately, they are not bred much. They tend to fly rather high and thus can best be kept in a closed run. The hens are good layers, but are seldom broody and not very dedicated as far as this goes, so one would do well to have one's eggs hatched by some other breed or in an incubator. The eggs are big and white. A relaxed owner, giving time to these birds, will be rewarded with reasonably friendly creatures. The large comb, long wattles and big ears are sensitive to frost. In winter, you will have to take precautions to prevent the naked skin from freezing. To do so, put vaseline on the head furnishings and buy special drinkers to prevent the wattles

from getting wet. In the breeding season, the white ears can shrivel a bit and become brownish.

PARTICULARS
• The breed is reasonably popular in England, but they are not bred much in other countries. The most frequently bred color is black. Notably in this color, the large red comb and big white ears show up well.

• Apart from the Minorca Bantam discussed here, there is also the large Minorca. Except for its size, this is no different from the miniature form and has enthusiasts in various countries.

Minorca Bantam chicks

Minorca Bantam cock

APPEARANCE

In everything, the New Hampshire Bantam should be a miniature of the large 'Hamps'. Of course this is not totally true, as a dwarf fowl's proportions are different from a large one's. The head and eyes are for instance relatively larger in a diminutive chicken. The smaller New Hampshire is a rather large bantam, giving a powerful and vigorous impression. The wings are held well tucked against the body. The tail is carried spread at the end of the back line's rising hollow sweep. The

New Hampshire Bantams, chestnut blue marked

Minorca Bantam hen

animals have nice yellow legs and red earlobes.

COLORS AND MARKING PATTERNS

The color in which the breed was raised originally is chestnut red, and in this color it is recognized all over the world. There are also chestnut red blue marked as well as white New Hampshire Bantams bred and showed, though there are but few countries where all three of these colors are accepted. The white animals are not recognized in the Netherlands, because they look the same as the white Barnevelder found there.

New Hamsphire Bantam

COUNTRY OF ORIGIN
The Netherlands

ORIGIN
The Netherlands claims the honor of creating the midget version of this breed. After a rather doubtful start, the breed has become immensely popular in many countries. In the Netherlands, it regularly appears in small numbers at exhibitions.

QUALITIES
New Hampshire Bantams, with their fast growth and big laying capacity, are real utility fowl. Apart from that, they are a craze at exhibitions. The hens of this breed lay about 130 to

145 eggs a year, with an average weight of 40g (1½ oz). Broodiness is not a great feature of the breed: This is inherent in its utility aspect, for when a hen is broody she does not lay any eggs. Thus, eggs are often artificially incubated or hatched by some other breed, like the Wyandotte Bantam. The birds are good flyers, but usually remain within a fencing of 1.8m high (6 ft). They are affectionate and have a placid character, even the cocks.

PARTICULARS

The color chestnut red is the Hamps Bantam's specialty. This color is not easy to breed and the basic color and markings of the New Hampshire Bantam's progeny are rather diverse. When breeding on, the chestnut red tends to become red. However, the cock has to be what is known as 'three-colored', meaning that it should have three different shades of reddish brown. The lightest shade is seen in the neck hackles (golden bay), the medium shade is found in the saddle hackles (deep chestnut red), while the darkest one is on the saddle (lustrous dark golden bay). Still, in most cocks the color of the neck and saddle hackles is the same. A disadvantage of the reddish brown color is that it is influenced by outdoor life (sun, rain) and by laying. Therefore a hen starting with a rather even, warm red chestnut color, at the end of the laying season has a color that is wan and patchy.

Orpington Bantam

COUNTRY OF ORIGIN
Germany

ORIGIN
This miniature breed was developed at the beginning of the twentieth century. For this, the German Herman Kühn mated up (British) Orpingtons with Cochin and Java Bantams. Later, Langshan Bantams were used, while at a further stage, Wyandotte Bantams, among others, were crossed into the stock to introduce new colors.

APPEARANCE
The first impression of an Orpington Bantam is that of a 'big small chicken'. This image arises due to its broad as well as deep build and full, profuse feathering. What is more, Orpington Bantams are a bit stocky. The breast line of an Orpington Bantam is deep, descending almost perpendicularly. The wings must be carried well tucked. The cocks often hold their wings a bit too low. The shanks are short, and as a result of this and of their abundant feathering, the birds have a very low stand. The breed has a broad skull and a single comb.

COLORS AND MARKING PATTERNS
This popular bantam breed is found in many different colors, including black, blue laced, white, buff, red, buff black laced, barred, buff columbian and birchen.

QUALITIES
This breed is preeminently suitable for beginners living in residential areas. The birds are usually hardy and, when well taken care of, soon become trusting. The cocks are generally friendly. They are not great crowers and, compared to other breeds, do so rather softly. The hens are excellent layers, even in the Winter months. They get broody easily and usually rear their chicks without problem. Orpington Bantams can be given the free run, as they are rather placid and seldom or never fly. Often, a fencing of a mere 60cm (2 ft) is sufficient.

PARTICULARS
The color buff that is less popular in the bantams than in the large Orpingtons requires precautionary measures, as does the color

Orpington Bantams black

Orpington Bantams, laced blue

Barred Plymouth Rock Bantam hen

Orpington Bantam hen, blue laced

Buff-colored Plymouth Rock Bantam cock

blue. Under the influence of sunlight and rain, it can fade greatly and lose its evenness, which is sometimes called the 'turning' of the color. If you keep your animals out of the rain and see to a run with a lot of shade, it will slow the discoloration process.

Plymouth Rock Bantam

COUNTRY OF ORIGIN
Various countries

ORIGIN
The Plymouth Rock Bantam is a miniature version of the Plymouth Rock, the preeminent American utility fowl. This smaller version was developed from Plymouth Rocks and bantam breeds by different breeders in various countries. At the beginning of the last century, the first Plymouth Rock Bantams were exhibited in Germany, the United Kingdom and the United States. By making use of the single-combed Wyandotte Bantams that were occasionally born, the number of varieties has been increased.

APPEARANCE
The Plymouth Rock Bantam has to be a good copy of the large Rock, so it is a rather big bantam with a long body. This elongated contour is further enhanced by the low carriage of the tail that, without showing any angle whatsoever, links up with the almost horizontal line of the back. The tail is quite short and is carried semi-spread. The cock's tail feathers are entirely covered by the main and lesser sickles. The breast is deep and well rounded. The legs are yellow. On the head, there is a medium-sized red single comb. The earlobes of this breed are also red. The eyes are large and reddish brown in color, having a lively expression.

COLORS AND MARKING PATTERNS
The breed is found in many different colors, including black, white, buff, columbian, buff columbian, multiple penciled partridge ('triple laced'), multiple penciled silver partridge, barred, red barred, blue laced and red porcelain. The barred variety is the original and most popular color.

QUALITIES

This is a very strong and reasonably popular breed. The hens start laying rather early, having a considerable laying capacity, though they do not tend to get broody often. The eggs are of a very light creamy color. Plymouth Rock Bantams hardly ever fly, but a fence of about a 1.50m (5 ft) is advisable. They are fairly placid animals that are not aggressive and soon become trusting, provided you treat them well. Young Rock Bantams are fast growers that afford few problems when rearing them.

PARTICULARS

In the barred variety of this breed, the hens look darker than the cocks do. This is because, in the hens, the black bars are broader than the white ones, while in the cocks the black and white crosswise stripes are of about the same width. The reason for this is the sex-related hereditariness of the barring factor ('linkage'). Birds differ from mammals as regards hereditariness in the sexes. Male birds have two sex chromosomes ('XX'), while the females must make do with only one ('X'). The factor for barring is found on the sex chromosomes. Because the cocks have two sex chromosomes, this barring factor is present twice, resulting in a narrower black bar in the cock than in the hen.

Rhode Island Bantam

COUNTRY OF ORIGIN

Germany/the United Kingdom

ORIGIN

This miniature breed was bred in both Germany and England by mating up Rhode Island Reds with bantam breeds. They were created at the beginning of the twentieth century.

APPEARANCE

Seen from the side, the fairly long body should have a 'brick shape', in which particularly the straight, horizontal line of the back is striking. The breast is well rounded and the tail is of medium length, being carried a little above the back line. The comb can be either a single or

Rhode Island Bantam cock

Rhode Island Bantam hen

a rose comb. The eyes are reddish brown, and the shanks are always yellow, often with a somewhat reddish line of pigmentation down the sides.

Rhode Island Bantam cock

COLORS AND MARKING PATTERNS

The 'standard color' in which the breed is found is red. Apart from this, there are also white birds with a rose comb, but these are not seen very often. The red color comes with either a rose comb or a single comb.

QUALITIES

The miniature form of the Rhode Island lays eggs throughout the year, even in Winter. The eggs are light brown. Rhode Island Bantams are calm and can be easily tamed. They can be free-range chickens, but may also be kept in a run. The animals are fast developers, the hens laying their first egg at about five months. Some – but certainly not all – stocks get broody often and are reliable sitters.

PARTICULARS

The Rhode Island's diminutive form, and notably its original red has many fanciers in both Europe and the United States. From country to country, there are differences of opinion as to the ideal color, but most judges prefer seeing a deep dark brown. This color continues into the fluff, and is inextricably bound up with a few black markings on the wings and tails of the cocks, and on the bottom part of the neck feathers in the hens.

Rheinlander Bantam

COUNTRY OF ORIGIN

Germany

ORIGIN

The breed was developed in Germany from large Rheinlanders and non-standard bantams, and was recognized there in 1932.

APPEARANCE

The 'ideal' Rheinlander Bantam is a miniature of its large namesake, though in practice this is always a bit different. Overall, the bantam gives a somewhat more elegant impression than the large, heavy-built Rheinlander. This has nothing to do with its weight, for, like most dwarfed forms, this breed weighs about a third of what its big brother does. The animals are of an elongated country fowl type with an almost horizontal carriage. The wings are held a little below the horizontal line and well tucked. The tail of this miniature fowl is abundantly feathered and is carried medium high and wide spread. The hen's upper main tail feathers mostly have a slightly curved shape. As his trademark, the cock has a richly feathered tail, with long, broad and well-curved main and lesser sickles. The head is small and sports a small rose comb, the spike (leader) of which follows the neck line. On the comb, there are fine, tiny rounded points. The ear is red and in the darker vari-

White Rheinlander Bantam cock

White Rheinlander Bantam hen

layers, and bantam hens acquit themselves excellently of this task, their eggs having a white shell. Broodiness is an issue, so that the eggs are usually hatched by either an incubator or a foster mother. The animals have a fairly placid nature. If you keep them in smaller, closed chicken coops and approach them in a relaxed way, these birds can become

Blue Rheinlander Bantam hen

Black Rheinlander Bantam cock

eties the eye is dark brown. Rheinlander Bantams do not stand very high and have dusky legs.

COLORS AND MARKING PATTERNS

The first color bred was black. Later on, white, blue laced, partridge and cuckoo-colored Rheinlander Bantams were developed.

QUALITIES

Large Rheinlander hens are known to be good

reasonably tame. They fly well, but do not avail themselves much of this capability. The chicks of this breed are usually very vigorous and grow up fast. However, it does take quite a while before the cockerels have their full tail. In positioning the perches, one must keep this long, abundant tail in mind. Place the perches high above the ground and not too close to a wall. In chicken coops where hygiene leaves something to be desired and the bantams are visited by mice, the tail feathers will soon show evidence of gnawing if the perches are not placed high enough. Apparently, they form an attractive source of protein for mice. Your ban-

Black Rheinlander Bantams hens

Partridge-colored Rheinlander Bantam hen

tams however will not look very nice after such nocturnal visits.

PARTICULARS

Due to breeding broad, full tails, it rather frequently happens that this breed has more than the normal number of main tail feathers. As a rule, chickens actually have seven main tail feathers on each side of their tail. By selecting them as regards full tails, one can easily achieve eight.

Twenthe Bantam

COUNTRY OF ORIGIN
The Netherlands

ORIGIN
Around 1940, the miniature form of the Twenthe Fowl was bred. To this day, it remains unknown precisely what breeds were used to develop this bantam, but probably Asian Game Bantams and Leghorn Bantams were among them. This assumption is logical, as the large Twenthes were developed from crosses between farmyard fowl and, among others, Malays and Leghorns. The breed was created by Siemerink, a Dutch breeder from the town of Almelo.

APPEARANCE
Appearance-wise, Twenthe Bantams clearly show that they are related to the Leghorn Bantam, though they also have game fowl blood in their veins. This miniature breed is of a slender build and has a fairly long back. The tail's carriage is rather below the horizontal and semi-open, while the cock has inherited its beautiful ornamental feathering from the Leghorn. The main sickles are long and well curved. The wings are carried nicely tucked against the body and pointing somewhat downwards. The leg color of Twenthe Bantams is intensely yellow. The head clearly has a game fowl look to it, the skull being short and broad, while the fairly short beak is powerful. The featherless skin of the head has a lively red color. The head sports a walnut comb, with fine points and furrows on the comb's flesh, reminding

Silver partridge Twenthe Bantam hen

Silver partridge Twenthe Bantam cock

The influence of game fowl is clearly present in the Twenthe Bantam.

one of the texture on the outside of a straw-berry. The comb itself is small and hardly de-veloped in the hens.

COLORS AND MARKING PATTERNS
This breed is found in partridge and silver partridge.

QUALITIES
The cocks are known for their loud crowing and some specimens are aggressive from time to time. Among themselves, the birds are rather fierce – a natural legacy of their game fowl progenitors. When treated well, these lively, active birds generally grow to trust the person taking care of them. Twenthe Bantams can fly well and high, making a roofed-in run necessary if you want to keep them on your premises. The hens regularly go broody, and one need not expect any problems rearing the chicks. They are good layers and have cream--colored eggs.

Welsummer Bantam

COUNTRY OF ORIGIN
The United Kingdom and Germany

ORIGIN
This attractive breed came about in the 1930s and 1940s by interbreeding various kinds of bantams with the original Welsummer. The British breeders used Rhode Island Red Bantams and partridge-colored Old English Game Bantams for this. The Germans availed themselves of Rhode Island Red Bantams and

Welsummer Bantam hen

Welsummer Bantam cock

Wyandotte Bantams. Since 1950, this miniature breed has also been bred in the Netherlands.

APPEARANCE
Welsummer Bantams have a rather sturdy build with a average long, fairly deep and well--rounded breast. The backside of the hen is deep and full. The breed has a tail that is carried fairly high and is somewhat folded in the hens. The cock's tail is nicely covered by broad and well-curved sickles. The animals have a single comb that is not particularly large. The ear-lobes are red. The leg color is yellow, although growing lighter in practice when the hens lay many eggs. Welsummer Bantams furthermore have lively reddish bay eyes.

COLORS AND MARKING PATTERNS
Originally, this breed was only found in red partridge. This is the color in which it is rec-ognized in most countries and is regarded as the breed's original color. In the 1960s, the breed was also bred in yellow partridge in Ger-many, and a little later on in silver partridge.

QUALITIES
Like their large ancestors, these attractively colored bantams are known for their relative-ly large eggs with a dark brown shell. The eggs weigh 50g (1¾ oz) or more. Welsummer Ban-tams are active, lively creatures and not shy.

You can keep them in an open-roofed run, provided it is higher than 1.8m (6 ft).
Because Welsummer Bantams are active, they soon get bored in small runs with little diversion, which might result in feather-pecking. This is why one should see to a bit of exercise in small coops. By hanging up greens in netting or a basket just above the animals, you will keep them occupied. When reared, the young cockerels can get into terrible fights with one another, so always run an old cock with them, to keep the youngsters in their place.

Wyandotte Bantam

COUNTRY OF ORIGIN
The United States of America

Eggs of the Welsummer Bantam

Welsummer Bantam cock

ORIGIN
This miniature breed was developed from the large Wyandotte. The diminutive form was already known at the beginning of the twentieth

Wyandotte Bantams, columbian

century in the United States, and soon afterwards found its way to other countries, including those in Europe. Nowadays it is one of the most popular chicken breeds in countries where chickens are bred and exhibited. It is, so to speak, the 'Golden Retriever' among chickens. Only in England does the breed has few adepts.

APPEARANCE
In the countries where this breed is raised, opinions differ as to its type. Thus, there is a big difference between a Dutch White Wyandotte Bantam and a German one. The German birds are far higher on their legs and have a different tail shape. The Dutch type corresponds with the American standard. The Wyandotte Bantam is a medium heavy miniature fowl with an almost round body. If you trace the body line, it is a circle from which only head and legs protrude. The wings are held well tucked. The back line ends with a smooth concave sweep in the tail, so that it is hard to tell where the back ends and the tail begins. The main tail feathers are firm and broad. Looking at a Wyandotte Bantam from behind, one should see a V-shaped tail. However, not all birds have this. The head is short, round and broad, and adorned with a rose comb of which the spike or leader follows the neck line. The color of the eye is a reddish bay, the ear-lobes are red, and the Wyandotte Bantam has yellow legs.

261

Four month old Wyandotte Bantams; golden blue laced (left), silver black laced (right)

The most favored variants of this breed are the white and the laced birds and the ones with columbian markings.

QUALITIES

Wyandotte Bantams have a friendly, very placid nature. If you approach them calmly, they will soon be tame and trusting, and can even be 'trained to the hand'. Because the cocks are not aggressive, they are also ideal for people who only want to keep a few birds as a hobby and find interaction with their animals important. They are also very suitable for kids. Wyandotte Bantams are hardly inclined to fly and usually stay put behind a fence of a mere 60cm (2 ft). Giving them the free run is usually not a problem, as they do not feel the need to wander far. The hens are good layers and are often reliably broody (and sometimes persistently so). They are excellent mothers, keeping a close eye on their chicks. Thus, they are regularly used as foster mothers for eggs and chicks of less reliable breeds.

Wyandotte Bantam hen, silver black laced

Wyandotte Bantam cock, silver black laced

COLORS AND MARKING PATTERNS

This highly popular breed comes in many different colors, including black, white, buff, red, self blue, blue laced, columbian, buff columbian, columbian blue marked, buff columbian blue marked, salmon, porcelain, red porcelain, multiple penciled partridge ('triple laced'), multiple penciled silver partridge, multiple penciled blue partridge, multiple penciled red partridge, barred, golden black laced, golden blue laced, silver black laced, yellow white laced, golden necked, silver necked and black white mottled. In spite of there being many colors, breeders are still working on new varieties, including lavender.

Wyandotte Bantam cock, silver partridge

Wyandotte Bantam cock, barred

Wyandotte Bantams, golden blue laced

Wyandotte Bantams, salmon

Wyandotte Bantam hen, barred

Barred Wyandotte Bantam chicks

PARTICULARS

Without a shadow of a doubt, Wyandotte Bantams are among the most popular bantams worldwide. They are not only loved for their 'cuddly' appearance, but also, among other things, for their hardiness, placid nature and vast color range.

Salmon Faverolles Bantam cock

19 Table Breeds

Breed Descriptions

Faverolles Bantam

COUNTRY OF ORIGIN
Various countries

ORIGIN
The miniature form of the Faverolles has been bred in various countries by different breeders independently and with diverse starting material. It is logical that in Germany and England a dwarf form was raised that corresponded with the breeding direction found there. In France itself, the birthplace of the Faverolles, a bantam version was never developed. The German Faverolles Bantam was created in 1922 from a Faverolles cock that had stayed too small, crossed with Bearded and Booted Bantams and columbian Brahma Bantams.

APPEARANCE
The Faverolles Bantam has a deep, heavy and long build. Its head is broad and round, with

Salmon blue marked Faverolles Bantam cock

Salmon Faverolles Bantam chicks

a relatively small single comb. The beard is large and fully feathered, clearly consisting of three clumps and a pendulant center piece. The eye color is a reddish bay. The birds stand low and have pinkish white feathered legs. As a typical Faverolles breed feature, they have a fifth toe. Like the large Faverolles, the bantam breed is raised in various types, for instance the German and the English type. The difference between these types is found for example in the rather short and broad tail. The German type carries this practically horizontally, while the English type does so at medium height. The English birds were developed by each time selecting the smallest animals from among the large Faverolles. Little, if any, use was made of true bantam breeds. Therefore they are considerably bigger than the Faverolles Bantams bred in Germany.

COLORS AND MARKING PATTERNS
The original color was salmon, but in the course of time other varieties were added, including blue marked salmon. In this, the black markings of the salmon-colored birds were replaced by blue. There are also white, black, buff, cuckoo, columbian and blue laced Faverolles Bantams. Both in the Netherlands and Germany, we find only the two salmon varieties. In England, there is more interest in colors apart from salmon, which is also popular there.

Faverolles Bantams have five toes.

Salmon Faverolles Bantam hen

QUALITIES

Faverolles Bantams are very pleasant, gentle and rather placid chickens. If you take good care of them and approach them calmly, they can easily become very tame. You can let them run free, for they are not inclined to fly and will usually remain in your garden. But take into account that then the feathering of their feet will become less fetching. Therefore exhibition specimens are better kept in dry, clean runs.

If you keep Faverolles Bantams in a small run, they tend to get fat easily, so you should make sore they have enough to occupy them. This you can do by getting them to work a little for their feed: Hang a rack with greens at a level that forces the birds to jump to reach it. Thus, you keep them in better condition. Faverolles Bantams grow and develop fast. The hens are reasonably good layers, often laying on into Winter. For a bantam, the eggs are large and they are light brown in color. Broodiness is rare in these non-sitters.

PARTICULARS

- In Germany the breed is called *Deutsches Zwerglachshuhn*, a clear reference to its original color.
- The fifth toe is an aspect that is hard to breed in, as this toe tends to grow together with the fourth toe. Even if you select with respect to this feature, you will always get a percentage of birds in which the fourth and fifth toe have grown together. Moreover, this factor brings with it a further bifurcation of nails and toes. Two nails on one toe is something that occurs quite frequently in this breed, as does a splitting of the fifth toe, resulting in a sixth one.

Houdan Bantam

COUNTRY OF ORIGIN
The United Kingdom

ORIGIN
Around 1940, this diminutive breed arose in England from Houdans that were too small and were crossed with small bantams and bearded and crested bantams. The breed has never been very popular and unfortunately is hardly ever raised in most countries.

APPEARANCE
At first sight, the Houdan Bantam reminds one of the Crested Bearded Bantam. However, its build is a bit fuller and the birds have a somewhat lower stand. The back line is rather long and carried almost horizontally. The wings are also practically horizontal, while the tail is

Black mottled Houdan Bantam hen

Head of a black mottled Houdan Bantam hen

Young Houdan Bantam hen, black mottled

Head of a black mottled Houdan Bantam cock

Head of a black mottled Houdan Bantam cockerel

rather well spread and of a medium high carriage. The cocks have abundant sickles in their tail. The shanks have five toes, the extra toe standing separately from the fourth and slanting backwards. The leg of the mottled variety that is bred most, is pinkish white and has tiny black mottling. On the rather short, thick neck there is an impressive head, adorned with a big crest and a full, three-clump beard. The globular crest grows on what is called a skull knob, a bulge on the skull's crown. In front of the crest, there is a comb made up of two upward growing comb leaves, that are fused at the bottom. Such a comb is sometimes called a 'leaf comb', as the two comb leaves are rather deeply serrated, somewhat resembling the leaf of an oak.

COLORS AND MARKING PATTERNS
Although in practice we only see black mottled Houdan Bantams, other colors are recognized. White and lavender birds of this breed are also accepted at exhibitions.

QUALITIES
Houdan Bantams are placid and calm by nature. That is why they are easily tamed and can even be taken care of by younger kids. Because of their crests and beards, the animals can really only be housed in roofed-over, dry chicken coops. The large crest and full beard require a number of special facilities. Because these birds are susceptible to lice in their crests, check the animals regularly, and curb the complaint as soon as it manifests itself. The large beard and crest need protection from damp and dirt. Not only should the coop be dry

because of this and preferably fully roofed, there should also be a special drinker. Jar waterers (little 'water towers') are the most serviceable drinkers here. Houdan Bantams are reasonably good layers of white eggs. The hens usually have no problem getting broody.

PARTICULARS
This breed's leaf comb is in fact a buttercup comb in which the two comb leaves have not grown together at the back. Such a comb arises when a bird with a V-shaped or horn comb is interbred with a chicken that has a single comb. As a Bearded and Crested Bantam, which originally had a V-shaped comb, collaborated in developing the Houdan Bantam, it quite often occurs that Houdan Bantams are born with V-shaped combs instead of the required leaf comb. This means that some animals do not breed true as to passing on the comb.

Kraienkoppe Bantam or Breda Bantam

COUNTRY OF ORIGIN
The Netherlands

ORIGIN
This small breed was developed during the 1930s, and is therefore one of the first Dutch miniature breeds. Unfortunately the

White Breda Bantam cock

White Breda Bantam hens

Kraienkoppe, better known as the Breda Bantam, soon fell into oblivion. It was not until the eighties that a few breeders of large Bredas picked up the thread of the Breda Bantam again. At that point there was very little material left, to put it mildly. With a handful of Breda Bantams a breeding program was initiated, in which the Dutch Booted Bantam and the Owl Beard Bantam were also involved. Nowadays, the breed has a small, but steady number of fanciers and breeders.

APPEARANCE
The miniature version of the Breda is about two-thirds of the size of its large counterpart. The animals on average weigh 800–900g (1¾–2 lbs). They have an upright carriage and are of a rather sturdy – though slender – build, with a slightly sloping back. They have quite a high stand, meaning that their legs are fairly long. The back is rather long and ends in

Black Breda Bantam cock

Breda Bantam chicks

Black Breda Bantam hen

a high-carried tail that is spread. On their heels the animals have long, stiff feathers growing askew, called 'vulture hocks'. There are feathers on the rather long legs as well as on the outer toes, so that they do not really have fully feathered feet. The wings of this miniature breed are held at a downward slant. The breed was not named for the sound of the cock's voice, but for the crowlike shape of its head, in which it is particularly striking that a comb is totally lacking. Only some red, featherless and level skin reminds one of a possible comb. The wattles are short and round. The animals have a small bulge on their skull with stiff, hairlike feathers on it, growing backwards. The nostrils are cavernous and the ear-lobes white.

COLORS AND MARKING PATTERNS
Black, white, laced blue and cuckoo.

QUALITIES
In spite of their fierce appearance, Breda Bantams are neither fighters nor aggressive types. Even the cocks are quite friendly as a rule. The hens are almost never broody. The eggs are usually hatched by a foster mother or an incubator. The egg production is not bad at all: On average a Breda Bantam hen lays about 200 white eggs annually, each weighing around 45g (1½–1¾ oz). As the birds do not have really densely feathered feet, they can be given free run without getting damaged very much.

PARTICULARS
Outside of the Netherlands, this breed is usually known by the name of the city where the large Kraienkoppe originated, to wit Breda.

North Holland Bantam

COUNTRY OF ORIGIN
The Netherlands

ORIGIN
Around 1960, the North Holland Bantams were developed in the Netherlands from crosses with Niederrheiners and various miniature breeds, including Wyandotte Bantams, English-type Marans Bantams, Sussex Bantams and Plymouth Rock Bantams. The main breeder working on this breed, Mr. Meijer, is an honorary member of the Dutch Poultry Association.

APPEARANCE
North Holland Bantams should be as identical to their large namesakes as possible. Because this is a sturdy breed, the miniatures are also rather big, the cocks weighing around 1kg (2 lbs). The resemblance to the large breed has been reasonably successful. How-

North Holland Bantams become tame easily.

lobes. The breed has reddish bay eyes and pinkish white legs.

COLORS AND MARKING PATTERNS

The only variety in which this breed is raised is cuckoo. There should not be too much contrast between the light and the dark bars in this color; it should be rather a dark gray alternating with a light gray, than a black bar alternated with a white one. The result of this is that, seen from a distance, it looks as if the birds are covered in a bluish gray haze, notably in the hens. That is why the breed is popularly termed 'North Holland Blue'.

QUALITIES

Like most table breeds, North Holland Bantams are very placid and calm by nature. They prefer not to fly, and therefore possible to house the breed in smaller runs. Also, they can be given the free run of your yard, as they usually remain close to home and their henhouse. The animals have a very pleasant character and are tolerant of one another. Even growing cockerels can be kept together in the same coop for a long time. A good, calm minder can tame these animals very quickly. As they are such placid bantams, you can also let kids take care of them. The hens are reasonable layers and also go broody. Once they get into the nest, they are good sitters and good mothers as well. The chicks grow up fast and are rather precocious.

PARTICULARS

This diminutive form is relatively young as a breed. That is why the breed's typical standard features are still insufficiently secured as regards heredity. As the Niederrhein Bantam has contributed a great deal to the development of this breed, one can see quite a bit of its influence in the North Holland Bantams. Not only are the carriage and spread of the tail often 'Niederrhein-like', the color and markings are also sometimes not truly North Holland, as the contrast between the light and the dark bars is too distinct in many birds.

ever, quite frequently the large breed's typical tail shape is lacking in practice. The ideal tail is carried well above the horizontal, is rather short and is only allowed to be spread a little. Many dwarfs tend to carry their tails a bit too low and to spread them too much. The animals have a deep breast that is well rounded. Their stand is medium high, though in the hens it seems to be lower because of their deep and full backside. The wings are carried well tucked. The head is rather large and has a medium-sized single comb and red ear-

Sussex Bantam

COUNTRY OF ORIGIN
The United Kingdom

ORIGIN
The Sussex Bantam, a dwarfed version of the Sussex, was developed around 1920 in England. The breed was created by way of large Sussex specimens that had remained too small and a few bantam breeds we never found out the names of. In its country of origin, the breed is very popular.

APPEARANCE
The Sussex Bantam is a miniature fowl with a medium high stand and a 'rectangular' body shape. This is enhanced by the tail's low carriage, hardly above the horizontal line. The tail itself is well spread and the main tail feathers are medium long. The cock has rather short main and lesser sickles, covering the tail feathers. Sussex Bantams have a broad, deep breast. The leg color is white, also called pinkish white. The ear-lobes are red, as is the featherless facial skin. The head sports a medium-sized single comb and the color of the eye is red.

COLORS AND MARKING PATTERNS
The first color shown in England was columbian. Afterwards, other colors arose, such as buff columbian, red columbian, gray silver, red porcelain, white and columbian blue marked.

Sussex Bantam cock, gray silver

QUALITIES
These birds have a placid nature and a strong constitution. Taming them is no problem at all, for if you offer them something good to eat every day on your outstretched hand, this is done in a jiffy. Also, these friendly animals are highly suitable for children. If you have sufficient room, you can even keep several cocks, should you so desire. The birds are affectionate and seldom aggressive. Sussex Bantams are excellent layers, often laying on throughout the winter. The hens are regularly broody and are good mothers.

PARTICULARS
A breed-related color only found in the Sussex is gray silver. This variant looks a little like the color birchen, with the difference that the black feathers of the back also have silvery white lacing. Moreover the feathers on the back and breast have a white shaft. This black-and-white pattern is exceptionally beautiful.

Sussex Bantam hen, buff columbian

Sussex Bantam hen, red columbian

20 Multipurpose Breeds

Breed Descriptions

Amrock Bantam

COUNTRY OF ORIGIN
East Germany

ORIGIN
The Amrock Bantam was bred from the large Amrocks. In 1972, the breed was recognized for the first time in what was formerly East Germany. More than ten years later, other countries followed the East German example.

APPEARANCE
Amrock Bantams are rather big miniature chickens. The hens of this breed weigh around 900g (2 lbs). This dwarf fowl's type is called 'bell-shaped'. The simile refers to the profile (silhouette or contour) formed by the hen's back and tail line in combination with the neck and this profile somewhat resembles a bronze church bell. The line of the back is medium long, ending in the tail with a concave sweep. The tail itself is broad at the base, is almost entirely spread and is carried medium high. The breast line is deep and well rounded. Amrock Bantams have a single comb and red ear-lobes. The color of the eye should be a reddish bay. The Amrock has a medium high stand and yellow legs.

COLORS AND MARKING PATTERNS
The breed only comes in a barred version. The hens look darker, because their black bars are broader than those of the cocks.

Amrock Bantams

Amrock Bantam hen

Amrock Bantam chicks

Amrock Bantam cock

QUALITIES

The breed is known for having fast growth and development. Moreover the hens are reasonably good layers, and start doing so at the age of five months. The eggs are relatively large and of a light brown color, weighing on average more than 40g (1½ oz) and sometimes even 50g (1¾ oz). The hens are not always reliable sitters; their eggs are often hatched by other breeds or in an incubator. As the attractively marked Amrock Bantams are not really keen flyers and are rather placid, you can keep them very well in a roofless run or leave them to wander about the garden. When approached calmly and taken care of well, they fairly soon become trusting. In order to achieve the nice yellow leg color, you should see to a bit of extra natural pigment. If you offer them a spacious run or let them grub about the lawn, they will ingest this pigment from the grass. In small runs, you can feed them extra grass, kale, carrots and La Plata corn.

Bielefelder Bantam

COUNTRY OF ORIGIN
Germany

ORIGIN
The Bielefelder Bantam is a miniature form of the Bielefelder. It was bred by the German Roth at the end of the 1980s. Roth created the breed by crossing Bielefelders with, among others, Amrock and Welsummer Bantams.

APPEARANCE
This miniature form of the large Bielefelder belongs to the bigger bantam breeds. Its body is of an elongated build. The breast is deep and

A study of the head of a Bielefelder Bantam hen

A study of the head of a Bielefelder Bantam cock

Bielefelder Bantam hen

well rounded, while the shape is 'rectangular'. The tail is well spread and is not carried very high, so that there is only a faint angle visible where the back ends in the tail. The main tail feathers themselves are broad. The Bielefelder has a single comb which is rather small compared to the bird's size. The ear-lobes are red and the eyes are a reddish bay. The legs are yellow.

COLORS AND MARKING PATTERNS

The breed is found in the original color cuckoo red partridge (*kennfarbig*) and in cuckoo silver partridge. The combination of red partridge with cuckoo markings sees to it that the red partridge's plain black feather parts become cuckoo, showing an alternation of light and dark bars. In the hens, the breast must be

without these cuckoo markings – something that is very hard to achieve.

QUALITIES

Like its big brother, the Bielefelder, this miniature breed is a 'layer cum table breed'. Among other things, this means that the animals grow and develop fast, and that the hens have a considerable laying capacity. Usually, you may also expect an egg in winter from these animals. The eggs are of a good size and are light brown in color. Bielefelder Bantams are by nature calm and friendly chickens. They can be easily 'trained to the hand', and can either be kept in a run or left to roam the yard.

PARTICULARS

In developing the large Bielefelder, one not only had in mind a good layer with quite a bit of meat on it, but also what is called an 'auto-sexing' breed. This means that, by their down, it is straight away possible to tell which chicks are hens and which are cocks. The bantams also have this feature. The down of newly hatched cock chicks is of a lighter brown and they have a bigger white spot on their head than the hen chicks do. Because of this quality, one is able to see right after the eggs have hatched how many there are of each kind.

La Flèche Bantam

COUNTRY OF ORIGIN
Germany

La Flèche Bantam cock

ORIGIN

The La Flèche Bantam is a miniature of the large La Flèche that is of French origin. It was bred in Germany by way of La Flèche chickens and bantam breeds like the Rheinlander Bantam. In 1970, it was acknowledged in Germany.

APPEARANCE

The La Flèche Bantam is a rather big, though nevertheless slender-built miniature fowl with a fairly high stand. Its body is long and rather broad. The tail is large and carried spread, and the cocks have well-developed ornamental feathers in their tail. In most varieties, the color of the legs is bluish gray or dark slate. The cuckoo and the white specimens have lightly colored shanks. Like their large counterparts, La Flèche Bantams have a V-shaped comb consisting of two little, round, parallel horns sticking upwards (also called a 'horn comb'). Right behind these horns, there are a few tiny, erect feathers, which in fact is a rudimentary crest. The 'nose caps' are prominent on the upper part of the beak and 'flared' ('cavernous'), implying kinship with the crested fowls. The ear-lobes are always white. The color of the eye, depending on the variety, is reddish brown to dark brown. There is some difference in shape as regards the various breeding directions. The build of French La Flèche Bantams is often a bit more hefty and plump than the elegant birds bred elsewhere, for instance in Germany.

COLORS AND MARKING PATTERNS

The breed is found in four different colors, to wit black, white, laced blue and cuckoo. The black variety is accepted in all countries where the breed is raised; the remaining colors are not always approved.

QUALITIES

La Flèche Bantams are lively birds that love to fly high and are very good at doing so. If you give them free run, they will be found all over the neighborhood and will look for a branch to spend the night on. You can only prevent this by keeping them in a closed run. However, please take into account that these animals need sufficient diversion. La Flèche Bantams are far from aggressive, but seldom become really tame. As is inherent in the color of their ears, they lay white, relatively large eggs. La Flèche Bantams are vigorous miniature fowl that are fast growers and reach adulthood early.

PARTICULARS

- The La Flèche's special V-shaped comb ('horn comb') and the breed's original black color has resulted in its nicknames 'devil-headed chicken' and 'Satan's fowl'.
- The breed is quite rare, and in many countries it is seldom or never seen.

Orloff Bantam

COUNTRY OF ORIGIN

Germany

ORIGIN

Around 1920, a successful attempt was made in Germany to create a miniature form of the Orloff. In order to develop this breed, Orloffs

Orloff Bantam hen, black white mottled

Orloff Bantam hen, red porcelain

that had remained too small as well as Malay Bantams were used. As was the case with so many other breeds, there was almost nothing left of this still young diminutive breed after the Second World War. By way of some 'remnants' and both Rhode Island and Japanese Bantams, the breed was built up again. Since

Orloff Bantam hen, red porcelain

1952, it has been accepted into the German standard of perfection.

APPEARANCE

Orloff Bantams are rather hefty dwarfs, the hens weighing approximately 1kg (2 lbs). The breed is clearly related to the game fowl. This kinship is betrayed by its erect carriage with the somewhat sloping back line and even more so by its head. The animals have a fairly high stand and yellow legs. The back is rather long, sloping and 'even'. The breast is broad and well rounded. The wings are carried well tucked. The Orloff's tail is not particularly large and is carried rather above the horizontal. Its plumage is considerably more profuse than that of real game fowl. This can also be seen in the abundant main and lesser sickles of the cock's tail. The neck is long, is carried upright and is fully feathered. Notably the upper part of the neck looks rather thick. This is enhanced by these chickens' full three-clump beard. The skull is rather short and broad, and due to this the bay eyes are deep-set under the so-called 'eyebrows'. The comb has the shape of half a walnut, with characteristic furrowing.

COLORS AND MARKING PATTERNS

The best known variety of the Orloff Bantam is red porcelain. The breed is also recognized

Orloff Bantam cock, red porcelain

277

in red, white and cuckoo. The latter two colors are however a rarity.

QUALITIES

By nature, Orloff Bantams are hardy and strong, and are quite indifferent to weather conditions. Thus, they are not very fussy as to their housing, thriving either in a closed run or when running free. They are not really keen flyers, so the run need not be roofed-in. Towards their owner, these chickens behave calmly and trustingly. However, among themselves, they show that they have game fowl blood in their veins. Thus, if you introduce new females into the flock, the hens might be quarrelsome as to their place in the pecking order because young cockerels are rather pugnacious, they are best placed under the supervision of an adult cock, so that fierce fights are prevented. In this way, growing cockerels can remain together for quite a while, provided that there are sufficient possibilities for escape and hiding. The hens lay a considerable number of eggs with a light-colored shell. Broodiness does occur in this breed, though they are not overkeen in this respect. However, if the hens do become broody, they are reliable, good mothers.

PARTICULARS

- The most common color found in this breed, red porcelain, has somewhat different markings than for instance the Sussex red porcelain. In the Orloff, the markings are a bit cruder and do not constitute such an important part of the animals' exhibition value. This is notably seen in the breast, which contains quite a lot of black feather parts. Generally, the black spangles and white mottling at the feather's tip do not have a very round shape and rather seem to overlap one another.
- Apart from the diminutive form discussed here, there is also a large Orloff, which is not as common as the dwarf form.

Sulmtaler Bantam

COUNTRY OF ORIGIN
Germany

Sulmtaler Bantam hen, wheaten

ORIGIN

The Sulmtaler Bantam is a miniature of the large Sulmtaler. The bantam breed was created by the German breeder Webers in the 1950s. To this purpose, he crossed Sulmtalers with various bantam breeds, including bearded and crested ones plus the odd game bantam and non-standard crested bantam. Later on other breeds were also bred in. Nowadays the type remains firmly fixed.

APPEARANCE

The Sulmtaler Bantam is rather big and has a somewhat elongated build. The body is deep and broad. The back is fairly long and is carried horizontally. The rather short tail is well spread and is held medium high. The legs are pinkish white. The neck is not very long and is rather abundantly feathered in the cocks. The Sulmtaler has a small tuft following the shape

Sulmtaler Bantam hens, wheaten

Sulmtaler Bantam cock, wheaten

Sulmtaler Bantams, wheaten

of the head. In front of this tuft, there is a single comb. The blade of this comb is rather short and the points are not deeply serrated. In the hen, the comb's anterior has a double wave or twist, so that it is S-shaped. The ear-lobes are white, the eyes bay.

COLORS AND MARKING PATTERNS
The breed comes in two colors, wheaten and blue wheaten. The latter is found in Austria, but is not as established in other countries.

QUALITIES
Sulmtaler Bantams are fairly calm and friendly chickens. It is certainly no 'dashing exploit' to tame these birds. They are excellent flyers and can therefore best be kept in a closed run that need not be very big. Sulmtaler Bantams are also very suitable for those who do not have much space. The hens lay rather small light-colored eggs, weighing 35 to 40g ($1\frac{1}{4}$–$1\frac{1}{2}$ oz). They are non-sitters; most breeders put their eggs under a hen of some other breed or use an incubator. However, sometimes there is no need for this, because once a Sulmtaler Bantam is broody she usually persists.

PARTICULARS
It is hard to breed the comb of a Sulmtaler Bantam hen up to standard. The hen must have an 'S-shaped comb', as the comb's length would interfere with the tuft that is placed rather far forward on her head. If a hen has a perfect comb, her brothers usually also have this longer comb. However, the texture of a cock's comb is a lot firmer, so that there is no

Sulmtaler Bantam chick

S-twist. The result is that the comb's blade lops sideways, which is not a pretty sight in the cocks one would therefore prefer a somewhat shorter comb. Because of all this, exhibition specimens tend to be taken from different breeding flocks, a flock for hens and a flock for cocks.

Vorwerk Bantam

COUNTRY OF ORIGIN
Germany

Vorwerk Bantam chicks

ORIGIN
This breed is a diminutive form of the Vorwerk, a well-known German utility fowl, with its highly characteristic belted markings (Lakenvelder) combined with a buff-colored instead of a white body. Fairly soon after the Vorwerk was developed, German breeders attempted to dwarf the breed. With a view to this, Vorwerks were mated up with various other miniature breeds. In spite of this, it took until 1963 before the Vorwerk Bantam was recognized in Germany.

APPEARANCE
This miniature breed falls into the country fowl category and has an average-high stand. The body is rather broad, with an elongated build. In the cock, the back tends to slope a little. Vorwerk Bantams carry their tail moderately spread and medium high. The cocks have well-developed ornamental feathers, which are seen in the averagely long and beautifully curved main and lesser sickles of the tail. The wings are carried nicely tucked. This bantam's head has a medium-sized single comb and white ear-

Vorwerk Bantam hens

Vorwerk Bantam cock

lobes. The color of the eye is a yellowish bay. The legs are clean and slate blue.

Vorwerk Bantam hen

COLORS AND MARKING PATTERNS
The breed is only found in a single variety with belted markings, in which the white has been substituted by buff.

QUALITIES
This breed is very popular in its country of origin, but also has a great following abroad. The Vorwerk Bantam is a chicken with a pleasant character. They can become reasonably tame and are moderately active. Usually, the birds get on well together, which is even true for the cocks when there is sufficient room available. The hens lay white eggs and do so frequently. Because of its unique combination of color and markings, among other things, this breed is also a great favorite with hobby breeders. It takes quite a while before one can evaluate the young animals as to color and markings. Only after the third molting, do the final markings appear.

Aseel Bantam hen, partridge mottled

21 Game Fowl Breeds

Breed Descriptions

Aseel Bantam

COUNTRY OF ORIGIN
The United Kingdom

ORIGIN
It can no longer be traced how this miniature form of the Aseel (also spelled 'Asil') was developed, though it seems that a few specimens of it were already exhibited in England at the end of the nineteenth century. In spite of having been around for a century, the Aseel Bantam has not gathered a large following among breeders, for it is only bred sporadically.

APPEARANCE
As an Aseel Bantam cock weighs about 1kg (2 lbs), it is not a very small bantam. In this breed, the weight is not so much a question of body volume, but of the body's width. The bantams have a provocative, upright carriage and their trunk is broad, short and deep. The back is short and steeply sloping. The wings are tightly tucked, with clearly defined shoulders standing out more or less prominently. The tail is very closely folded and is carried below the horizontal, almost in line with the back. The legs are quite short, are set wide apart and their color is yellow.

Aseel Bantam cock, partridge mottled

The Aseel Bantam has a small, short and broad skull with the 'eyebrows' characteristic of game fowl. On the head, there is a small comb with three low lengthwise ridges. The breed is muscular and tight-feathered.

COLORS AND MARKING PATTERNS
Aseel Bantams are primarily bred for their shape, condition and character. In doing so, color and markings are not really important. The breed does not come in many varieties, but white, black, wheaten and partridge mottled are sometimes seen.

QUALITIES
The great advantage of this breed is that bantams can be easily housed in smaller coops. Furthermore, these animals become very affectionate and trusting towards those taking care of them. However, among themselves they are terrible trouble-makers. At a very early age, the cocks want to see who is the strongest and top of the order of rank. The result is fierce fighting, in which the cocks do not give up quickly. That is why it is best to run young specimens together with an adult cock, who will still have natural authority for a considerable time. Still, the moment will come when all of the cockerels will have to be housed individually. Because the hens are not very tolerant among themselves, keep these animals in rather small flocks. As layers, Aseel Bantams are not a success, and only in spring do the hens lay reasonably. They do get broody and bring up their chicks in an exemplary fashion. The breed is hardy and vigorous and is not fussy about how it is housed.

Indian Game Bantam or Cornish Bantam

COUNTRY OF ORIGIN
The United Kingdom

Cornish Bantam cock, double laced

among bantams'. It is unquestionably a very broad and short bird. Seen from the front, the enormous wide breast is striking. Its short, thick, round legs, yellow in color, are fitted so to speak at the side of the body, resulting in a rather straddle-legged stand. Seen from the side, the body's shape is almost square and is sometimes called 'cube-shaped', meaning that the body is as broad as it is deep and long. The wings are carried well tucked and the shoulders project a little above the back line. The short tail is folded and is carried a little below the horizontal line. The short neck is held a bit backwards. The breed has a broad, short head and a pea comb with three low lengthwise ridges. Above the eyes, there are the 'eyebrows'. The eyes have a somewhat cruel expression and are pearl-colored. The feathering is hard and tight. The muscles are highly developed and extremely powerful.

COLORS AND MARKING PATTERNS

The breed is found in, among others, double laced, blue double laced, red white double laced ('jubilee'), buff, black and white. The double laced variety is, without doubt, the most popular.

QUALITIES

The Cornish Bantam is one of the most remarkable bantam breeds. With their broad bodies, hardy constitution and characteristic facial expression, they are unmistakably of game fowl stock and make an unforgettable impression on many people. However, due to their game fowl blood, the cocks can be quite aggressive towards each other. Also the fe-

Head of a Cornish Bantam hen, double laced

Cornish Bantam hen, double laced

ORIGIN

The breed has been developed from large Indian Game or Cornish (as they are usually called in the United States) by way of Aseel Bantams. Around 1900, the first specimens were exhibited at British shows.

APPEARANCE

The Cornish is sometimes called the 'bulldog

Cornish Bantam hen, red white double laced

Cornish Bantam hen, red white double laced

males can pester the life out of one another, though this often has to do with the amount of space the birds have. As a rule you had better not keep more than one cock together with one or two hens of this breed, for that way they are easier to tame. Towards their owner, these animals are usually friendly and responsive, even the cocks. The hens of this breed do not lay very many eggs. The chicks are slow growers and take a long time to reach adulthood. Their hard feathering means that flights and main tail feathers break easily. It is very possible to house Cornish Bantams in a coop, now

Cornish Bantam cock, red white double laced

and then giving them a limited free run. They do not fly, and are not good at jumping. Thus you should not fix the perches too high above the ground, and these should be thick enough to offer the birds sufficient support.

PARTICULARS
- Cornish Game Bantams are not so very popular, but do have a circle of advocates in almost every country where chicken breeds are raised and shown.
- When cocks have a very low stand, they can sometimes be bad fertilizers. With their heavy body and short legs, they simply cannot manage to tread the hens. So, in breeding, one should use a cock with a somewhat higher stand.

Shamo Bantams

COUNTRY OF ORIGIN
Japan

ORIGIN
The Japanese word 'shamo' translates as 'fighter'. Sometimes the word 'ko' is added to indicate the diminutive, 'Ko-Shamo' meaning 'little fighter'. It is not known how the Shamo was developed in Japan. However, it is certain that this is an old breed. During the 1970s, these true bantams were imported to Europe.

APPEARANCE
It is evident that Shamos belong to the game fowl breeds, as one can clearly tell from their carriage and head. When coming into action, particularly the cocks have a practically up-

The eggs of the Shamo Bantam are very small.

Shamo Bantam hen

Shamo Bantam chicks

right station, in which the length of the neck and legs is striking. If you compare these two body parts with the trunk's length, you will see

Wheaten Shamo Bantams

that each part takes up about a third of the body's total length. The animals are tight-feathered and hard-muscled. The tight feathers are seen in the breast, among other places, where the featherless breastbone is clearly visible. Also the neck is tight-feathered, and the cock's hackles do not even reach to the base of the neck. The tail is carried folded in line with the back. It is also striking that the lower main tail feathers stick out sideways a little and bend upwards, thus enveloping the tail. This particular tail shape is called 'shrimp tail'. The wings are held well tucked. The shoulders are slightly prominent, standing out from the body and are carried a little above the back line. The skull is short and broad, with a 'beetling' brow, a ridge above the eyes making them look deep-set. On top of the head, there is a small walnut comb – also described as a 'pea comb' – and the wattles are very short. The face is protected by thick red skin that is bare of feathers. The legs are round and yellow and have tiny scales.

COLORS AND MARKING PATTERNS
Shamos are recognized in various colors, including wheaten, silver wheaten, white, black and red porcelain. The wheaten variants are bred most frequently.

QUALITIES
Shamo Bantams are suitable for those who like their chickens to have a distinct character. Although in Europe they were never bred for cock fights, this quality is firmly embedded in the breed. However, towards their owners these birds grow very trusting and tame, while carrying intolerance to extremes among them-

By nature Shamo Bantams are very tame and trusting.

Shamo Bantam cock, silver wheaten

selves. The cocks fight each other to the death; they will not give up any sooner. The fights sometimes start when young cockerels are no more than six weeks old. In that case, the only solution is to house them separately. Also the hens are particularly intolerant. Once the precedence within a certain flock has been established, you must not disturb it by taking animals out of the flock or adding any to it. This ineritably results in fierce fights, in which the animals hurt one another seriously. An advan-

tage of this breed is that they are quite happy when kept within a limited space. Laying does not amount to much. The hens only lay eggs for a brief period, though they lay more than enough to keep up the breed. If you appreciate a lot of contact with your birds and don't have plenty of room, you might consider a pair of these bantams. However, never combine them with other chickens, for it won't work.

PARTICULARS

There are several 'little fighters' hailing from Japan, and they resemble one another to a certain degree. Due to this, some variety has arisen as regards the ideal image in Europe. The original Japanese imports were very tight-feathered, sometimes not even with their wing plumage intact. In that case, birds lack a number of secondaries, so that primaries and secondaries no longer fit closely.

Malay Bantam

Wheaten Malay cock

COUNTRY OF ORIGIN
The United Kingdom

ORIGIN
At the end of the nineteenth century, the English Bantam fancier Mr. Entwisle bred miniature forms from a great deal of large fowl. As there were very few true bantams available at that time, each one of these creations was a masterly example of the breeder's art as well as of perseverance. The diminutive Malay was bred by way of large Malays that had remained too small, Modern English Game Bantams and Aseel Bantams. As early as 1893, white Malay Bantams were exhibited in England.

APPEARANCE
Malay Bantams are sturdy, heavy game bantams with a high stand. The cocks weigh about 1400g (3 lbs) and so cannot be said to be really small. This breed's type is sometimes referred to as 'triple-arched'. The first arch is

Young Malay cockerels

Wheaten Malay cock

formed by the long, slightly curved neck. The second arch is seen in the wings that are carried well tucked and high, with their pinions resting on top of the saddle. The third arch is made up of the tail's low carriage, forming a faint angle with the body. This fighter's station is very erect, with a clearly sloping back line. The shoulders are a bit angular and are set well apart, standing out from the body. The thighs are long and powerful, forming a faint angle with the yellow shanks. Malay Bantams have a short, broad head with clearly developed 'eyebrows' that give good protection to the eyes. On top of the head there is a small walnut comb, the wattles are very short, and the head and ear-lobes have a bright red color. Under the head, there is a naked skin fold, called a 'dewlap'. The eyes are deep-set, of a fierce expression and preferably pearl-colored. The animals have highly developed, hard muscles and are tight-feathered.

COLORS AND MARKING PATTERNS
Malay Bantams can be white, wheaten, bloodwing white or partridge mottled as regards their varieties. However, in judging the breed at shows, colors and markings are only a small part of the evaluation. Far more important are type, station, musculature and feathering.

QUALITIES
Malay Bantams need a minder who is interested in the bird's extreme shape. In order to bring out this shape to best advantage at exhibitions, the animals need training. During this training, the owner uses his hands to put the birds in the best possible station. Thus, wing carriage and a high leg stand are emphasized even more. The advantage of correcting them

Wheaten Malay hen

by hand is that they become very tame and start trusting the one taking care of them. Among themselves, they are not very tolerant. Because of the urge to fight for their place in the order of precedence, the cocks do not avoid each other, but seek confrontation. As the hens can squabble quite a lot among themselves, it is best for this breed to be housed in pairs or threesomes. These are hardy birds that are not fussy as regards their housing. Malay Bantams are hardly able to fly, so the runs do not necessarily need roofing over. As their stand is so high and they have such a long body, the feeder bowls and drinkers should be placed a little above ground level. Malay Bantams are certainly no layers, but produce a reasonable number of eggs in a couple of months' time.

Modern English Game Bantam

COUNTRY OF ORIGIN
The United Kingdom

ORIGIN
The Modern English Game Bantam (or 'Modern Games Bantam' as the jargon has it) is a fairly old breed. It was shown for the first time at the end of the nineteenth century at an English show and its name was derived from its large namesake. As a breed, the Modern English Game Bantam is in fact older than the Old English Game Bantam. The English bantam specialist Entwisle developed the breed by way of Cornish Bantams and Malay Bantams.

APPEARANCE
The Modern English 'little fighters' are sometimes irreverently called 'skinny' by laymen. This refers to the body's very high station, which one perhaps considers out of proportion. If you compare their body and stand with that of country fowl, you will see that these creatures indeed look lean and lithe. This bantam's trunk is short and slopes backwards. The abdomen is tucked up well and the birds have an upright carriage. The wings are held tightly against the trunk. The shoulders are wide and stand out from the body

Modern English Game Bantam cock, yellow birchen

a little. The tail is very much folded (called 'whipped' or 'gamy'), rather short, and carried slightly above the horizontal line. The neck of this miniature breed is long and thin. The head is long and slender, sporting a small single comb and red ear-lobes. The eyes are lively; their color depends on the color of the feathers and can be either bay or a very dark brown. Their extremely high stand is due to the long thighs and shanks. The legs are clean and round. The leg color of this breed depends on the variety. White animals have yellow legs, the partridge variants have green legs and the black and birchen marked animals have black legs. These small, lithely built creatures are hard and very muscular to the touch, not repudiating their descent as a game fowl breed. They are fairly tight-feathered.

COLORS AND MARKING PATTERNS
The breed is found in many colors, including white, black, laced blue, self blue, birchen, blue birchen, golden birchen, blue golden birchen, cuckoo, partridge, cuckoo partridge, silver partridge, blue partridge, silver blue partridge, wheaten, lavender, golden necked, golden necked blue, silver necked, silver

Modern English Game Bantam hen, birchen

Modern English Game Bantam cock, partridge

necked blue, bloodwing white and bloodwing silver partridge.

QUALITIES

This breed, in regards to weight one of the lightest ones we know, is mainly kept by people who admire the birds' shape. As exhibition fowl, Modern English Game Bantams are rather popular. The hens lay, although their build might lead one to expect differently, quite a lot of eggs, and also become broody rather easily. Because of their long legs and tight feathering they are not very suitable as sitters. It is better to call in the services of a broody of some other breed. The breed is famed for being really tame. The animals are trusting and can very easily be 'trained to the hand'. Exhibition breeders make use of this quality to train the birds as to their most favorable 'station'. You can easily do this by putting the birds in the correct station using both hands. After only a couple of times, the animals know what is expected of them and stretch their legs as well as their necks even at the slightest touch. These small and easy-going bantams can be housed in small coops with limited space. The cocks are certainly

Modern English Game Bantam hen, bloodwing white

not rowdy crowers. All of these qualities make the Modern English Game Bantam very suitable for a small city garden. Because they are tall, one should place feeders and drinkers a bit higher than usual. Although these bantams look delicate, they certainly are not. They grow up fast and easily, affording few problems rearing them. Among themselves, they are fairly tolerant. The young cocks are certainly no fiercer than most country fowl breeds.

Old English Game Bantam

COUNTRY OF ORIGIN

The United Kingdom

ORIGIN

In spite of the name 'fighting bantam', it is a question here of exhibition birds, and as such they are popular with a circle of fanciers. It is unknown how the breed arose. Although it seems obvious to say that the breed was developed from the large English Game Fowl, there is no evidence for this.

APPEARANCE

Old English Game Bantams are extremely popular. This is probably due to their very typical shape, that cannot be compared to that of any other breed. If you pick up an Old English Game Bantam, the first thing that strikes you is its enormous muscular bulk and the hardness of its body. Moreover, seen from the front these animals are of a very broad

Partridge-colored Old English Game Bantam cock

291

build. Their body is not only broad, it is also very short, which is even evident in the breastbone, being clearly shorter than in other chicken breeds. The body, starting out really broad at the front, tapers at the saddle. Regarded from above, its shape is somewhat triangular, the so-called 'clothes iron shape'. The back line is sloping. The wings are held tightly to the body, and the shoulders are well rounded, jutting out a little above the back line. What is more, the shoulders stand out from the body slightly. With a smooth hollow sweep, the line of the back ends in a tail that is carried semi-high and somewhat folded. As is typical of game fowl, the cock's ornamental feathers are hard. In the tail, we find rather

Cuckoo partridge-colored Old English Game Bantam, cock

292

short sickles, that already start curving before reaching the end of the main tail feathers. The bantam's stand is medium high and its shanks are at a clear angle with the thighs. The head has a single, rather small comb, red ear-lobes and fierce eyes.

COLORS AND MARKING PATTERNS

Starting out from the idea that 'a good fighter cannot have a bad color', one tends to worry less about a game bantam's color at exhibitions than about that of other breeds. Many colors are recognized, including black, white, splashed, self blue, partridge, silver partridge, blue partridge, dark partridge, silver blue partridge, cuckoo partridge, partridge mottled, bloodwing silver partridge, yellow shouldered blue partridge, birchen, blue birchen, golden birchen, blue golden birchen, three-colored (spangled), brown, wheaten, blue wheaten, black with a brassy back called 'furness' (also spelled 'furnace'), blue with a brassy back ('blue furness'), cuckoo, red necked blue, red necked black, red necked silver blue and bloodwing white. The partridge-colored variants are the popular ones in most countries.

Silver partridge-colored Old English Game Bantam cock

Typically English are what are called the furness-colored birds: black or blue animals with brassy touches. 'Splashed' is a color pattern that inevitably crops up when breeding blue. In most countries such a bird only has value as a 'breeder', so this is a non-standard variant.

QUALITIES

Old English Game Bantams are very tame towards their minder. One can get a young animal tame and trusting in no time. Due to this, it is a very suitable breed for kids. In name they are fighter bantams, but in practice the fighting spirit is not really in evidence. From the time it was developed, the breed has only been bred as to its game bantam appearance, not as to fighting spirit. Young growing cockerels may now and then get into scrapes, but this behavior is no different than that of most country fowl breeds. Among themselves, the hens are remarkably tolerant. If you like this breed, but like other breeds as well, then there is no objection to keeping a few hens of this breed together with some other bantams. Old English Game Bantams are mainly kept by those who find the birds' type and character attractive. As layers, the hens are not so hot, usually only laying a few eggs in spring and summer. Still, they do get broody regularly, so you can let them hatch their own eggs. However, do not run hens that have chicks with the rest of the flock, but keep them in a separate coop. As soon as the mother's task is done, you may carefully introduce her into the flock again. These bantams are very hardy and vigorous. They are not fussy as to their housing and are satisfied with little. Because the cocks are not loud crowers; they crow rather softly and infrequently, this is an excellent breed for keeping in residential areas.

PARTICULARS

- Old English Game Bantams as a rule do not have beards or tufts. However, such variants do exist.
- There is also a large English Game Fowl, though it is extremely rare.

22 Ornamental and Long-tailed Breeds

Breed Descriptions

Antwerp Belgian or Belgian Bearded D'Anvers Bantam and Belgian Bearded de Grubbe Bantam

COUNTRY OF ORIGIN
Belgium

ORIGIN
The Antwerp Belgian (also referred to in English-speaking countries as Barbu d'Anvers or Belgian Bearded d'Anvers Bantam) is one of the oldest true bantam breeds. This means that the breed has no large variant and is therefore not a dwarf form. One of the first recordings of an Antwerp Belgian is from the seventeenth century, being a quail-colored hen in a painting by Albert Cuyp. The first written record is found in a French book published at the beginning of the nineteenth century. This book mentions 'the Netherlands' as the bird's origin, but this is nowadays considered to be the Flemish-speaking part of the Netherlands (the north of Belgium). The breed probably takes its name from the fact that breeding this tiny bearded bantam was concentrated in the vicinity of Antwerp. In 1904, the Belgium Bearded Bantam breeder Robert Pauwels wrote that, spontaneously, a tailless bearded bantam had been hatched at his breeding farm. He named this spontaneous mutation after its place of origin Grubbe, close to the small Belgian town of Kortenberg. The Belgian Bearded de Grubbe Bantam (Barbu de Grubbe) only differs from the Antwerp Bearded Bantam in one detail: The sub-breed lacks a tail and is therefore what is called a rumpless bantam.

Belgian Bearded de Grubbe Bantam hen, quail-colored

Belgian Bearded de Grubbe Bantam hen, porcelain

295

APPEARANCE

Antwerp Bearded Bantams – called 'Beards' by many fanciers – are among the smallest of bantams. The first impression is that of a perky little chicken. The type is short and stocky, with wings that are carried low. A true breed feature is their full beard, preferably consisting of a 'throat beard' and muffs. The Antwerp Bearded Bantam has a very full-feathered neck. The neck is often so thick that, in the cocks, one can hardly see anything of the back. The neck feathers almost touch the tail. The animals have a rose comb, the spike or leader of which follows the back line and has tiny rounded points. This is sometimes called the 'comb work'. Striking are the very dark brown eyes. The tail is carried somewhat folded. In the cocks, the main sickles are only slightly longer than regular tail feathers and faintly curved. The Grubbe Belgian is similar to the Antwerp Belgian in everything, except that it lacks a tail, and due to this, its saddle looks as round as a little ball. Usually, these birds tend to stand a bit more upright than their 'tailed' congeners.

COLORS AND MARKING PATTERNS

The Antwerp and Grubbe Belgians are found in many different colors, including black, white, self blue, laced blue, red, cuckoo, partridge, silver partridge, porcelain, isabella-colored porcelain, columbian, buff columbian, quail, silver quail, blue quail, black white mottled, blue white mottled, lavender white mottled, ochre white mottled and red marked white. These colors are recognized both in the country of origin and in the Netherlands. In other countries, the color range is usually a bit more limited, but they tend to have different colors again. Thus, there is a buff in Germany, a lavender quail in England and a porcelain blue marked one in Denmark. Notably the color quail and its variants are characteristic of this breed. It is remarkable that in origin the quail color is typically Belgian. In no other country has this color arisen as a mutation of the color fawn. The quail color is a beautiful combination of a warm golden brown with a velvety black. Cocks and hens have entirely different markings. As chicks, the quail-colored Antwerp and Grubbe Belgians stand out a mile. They are almost entirely brownish black and have a striking yellow-brown beard.

QUALITIES

Antwerp Belgians are very popular. The hens are good layers, but due to their size the eggs are of course also quite small, weighing about 35g (1¼ oz). Some stocks produce hens that are good sitters, but that is not a hard and fast rule. They are friendly, active animals that can be kept in a run or coop that is not very large. When well taken care of, they easily become

Antwerp Belgian cock, quail-colored

Antwerp Belgian cock, porcelain

Antwerp Belgian hen, porcelain

Antwerp Belgian cock, quail-colored

tame and trusting. As is inherent in their jaunty, plucky spirit, the cocks often react rather fiercely towards their owner during the breeding season. Then they might start pecking at the hand that feeds them and attacking it. If you have children, you will have to keep this in mind. As crowers the cocks are practically unsurpassed, starting to crow fanatically at an early hour and doing so often and piercingly. That these bantam cocks are regular winners at crowing competitions says enough. You will have to insulate your roost thoroughly, so that this does not disturb your neighbors. Furthermore, in connection with their full head feathering, you should provide your animals with a special drinker. A jar waterer (little 'water tower') is usually satisfactory. As they can only get a little bit of water at a time, it prevents the beard from becoming wet and the animals from looking less attractive.

PARTICULARS
- The Antwerp Belgian is the national bantam breed of Belgium. In the past, the Belgian postal service has given out a stamp showing a quail-colored cock of this breed. The breed is sometimes called Belgium's most important export product in the field of chickens. Even in Australia and South Africa we find these 'Antwerp Beards'.
- That the breed is known and loved all over the world appears, among other things, from the fact that in countries like the Netherlands, Germany, England and even Australia, specialist Antwerp Belgian breed clubs have been founded. Although they all tend to breed as much as possible according to the standard of the country of origin, there are also small differences. Thus, in Germany, Antwerp Belgians are a bit bigger than the Belgian birds.
- A striking standard feature of the breed is that most cocks have no spurs. However, that this male symbol is lacking does not result in negative fertility in practice. The reason is probably that the cocks are required to have little ornamental plumage, a rather small comb and no wattles. Due to this, breeders very much select for female features in male animals.

Brabanter Bantam cock

A study of the head of a Brabanter Bantam hen

Brabanter Bantam

COUNTRY OF ORIGIN
The Netherlands

ORIGIN
This miniature breed was developed from a cross between Crested Beards and Antwerp Belgians. One bred on with the offspring of this, and by way of a focused selection the Bra-

banter Bantam arose. This dwarf form of the Brabanter was first shown in 1933 at a large exhibition in the Netherlands. Although in the Netherlands the breed has a small yet solid basis, one seldom sees it abroad.

APPEARANCE
Brabanter Bantams are a striking phenomenon among bantams. This is notably due to their characteristic head. On this, there is a crest that is sometimes described as a 'shaving-brush crest'. It consists of vertically growing feathers rising up in a dense mass, flattened at the sides. A skull knob, like in crested fowl, is an absolute no-no in this breed, as the crest would then become too high and globular. Furthermore, Brabanter Bantams have a three-clump beard with clear gaps between beard and muffs. Another typical crested fowl feature is that the nostrils stick out a bit and are flared. The comb is V-shaped (horn comb). The breed is of a country fowl type, having a fairly elongated build with a rather upright carriage. The wings are long and well tucked. The carriage of the tail is above the horizontal, and the animals spread it amply. In most colors, the legs are slate blue. The breed has white ear-lobes and reddish bay eyes.

COLORS AND MARKING PATTERNS
The first specimens of this breed were probably black. Later on self-colored whites were bred and colors were developed like blue

Brabanter Bantam chicks: to the left a golden black half-moon spangled specimen, to the right a yellow white half-moon spangled one

Still, these are pleasant birds of a fairly placid nature. Usually, they are not truly tame, though not shy either. Like all country fowl, they are good flyers. The run should be roofed-in to prevent them from flying off.

PARTICULARS

Brabanter Bantams are closely related to the Owl Beard Bantams. Originally, they were bred from the same crosses. Nevertheless, in breeding them, one should beware of frequently mating up these two breeds. For, due to this, the Brabanter's typical three-clump beard is lost, while the Owl Beard Bantam's rounded beard in fact starts to show clefts or gaps.

Brabanter Bantam cock, yellow white half-moon spangled

Brahma Bantam

COUNTRY OF ORIGIN
The United Kingdom

ORIGIN
Soon after the introduction of the large Brah-

laced, cuckoo, golden black half-moon spangled, silver black half-moon spangled and yellow white half-moon spangled. Lavender is the most recent color in this breed.

Columbian Brahma Bantam chicks, three days old

QUALITIES

One of this breed's greatest advantages is that the crest sticks right up into the air and leaves the eyes free. Thus, it does not get soiled as quickly and does not interfere with the Brabanter Bantam's vision. They are mainly kept as ornamental chickens. The hens usually do not lay many eggs and are also seldom broody.

Brahma Bantam hen, buff columbian blue marked

Brahma Bantam cock, buff columbian

ma, the first Brahma Bantams were developed in England around 1870. The initial attempt was made by way of a selection of large Brahmas that had remained too small, but this was unsuccessful. Entwisle, an English breeder who stood at the cradle of a great many bantam breeds, successfully developed the Brahma Bantam from a cross of Aseels, Cochin Bantams and Booted Bantams. Later on they were mated up again with Japanese Bantams. As early as 1887, the birds were shipped to the United States and Europe. The breed soon became very popular in many countries.

APPEARANCE

Like their large brothers, Brahma Bantams are true giants. A Brahma hen weighs around 1200g (2½ lbs), and thus has the same weight as the large penciled Holland fowl. These are chickens with character. The breed's stand is medium high and its build is sturdy and broad. The latter is emphasized again by its full and abundant plumage. The back is fairly short, running with an uninterrupted sweep towards the tail. The tail's carriage is fairly high, and it is short and amply spread. The cocks have short, broad and rounded main and lesser sickles, entirely covering the main tail feathers. Due to profuse feathering, the neck looks thick and short, be-

ing elegantly arched. The head is on the small side, though round and broad. Their broad skull protrudes over the eyes, forming what are called the 'eyebrows'. The comb has three low lengthwise ridges, the ear-lobes are red and the eyes reddish bay. Brahma Bantams have yellow, densely feathered legs. Also the feet are fully feathered.

COLORS AND MARKING PATTERNS

The breed is raised in multiple penciled partridge ('triple laced'), multiple penciled silver partridge, multiple penciled blue partridge, columbian, buff columbian, columbian blue marked, buff columbian blue marked, birchen, buff and white.

Brahma Bantam hens, columbian

Brahma Bantam cock, columbian

QUALITIES

The Brahma Bantam is quite a popular breed and also suitable for beginners. The hens are excellent sitters and rearing chicks is as a rule not a problem. Still, the hens can take longer

Brahma Bantam cock, multiple penciled
blue partridge

than other breeds before they start laying eggs and have developed entirely. Brahma Bantams are very tame and placid, and can even be 'trained to the hand'. They are not really inclined to fly, so it is quite easy to keep them behind a relatively low fence: about 60cm (2 ft) usually suffices. The cocks are as a rule friendly and hardly aggressive. Exhibition specimens should be kept in clean, roofed-in runs, so that the feathers of feet and legs do not get dirty or damaged. Usually it is necessary to wash them before shows. Due to their placid nature and good appetite, Brahma Bantams easily turn to fat. That is why they should be rationed, meaning that they should not have feed at their disposal all day long.

PARTICULARS

Saying that the breed has a broad skull is rather a question of wishful thinking, as in fact this skull shape is lacking in most colors. In practice, this standard feature of the breed is only found in the birchen or the columbian marked specimens. All other colors have long, narrow heads.

Burmese Bantam

COUNTRY OF ORIGIN

Burma

ORIGIN

The Burmese Bantam is an old breed which, according to tradition, English sailors now and then brought from Burma to England. This bantam is probably the archetype of many different old bantam breeds, like Booted Bantams and Japanese. Until about 1990, there was a vague standard description of this breed in the Netherlands. As the animals had not been seen for at least fifty years, the breed was no longer mentioned in the standard of perfection. Also in Britain, there was no more than a breed description, while the birds were extinct. Various breeders attempted to bring back the breed, using different breeds to achieve this purpose. In 1990, an attempt finally met with success. With the help of Japanese, Cochin, Belgian Bearded d'Uccle and Crèvecoeur Bantams, the breed was recreated.

Burmese Bantam hen, black

Burmese Bantam cock, black

APPEARANCE

Burmese Bantams are akin to the Booted Bantams and the Japanese Bantams. From the former they got their feathered feet and vulture hocks, from the latter their low leg stand. Their build is deep and looks even deeper due to their rather low stand and full feathers. The feathering of their feet is highly developed. On either side of their thighs the feathers lengthen into vulture hocks, largely covered by the rather big wings that are carried low. The fairly compact and not even medium-sized crest is placed on the back of the head. The beard is full, consisting of three clumps. The animals have a V-shaped comb (horn comb) and short wattles, in part covered by the beard. The color of the eyes is reddish brown. The tail's carriage is high and it has well-developed curved sickles and innumerable tail coverts or side-hangers. The shanks are yellow. In the color black, there is so much pigment in the shanks and toes that the yellow is only seen on the soles of the feet and between the toes.

COLORS AND MARKING PATTERNS

Up to now, black is the only recognized color. Colors like white, black tailed yellow and golden necked black are at this point in time 'under construction'.

QUALITIES

Burmese Bantams are little chickens and suited to being housed in smaller coops. Because of their crest, beard and full-feathered feet, such housing must be dry. You can let them run free in your yard, as with their feathered feet they do not cause much damage. This is a great advantage if you like your chickens to wander about, but also appreciate a well-tended garden. However, when it rains you will have to provide a dry place for them. Burmese Bantams are calm and trusting by nature. The hens in particular get very tame. They are good layers and, compared to their body weight, lay big eggs of a light brown color. The Burmese is a vigorous and fertile breed of which the chicks grow up fast and without problem.

PARTICULARS

Originally, the Burmese was recognized in several comb shapes. The single comb was regarded as the most common one. The present standard of perfection is based on animals from one breeding farm. Other breeders are at this point in time involved in breeding single-combed Burmese.

Japanese Bantam hen, blue tailed white

Golden birchen Japanese cock with long legs

Japanese cock, porcelain

Chabo or Japanese Bantam

COUNTRY OF ORIGIN
Japan

ORIGIN
The Japanese – its other name, Chabo, is not often heard – is a true bantam, so not, like most so-called bantams, a miniature form of a larger breed. Its progenitors hail from China and were exported from there to Japan. They are also said to have been imported from Indochina, particularly from Vietnam. However, in Japan the breed was perfected to its present form, and Japanese Bantams are still highly popular there. It is an ancient breed, and probably the first Japanese Bantams came to Europe as early as the sixteenth century.

APPEARANCE
This bantam breed comes in various varieties, and thus there are frizzle-feathered, silk-feathered, rumpless and bearded Japanese. There is also a large-combed variant, a 'subspecies' in which notably the cocks have enormous combs. Alongside of these variants, there is another one with a black head. These black-headed birds have lots of dark pigmentation, so that heads and combs are purplish. All va-

rieties have very short legs, and their feet are sometimes hidden from sight by all the down. The large, broad tail as a rule is set at a right angle to the body. Due to this and the high-held head, the body acquires a kind of U-shape when seen from the side. The wings are held low. Due to the combination of short legs and wings that are carried low, the wing tips tend to touch the ground. Japanese are full-feathered and therefore look larger than they are in reality. The short legs are yellow.

Japanese cock, black tailed white

Black mottled Japanese cock

COLORS AND MARKING PATTERNS

Many different colors of Japanese are bred, including blue laced, blue tailed yellow, black tailed yellow, blue tailed white, black tailed white, cuckoo, black, white, self blue, buff, wheaten, silver wheaten, yellow wheaten, golden necked black, silver necked black, birchen, blue birchen, golden birchen, buff columbian, black white mottled, blue white mottled, red white mottled, ochre white mottled, bloodwing white, porcelain, partridge, silver partridge, blue partridge, multiple penciled partridge ('triple laced'), multiple penciled silver partridge, lavender, blue mottled and light yellow.

QUALITIES

Japanese are ideal bantams for kids. As these are small birds, children can easily manage them, and moreover they are very placid and trusting by nature. Due to their very short legs, they cannot run fast. The chickens lay few eggs; these are moreover tiny. However, they do tend to get broody. Both cocks and hens are very considerate towards chicks. It is even possible to run a mother with chicks together with other Japanese. Among themselves, these are tolerant creatures. The cocks are not very shrill crowers, nor do they do so very loudly. The birds need little room and are therefore a good idea if you are not capaciously housed. They are very suitable for keeping in a city garden, provided you see to a roost with good sound insulation. With this

Black mottled Japanese hen

Day-old white Japanese chick

Rumpless Japanese hen, black

Japanese cock, black

Frizzle-feathered Japanese hen, blue tailed yellow

Frizzle-feathered Japanese hen, silver wheaten

kind of breed, one should really always keep a cock, as the male animals are unique in shape and character. If your kids are the ones taking care of them, this breed is an excellent choice.

PARTICULARS

The hallmark of the Japanese are their short legs. This has also given the breed the name of 'the clown among chickens'. The animals have a somewhat shuffling gait. These short legs however do need special care. In the roost, the perches should of course not be fixed too high, and also the level of the feeders and drinkers should be adapted. The roost's pop-hole should not be too high either; more or less at floor level is in fact the best solution. You can let your Japanese run free in your garden. They will not do much damage to your lawn as they are not expert diggers. During rainy weather, the animals should be kept in a dry coop, as their breast almost touches the ground and so gets wet easily. This henhouse should be kept very clean, as the wing tips or pinions touch the ground. Japanese have large combs and wattles that require extra care during frosty

weather. Put some acid-free vaseline on them in good time. The factor ruling the short legs sees to it that a true-breeding Japanese is never hatched. From every 100 fertilized eggs of a breeding flock of short-legged Japanese, on average 50 chicks are short-legged, 25 have normal legs and 25 eggs never hatch. You can prevent this premature dying by mating up a short-legged Japanese with a partner with long legs. The outcome of this combination is 50% short-legged chicks and 50% normal-legged ones.

Cochin Bantam

COUNTRY OF ORIGIN
China

ORIGIN
Although the breed's name implies that it is a question here of a dwarf form of the large

Cochins, Cochin Bantams do not resemble Cochins enough to be regarded as such. The breed was already being raised and kept in

Cochin Bantams around 1900

England in the nineteenth century, but long before that time was found in China, whence many animals were fetched.

APPEARANCE

One's first impression of a Cochin Bantam is that of 'a feathery ball with legs'. The birds are short, broad and of very low stand. Their plumage is abundant, soft and richly fluffy. The animals have full-feathered feet, so that a Cochin Bantam's legs are hardly visible. The tail is a downy, rotund mass of feathers, covered by soft ornamental feathering in the

Cochin Bantam cock, red porcelain

Cochin Bantam cock, white

cock. As the saddle is broad and also fully feathered, it looks as if the tail starts where the neck hackles end. The back line cannot be discerned. The tail's highest point is not the tip, but is closer to the saddle. Cochin Bantams emphasize their low stand even more by 'bending forwards'. If we draw a horizontal line from the head, we end at the tail's highest point. The breast is full and deep. The Cochin Bantam has a single comb, red ear-lobes, reddish bay eyes and yellow legs. The breed is found both with normal feathers and with frizzled feathering.

COLORS AND MARKING PATTERNS

This breed is raised in a great many colors and markings, including black, self blue, white, buff, red, birchen, golden birchen, columbian, buff columbian, cuckoo, yellow cuckoo, wheaten, silver wheaten, lavender, porcelain, black white mottled, blue white mottled, multiple penciled partridge ('triple laced'), multiple penciled silver partridge, salmon and blue laced.

Cochin Bantam hens, red porcelain

Frizzle-feathered Cochin cock, black

White Cochin Bantam hen

Cochin Bantams lay very small eggs.

QUALITIES

Cochin Bantams are very popular indeed, not only because of their placid, tame character, but also because they look so round and cuddly. These bantams in fact should have a roofed-in run. As there are far too many feathers on their feet and they have a low stand, their leg feathers tend to get soiled and wet easily. However, they do not fly, so strictly speaking a roof is not necessary. As they need little space and are rather tame, they are pleasant animals for people with small gardens. The hens lay few eggs, which moreover are small. The eggs have a light beige shell. A disadvantage of this breed is that it is often broody and for a prolonged time. Even without laying-nests and in a brightly lit henhouse, they decide at a certain moment that it is 'time to sit'. The hens are good mothers and will rear chicks of a large variety of species, including ducks and pheasants. Among themselves, these very tame and calm chickens are not always so tolerant. Putting strange animals together can lead to violent clashes, even among hens, and certainly young cockerels do not avoid getting into scrapes. Also, the cocks can react very fiercely towards the person taking care of them, though this phenomenon is not found in all strains. An advantage of this breed is that the cocks crow relatively softly.

PARTICULARS

The Cochin Bantam found in most European countries is of the American type. In the United Kingdom, these birds are called 'Pekin Bantams', and they are smaller and less broad than the American type. Also, their feathering is not as abundant.

Black Cochin Bantam cock

Tournaisis

COUNTRY OF ORIGIN
Belgium

ORIGIN
From the farmyard bantams living along the French-Belgian border, a regional breed was developed in the nineteenth century called *Mille Fleurs du Tournaisis*. In the past, the breed was also known as *Naine du Tournaisis*, a name that is still sometimes used in English and means 'Dwarf of the Tournais Region' or simply 'Tournais Bantam', though nowadays it is usually called the Tournaisis. Nothing is known about the breed's origin, but one surmises that the old French breed *Mantes*, a black mottled fowl, collaborated in this respect. The latter is certainly a possibility, as the Mantes was kept as a utility fowl in the same region.

The breed is mentioned for the first time in *Chasse et Pêche* from 1923. Previous to the First World War, one had already started recording the breed's features, but due to the war most of this effort was lost. The breed was redeveloped from the remnants and from partridge mottled Old English Game Bantams.

Tournaisis hen

Tournaisis cock

Tournaisis Bantams

APPEARANCE
The Tournaisis is a true bantam with a small body. The breed's type is that of a country fowl, with a tail carried rather above the horizontal and wings held low. The wings are held at a somewhat downward slant, but should not be droopy. The tail is reasonably spread and has long, well-curved main sickles in the cock. The ear-lobes are red and the single comb is rather small. The eyes are reddish bay; the legs pinkish white.

COLORS AND MARKING PATTERNS
There is only one color, to wit mille fleurs.

QUALITIES
These small bantams, with an average weight 700g (1½ lb), have a small though steady following in Belgium and its neighboring countries. Outside of these, it is hardly ever seen. The Tournaisis is a vigorous and hardy breed. If the animals are left to run free, they prefer spending the night in a tree, when given a chance, instead of in their roost. In spite of

their freedom-loving nature, they can be very well kept in smaller, closed coops. This is a trusting and active little bird. For a bantam breed, the eggs are reasonably sized. The Tournaisis is a good, reliable broody, originally also used for hatching the eggs of pheasants and partridges.

PARTICULARS

- Due to its rather calm nature and small size, this breed was also kept on board of the barges sailing the river Scheldt. That is why it is sometimes called 'the Skipper's Little Chicken'.
- The color and markings of the Tournaisis are unique. In all breeds, markings that are as regular as possible are appreciated, but in the Tournaisis the markings should on the contrary be irregular. Thus, the breed can have feathers with three different colors on them as well as self-colored feathers. Unfortunately, there is a difference of opinion about the color in its country of origin. In the Walloon part of Belgium, one would rather see a brownish yellow ground color, while the Flemish prefer a ground color that is chestnut.

Dutch Bantam

COUNTRY OF ORIGIN
The Netherlands

ORIGIN
The Dutch Bantam was developed from a tiny bantam of a country fowl type that was of old found in Europe. So, it is a true bantam and not a dwarf version of some large breed. Later on, it was mated up with various other breeds to acquire new colors. The Dutch Bantam was officially recognized in the Netherlands in 1906, and was also proclaimed the Dutch national bantam breed. Originally, there was also a rose-combed Dutch Bantam, alongside the single-combed variant. However, this has been lost entirely. From gene research in 1997, it appears that the Dutch Bantam is closely related to the old Dutch Country Fowl.

Lavender Dutch Bantam hen

APPEARANCE
The Dutch Bantam is the smallest bantam breed known. The cocks only weigh 500g (17½ oz), while the hens are as light as 450g (16 oz). Their type is that of the country fowl. This we can tell from the fact that the tail's carriage is fairly high, while the back is short and concave, ending with a sweep in a well-spread tail. The breast is prominent and well rounded. The stand is rather low and the shanks are slate blue. Dutch Bantams carry their wings low. The wings are held at a backward slant, but should not touch the ground. The head is small and delicate, and has a small single comb. The ear-lobes are white and the eyes reddish bay to brownish red. The cocks have profuse ornamental plumage. The saddle is abundantly feathered with lots of long saddle hackles. The tail is

Dutch Bantam hen, yellow partridge

Dutch Bantam hen, silver partridge

Black Dutch Bantam hen

White Dutch Bantam cock

a true showpiece with broad, long as well as nicely curved main and lesser sickles.

COLORS AND MARKING PATTERNS
Nowadays, the breed is found in many different colors and patterns of markings, including black, self blue, white, partridge, silver partridge, blue partridge, silver blue partridge, yellow partridge, bloodwing silver blue partridge, bloodwing silver partridge, cuckoo partridge, cuckoo, lavender cuckoo, buff columbian, buff columbian blue marked, wheaten, salmon, lavender, bloodwing white, quail and silver quail. And still colors are being added to this popular breed. Thus, in England, a columbian Dutch Bantam was bred, while in the United States a penciled variant arose coincidentally.

QUALITIES
Dutch Bantams are active animals, which due to their small size need little space. You can keep them very well in a 'rabbit hutch-type henhouse' and even breed them in a small garden. The hens lay white eggs. They are good

sitters and it is nice to watch such a tiny chicken pottering about in the run with her minute chicks. Still, carefully consider the wire netting's mesh size, for young chicks walk out through most meshes just like that! The breed will make nice pets for your kids. Because of their size, they are easy to manage. Moreover, they become absolutely tame. Among themselves, these birds are tolerant.

PARTICULARS
The Dutch Bantam is a highly popular breed all over the world. It has specialist breed clubs in many countries, and there is even a Dutch Bantam Association in the United States.

Dutch Crested Fowl Bantam

COUNTRY OF ORIGIN
The Netherlands and the United Kingdom

ORIGIN
The miniature form of the Dutch Crested Fowl was created in both England and the Netherlands independently. At the end of the nineteenth century, the English bantam expert Entwisle crossed Crested Fowl that had remained too small with Java Bantams. The final product was a diminutive breed that was far too big. In the Netherlands, poultry park De Nijverheid in Vlaardingen made a successful attempt as well, but unfortunately the breeds used cannot be traced. The present Crested Bantams are descendants of this creation. Round about 1915, they were first exhibited in the Netherlands.

Dutch Crested Bantam hen, black

Dutch Crested Bantams

APPEARANCE

Dutch Crested Bantams belong to the country fowl type. These are fairly svelte, slender creatures with an elongated build. The tail is carried above the horizontal and is spread amply, while the cocks have broad, long and well-curved sickles. The fairly long wings are carried tucked against the body at a downward slant. The legs are clean and slate blue. The breed's outstanding standard feature is its large, globular and full crest. This 'topknot' grows on a lump on the skull's crown, called the skull knob. In the hens, the feathers of the crest are short and round, resulting in a globular crest. The cocks have somewhat longer and narrower crest feathers, so that the crest leans backwards more. The birds do not have a comb. The ear-lobes are white and the eyes reddish brown. Two varieties of this breed are recognized: birds with a white crest and those with a crest that has the same color as the body. The most commonly bred one that has most contrasting color is the white-crested bird. This has a crest as white as a sheet, except for a few 'supporting feathers' at the front, which have the color of the body.

COLORS AND MARKING PATTERNS

The following colors are found in this breed: black, white, laced blue, cuckoo, black mottled and buff. Since the turn of the last century, one has also been working on white crested bantams with a black crest.

QUALITIES

Dutch Crested Bantams are fairly placid chickens that require extra attention. The crest is an ideal breeding ground for lice, so it is necessary that you regularly check it and give it preventive treatment. If crests get wet, not only the breed's good looks are lost, but the birds are bothered by the wet, 'stringy' feathers around their head. A dry, roofed-in abode is therefore an absolute necessity here. If the minder approaches these animals calmly, they are fairly easily tamed. Because of their crests, the birds can only look sideways and downwards. Therefore do not all of a sudden pick up these chickens from above, as this will startle them. The hens lay a reasonable number of white eggs, and do get broody, though this trait is not

Black Dutch Crested Bantam hen

311

popular true bantam originated. Many people assume that the breed was brought from Java to Europe, though at that time it did not have its present uniform type. The first specialist breed club for the Java Bantam was founded in Germany in 1909. In England, the breed is called 'Rosecomb', which indicates that it is very old, and was probably one of the first rose-combed bantams imported.

APPEARANCE
The Java Bantam has a number of striking breed features. The type is short and upright, while the plumage is very broad and rounded at the end, which is mainly conspicuous in the cock's sickles. These are long and broad, are carried well curved and have a rounded tip. The head is another striking feature of the Java Bantam. The head itself is small, short and broad. It has a rose comb with small well-defined points, and this tapers off into a rounder spike or leader, projecting horizontally. The color of the eyes depends on the variant, but is dark brown in the darker varieties. Striking are its large, thick, round ears, that are white. The Java Bantam carries its wings low and at a backward slant. The breast is well rounded and rather prominent. The back is short and hollow. The color of the legs depends on the

very strong in this breed. From the start, the chicks show the contrast between the crest's and the body's color, while the skull knob is still clearly visible at that time.

PARTICULARS
Crests are intermediary heritable in regards to size. This means that from two animals with medium-sized crests, larger but also much smaller crests can be bred. If crests get too big, they block the chicken's view, therefore breeders take this into account and also use animals with smaller crests for breeding. Moreover, they see to it that the crest's structure does not get too loose. If, in spite of all precautions, chicks are born that cannot see very well, then it is necessary to clip away the feathers around the eyes now and then.

Java Bantam

COUNTRY OF ORIGIN
Probably Indonesia (Java)

ORIGIN
One cannot tell with any precision where this

Cuckoo-colored Java Bantam hen

Cuckoo-colored Java Bantam cock

Java Bantam hen, black

Black Java Bantam cock

variety, but in the dusky ones – which are most common – it is slate blue. These small bantams are not very heavy: the cocks weigh about 650g (23 oz) and the hens 550g (19½ oz).

COLORS AND MARKING PATTERNS
Java Bantams are bred in many different colors. These include black, white, buff, self blue, laced blue, partridge, blue partridge, silver partridge, yellow partridge, cuckoo partridge, lavender, columbian, buff columbian, cuckoo, porcelain, lemon porcelain, black white mottled, blue white mottled and birchen. The black color is the most common.

QUALITIES
The breed is rather calm and easily tamed. Java Bantams can be kept in a smaller space, so that a small city garden will suffice. Unfortunately the males are very temperamental and have shrill voices. Thus they are great for cock-crowing matches, but usually not so popular with the neighbors, making it necessary to have a roost with good sound insulation. Among themselves, the cocks are rather fierce, and in such fights their lovely white ears are easily damaged. This can only be prevented by housing the young cockerels separately, as

soon as they start getting into scrapes. The hens lay a moderate number of eggs with a white shell.

PARTICULARS
A black Java with broad feathers that have a green luster on them is as pretty as a picture. However, for this effect a broad feather is an absolute requirement. This means that in rearing the breed a bit more animal protein is required. Extra feed in the form of mealworms or something of the kind is a sensible thing to provide.

Naked Neck Bantam

COUNTRY OF ORIGIN
Germany

ORIGIN
At the end of the nineteenth century, an initial attempt was made to breed a miniature form of the Naked Neck Bantam without success. Various attempts at the outset of the twentieth century came to nothing, due to lack of interest as well as the First World War. Around

1935, one tried again and succeeded this time. Large Naked Necks were crossed with various small bantam breeds of the country fowl type, and this eventually resulted in the recognition of the Naked Neck Bantam.

APPEARANCE

A lot of people are prejudiced upon seeing this extraordinary breed. One finds the red naked neck unnatural or even pitiful. Actually, this is odd, for Naked Necks are certainly not to be pitied. For centuries, they have been around in some very cold parts of Europe, without their naked necks giving them any trouble. This lack of feathering is certainly not unnatural: Game fowl are usually also very tight-feathered and lack plumage in some parts, while there are also wild birds with featherless necks (for instance vultures). This bantam breed has a country fowl type, the birds having a rather elongated build with a somewhat sloping back and a well-spread tail of medium high carriage. The wings are carried well tucked. The legs are featherless and slate blue in color. The neck is totally naked and bright red in the cocks. In the hens, the necks have a much lighter color. Due to the lack of feathering, the neck seems rather long, while the nakedness continues into the facial skin. However, the crown of the skull has feathers on it again. The animals have a medium-sized single comb and red ear-lobes. The color of the eyes is a reddish bay.

COLORS AND MARKING PATTERNS

The breed is acknowledged in white, black, laced blue and cuckoo.

QUALITIES

Although one supposes differently at first sight, the Naked Neck Bantam is a strong and hardy breed that does not need extra facilities in regards to its housing. Even during hard frost, these animals feel 'as fit as a fiddle'. Furthermore, they are very pleasant company and can become very tame for birds of the country fowl type. As the bantams are not very particularly big, they take up little space in the henhouse. The hens are reasonably good layers and sometimes go broody. However, due to being so tight-feathered, they have trouble keeping warm the eggs you entrust to them. So if you

A study of the head of a Naked Neck Bantam cock

Naked Neck Bantam cock, black

select a Naked Neck Bantam as a sitter, do not give her more than five eggs.

PARTICULARS

- In Europe, there are two varieties of Naked Necks: the Transylvanian variety of which the Naked Neck Bantam is the miniature form and the French Naked Neck. The difference is mainly found in the neck. In the Transylvanian kind, this should be totally featherless, while in the French Naked

Naked Neck Bantam chick, one week old

Neck there is a tiny bunch of feathers at the front of the neck, the 'bib'.
- The genetic factor ruling 'naked-necked-ness' is dominantly heritable. This means that when mating up Naked Necks with other chickens, the chicks are hatched with naked necks straight away. The factor tends to influence all of the body's plumage. By breeding from animals that have entirely featherless necks, chicks are born in which the breast is in part featherless. This is undesirable. Therefore, breeders assemble their breeding flocks from birds that do not always meet the ideal, but do produce chicks that are up to standard.

Naked Neck Bantam hen, black

Crested Bearded Bantam

COUNTRY OF ORIGIN
The United Kingdom

ORIGIN
Around 1870, the English breeder Entwisle started a breeding program with the aim of achieving a diminutive form of the Crested Bearded Fowl. This very successful and well-known breeder crossed large Crested Beards with Sebrights and Javas. By interbreeding these crosses, he succeeded in getting Crested Bearded Bantams.

APPEARANCE
Crested Bearded Bantams fall into the country fowl category, just as the Crested Bantams do. However, they look a bit fuller and shorter in build than the Crested Bantams. Their somewhat more profuse feathering and their far thicker neck contribute a great deal towards this look. The body is broad and has a well-rounded, fairly deep breast that is carried rather prominently. The tail's carriage is medium high and the tail itself is well spread. The cocks have broad, long sickles that are handsomely curved. The wings are held at a slightly downward slant and tucked against the body, and the legs are slate blue. The head is a real gem. The hens sport a large, full, globular and firm crest. As a result of a somewhat longer and narrower feather shape, the cocks do not have such a round crest, but one that looks a little looser and points more backwards. Under the head, there is a full, three-clump beard. There is a clearly discernable gap between

Crested Bearded Bantam, chicks of various colors

Crested Bearded Bantam cock, silver black laced

Crested Bearded Bantam cock, silver black laced

Crested Bearded Bantam cock, yellow black laced

Crested Bearded Bantam cock golden black laced

A study of the head of a Crested Bearded Bantam cock

the beard and the muffs or whiskers. The full beard pushes the neck feathers back a bit, resulting in an optically thick neck. These bantams should have neither comb nor wattles. Still, sometimes they do have them, though these are very small and should be entirely lost among the feathers. Apart from normally feathered Crested Bearded Bantams, there are also specimens with frizzled feathers.

COLORS AND MARKING PATTERNS
The colors in which this breed is raised are: golden black laced, silver black laced, yellow white laced, black, white, laced blue and cuckoo.

QUALITIES
This bantam is not only attractive to look at, it also has a pleasant character. Some cocks, but by far not all of them, can occasionally be a bit 'mischievous' towards their owner, though the hens are trusting, tame and placid. Due to the full, abundant head plumage they can be a little jumpy when approached from above, as they cannot see you coming. So, always approach the birds with your hands at their eye level. Due to the head's extra feathering, it is sensible to provide them with drinkers and feeders that are specially designed for bearded

Crested Bearded Bantam hen, golden black laced

Crested Bearded Bantam hen, yellow white laced

and crested fowl. These prevent too much damage to or soiling and wetting of the beard and crest. It is necessary to keep these chickens in a dry, roofed-in coop. Furthermore, extra checks for lice that may have gotten into the crests of these profusely feathered bantams are indispensable. The hens of this ornamental breed lay a reasonable number of eggs, but are non-sitters.

PARTICULARS

- For a long time, it was the fashion for all large crested fowl and bantams to develop bigger and bigger crests. This was done at the cost of the animals well-being, for they had too little vision. In the last couple of decades, this has clearly changed. Breeders would like to retain this breed and want to take care that their chickens see enough in a natural way. They do this by strictly breeding as to the crest's shape and firmness, to wit: the firmer the feathers are, the more erect they stand, instead of hiding the eyes. Moreover, breeders want crests that are a bit smaller. If you yourself would like to breed a few chicks, you had better seek the advice of an experienced breeder first.
- There is also a larger version of the Crested Bearded Bantam. This is not discussed here, but has a circle of advocates in several countries and – except for its size – is hardly any different from the miniature form.

Booted Bantam

COUNTRY OF ORIGIN
The Netherlands/Europe in general

ORIGIN
This breed has been around in Europe for centuries, though not in its present standard form. It is not entirely clear where these small birds with feathered feet came from, but one supposes from Asia. In 1902, the animal acquired the breed name *Nederlandse Sabelpootkriel* ('Dutch Booted Bantam') in the Netherlands, but – with the exception of the Flemish-speaking part of Belgium – the attributive 'Dutch' is not used elsewhere.

APPEARANCE
The Booted Bantam is a true bantam and these are small animals. The cocks weigh around 750g (26½ oz) and the hens about 650g (23 oz). They are short bantams with a fairly stocky build and an upright carriage.

Dutch Booted Bantam cock, porcelain blue marked

The back is short and makes a rather sharp sweep into a tail that is carried above the horizontal. In the cocks, it has firm main sickles that are not curved, projecting over the tail feathers. The wings are carried at a downward slant. The bantams have strong feathers, notably seen in the plumage of the hocks, where there are long and stiff, sticking backwards. These vulture hocks or 'boots' is what the breed takes its name from. The leg color is grayish blue and the feet are very fully feathered. The Booted Bantam has a medium-sized single comb and large ear-lobes. The color of the eye is a reddish bay.

COLORS AND MARKING PATTERNS
The breed is found in many colors, but, as is often the case, these are not recognized in all countries. Among others, the colors include porcelain, isabella-colored porcelain, silver

Dutch Booted Bantam hen, porcelain blue marked

ularity. It is quite hardy and can be kept very well by beginners. As they have feathered feet, they cannot do much damage to your garden if you let them run free. However, should you want to go to exhibitions with them, then you had better keep them in a roofed-in, dry and clean run, for otherwise the feathered feet will soon look awful. Booted Bantams are small in size and do not need much room. Moreover, they can become reasonably tame. The hens of this breed lay quite a lot of eggs, with a medium weight of 38g (1.35 oz). Apart from this, they are excellent sitters and often rear their chicks effortlessly.

PARTICULARS

The breed has been around in Europe for centuries, and there are various related breeds on this continent. Thus, there is the Booted Bantam in Great Britain, Germany has its *Federfüssige Zwerg* and Belgium the Belgian Bearded d'Uccle Bantam. The original form is akin to the Japanese and Burmese Bantam, among others. Booted Bantams have blue legs, unlike their Asiatic ancestors. This probably arose due to a cross with local breeds. The typical Asiatic yellow leg color was still found in this breed at the end of the nineteenth century.

A study of the head of a Dutch Booted Bantam cock

Dutch Booted Bantam hen, black

porcelain, blue porcelain, lemon porcelain, partridge, silver partridge, bloodwing silver partridge, black, white, self blue, buff, birchen, buff columbian, black white mottled, blue white mottled, ochre white mottled, barred and lavender.

QUALITIES

The Booted Bantam is one of the best known bantam breeds. Thus, it has considerable pop-

Head of a lavender Dutch Booted Bantam hen

Owl Beard Bantam

COUNTRY OF ORIGIN
The Netherlands

ORIGIN
Apart from large Owl Beards, there are probably Antwerp Belgians and Crested Bearded Bantams at the basis of this bantam breed. The bantam was recognized in the Netherlands in 1935.

APPEARANCE
Owl Beard Bantams are about two thirds of the size of their large congeners and weigh on average 700g (1½ lb). The head is the hallmark from which the breed takes its name, more in particular the beard and comb. This full, rounded beard and erect V-shaped comb (horn comb) give the face an expression which may indeed remind one of an owl. As a typical characteristic of crested bantams and related breeds, this breed also has slightly cavernous nostrils placed right at the top of the

Owl Beard Bantam cock, silver black spangled

upper mandible. Behind the comb, there is the remnant of a crest, in the form of a few tangled feathers. This dwarf's eye color is a reddish brown and its ear-lobes are white. The breed is clearly of the country fowl type. This means that the birds have an elongated build and a tail carried fairly high. The tail is well spread and in the cock has a great many ornamental feathers. The breast is well rounded, and a laying hen has a rather deep and downy backside. The breed's leg color is slate blue in most variants.

COLORS AND MARKING PATTERNS
Black, white, blue laced, cuckoo, golden black spangled, silver black spangled, yellow white spangled, golden penciled, silver penciled, moor's head golden yellow and moor's head white. A relatively new color, accepted in the year 2000, is silver lavender spangled. Here, the black spangling, as seen in the silver black spangled markings, has been replaced by lavender. The moor's heads or *moorkops* are distinguished from other marking patterns by the color of their heads, which are black – including the upper part of the neck. This is a very attractive variant that is highly typical of the breed, but is unfortunately no longer seen in practice.

QUALITIES
Like their large counterparts, Owl Beard Bantams are alas not commonly encountered. This is a pity, for the breed is vigorous and

Owl Beard Bantams

strong, the hens are excellent layers and the animals – when calmly approached – can become very tame. They have white eggs. In spite of their active nature, these bantams can also be kept successfully in smaller abodes, provided you offer them sufficient diversion. Due to their vitality, it is fairly easy to breed these birds, but raising a beautiful Owl Beard Bantam nevertheless remains difficult. The specific shape of the comb, upon which high requirements are made, sees to quite a bit of variety in their progeny.

Phoenix Bantam

COUNTRY OF ORIGIN
Germany

ORIGIN
At the outset of the last century, very soon after the large Phoenix had been imported from Japan, an attempt was made in Germany to breed a miniature form of this fowl. Crosses between Phoenixes and Old English Game Bantams of the old type as well as small bantams of the country fowl type, formed the basis for this new dwarf breed. Although the breed never really became popular, more Phoenix Bantams are bred than is the case with their large namesakes.

APPEARANCE
Phoenix Bantams have a svelte, elongated and lean build. This image is enhanced by the long tail section which is carried fairly low and in line with the long back. The breast is full and well rounded. The wings are carried at a downward slant. Hens of the breed have a long and well-spread tail, in which the top feathers are highly curved. The cock has a wealth of long, narrow feathers on the saddle and in the tail. The saddle hackles are so extended that they touch the ground. Also the sickles are very long, dragging along the ground. Contrary to other chicken breeds, these sickles are not molted every year, but grow on for several years. This is the reason they get so long, provided they are taken care of in the right way. On its head, the Phoenix sports a small single comb. The ear-lobes are white and the eyes are a reddish bay. The legs

Owl Beard Bantam hen, golden black spangled

Silver partridge-colored Phoenix Bantam cock

are of medium length and either slate blue or olive green.

COLORS AND MARKING PATTERNS
Phoenix Bantams are recognized in the colors partridge, silver partridge, white and black.

QUALITIES
These truly ornamental birds in fact require an owner that has a special quality too, to wit

Silver partridge-colored Phoenix Bantam hen

White Phoenix Bantam cock

Partridge-colored Phoenix Bantam cock

dedication. Cleaning their henhouse takes a great deal of time and attention, for it has to be dry and spick and span. Only then will the cock's long tail remain in perfect condition. In the roost, the perches should be fitted in such a way that the tail can always hang free, without touching a wall. As taking care of a Phoenix involves far more work than with an ordinary breed, these chickens are not often seen. The advantage of such an intensive contact with the birds is that they become very tame and calm. In order to optimize the tail's abundant growth, you should also see to it that these birds get more animal protein. The Phoenix Bantam hens are reasonable layers and their eggs are white.

PARTICULARS
The original form of the Phoenix Bantam, the Phoenix, rarer than the dwarf form discussed here.

Black Phoenix Bantam hen

Sebright

COUNTRY OF ORIGIN
The United Kingdom

ORIGIN
Contrary to most bantams that are mere small variants of large counterparts, the Sebright is in origin a true bantam. The Englishman Sir John Sebright created the breed around 1800, wanting to develop a bantam with laced markings, and in this he was highly successful. Unfortunately, it is not quite clear which breeds formed the basis of the Sebright.

Partridge-colored Phoenix Bantam hen

APPEARANCE
Typical of the breed is that cocks and hens are much alike – a brilliant idea of the person who originally developed them. He achieved this by using 'hen-feathered' cocks, meaning cocks that lack the secondary sexual characteristics in regards to plumage. As, there are no ornamental

Sebrights around 1900

A study of the head of a black Phoenix Bantam cock

feathers, the cocks have beautifully lacing all over their bodies. The Sebright is one of the smallest bantams we know, with the birds on average weighing only 550g (19½ oz), while the majority of bantams weighs almost twice as much. The Sebright has a very short back and a jaunty appearance, in which the breast is quite prominent. The tail is carried above the horizontal and is well spread. The shape of a Sebright's feathers is broad and rounded. The neck is carried a bit backwards. The head is fairly short and has a rose comb, the leader or spike of which points straight backwards. The comb's color is purplish, though this is less striking in the cocks than in the hens. The color of the eyes is dark brown to brownish black.

COLORS AND MARKING PATTERNS
The first Sebrights were golden black laced and silver black laced. For a long time, these were the two only colors they were bred in, but in

the last century a number of colors were added outside of the Sebright's country of origin, like yellow white laced and lemon black laced. In spite of this, the two original colors are still the most popular ones.

QUALITIES
Sebrights are active, spunky birds that become tame rather easily. They are truly ornamental chickens. Thus, the hen is not a great layer and the size of the eggs is moreover small. The advantage of their limited measurements is that these birds fit very well into small henhouses. A couple of Sebrights may be held in any small garden. The animals are tolerant among themselves. Another great advantage is that the cocks are not really rowdy or shrill crowers. With a few precautions, you can even keep

a cock in a densely populated residential area. They do get broody, but this factor is not excessively present. Remarkable is their need for warmth in order to procreate, so that eggs usually remain unfertilized early in the year. The cocks only become active when it gets a bit warmer. Thus, the best time to breed these ornamental chickens is in April, May or June.

PARTICULARS
Most Sebright stocks are very susceptible to Marek's paralysis. It is a pity that this disease cannot be suppressed and always results in the chicken's death. It usually strikes when the animals are adult and the hens start laying their first eggs. Preventive vaccination is the only solution to this problem. If you buy young Sebrights, always inquire whether the animals have been vaccinated.

Spanish White Faced Black Bantam

COUNTRY OF ORIGIN
The United Kingdom

Sebright cock, golden black laced

Sebrights, silver black laced

Sebright hen, golden black laced

*Sebright chicks; a golden black laced specimen (left),
silver black laced (right)*

ORIGIN

As early as the end of the nineteenth century,
the diminutive variant of the Spanish White
Faced Black was first shown in London. However, the animals did not prove very strong and
there was not much interest in them. Due to
this, the breed was extremely rare and almost
passed into oblivion, until it came into the
limelight a bit more during the 1990s. Both in
England and in Germany, a few breeders specializing in the Spanish White Faced Black had
promoted the breed in the previous decade.
Now enthusiasm is somewhat on the increase.

*A study of the head of a Spanish White Faced Black
Bantam cock*

APPEARANCE

The most eye-catching features are the large
enamel-white ears and white facial skin. The
Spanish White Faced Black Bantam has a single comb that should have five points. The eyes
are dark brown to brownish black. The body
has an elongated build, with a slightly sloping
back line in the cock. The tail's carriage is
medium high. The hen wears her tail somewhat folded. The legs are slate blue.

COLORS AND MARKING PATTERNS

The Spanish White Faced Black Bantam is
only found in black.

QUALITIES

Originally, the Spanish White Faced Black
came under the category of layer breeds. Because of a focused selection for striking enamel-white ears and facial skin, being a good layer is no longer of importance, as now they have
turned into an ornamental breed. The hens lay
white eggs of a considerable size. Broodiness
is not a particularly marked feature in this
breed. For a breed that in origin is a layer,
these animals have a placid and trusting nature. The large white ears and the white facial
skin are present in rudimentary form at birth.
As the birds grow older, the facial skin becomes increasingly thick and white. Only
when they are well into being 'yearlings' are
the typical breed features fully present. It is
important to take care of this white skin well
and clean it regularly. In winter, put some acid-
-free vaseline on it. If you start breeding them,
the cocks should be housed separately as soon
as they begin to fight. If they damage one

Spanish White Faced Black Bantam chick

another's white ears, it will always remain visible, as the scars are brown.

PARTICULARS

There is also a large form of the Spanish White Faced Black. This form is hardly any different from the dwarf form discussed here, except for

Spanish White Faced Black Bantam cock

Spanish White Faced Black Bantam hen

the size and the fact that large specimens are even rarer.

Belgian Bearded de Watermaal Bantam

COUNTRY OF ORIGIN

Belgium

ORIGIN

One of the suburbs of Brussels is the borough of Watermaal-Bosvoorde. This is where, at the beginning of the last century, Antoine Dresse's breeding farm 'Les Fougères' was situated. In strict secrecy, the Belgian Bearded de Watermaal Bantam was hatched there, developed from a cross of an unknown number of breeds. What its progenitors were, Antoine Dresse always refused to disclose, as has his son Oscar after him. However, it is certain that Antwerp Belgians, among others, formed the basis of this breed. The Belgian Bearded de Watermaal Bantam or Barbu de Watermael certainly falls into the category 'rare'. Apart from Belgium and the Netherlands, the breed is only found

Black white mottled Belgian Bearded de Watermaal Bantam cock

in England, France and Germany. In the rest of Europe, it is hardly ever seen.

APPEARANCE

The Belgian Bearded de Watermaal Bantam is a small bearded bantam that on first sight reminds one of the Antwerp Belgian. Still, there are a number of obvious differences. Generally, the De Watermaal variant's build is more delicate, svelte and rather more graceful. The carriage is upright and the animal holds its wings at a downward slant. The body is slender with a full-feathered neck, which, however, is not as thick-set as that of the Antwerp Belgian. The back is short and makes a hollow sweep into a tail of a rather high carriage. The tail itself is broader at the base than at the end, so that it acquires a triangular shape. The cock has fairly hard ornamental feathers in its tail. Thus the main sickles are only a little longer than the main tail feathers, and hardly curved at all. This bantam's hallmark is its head, the skull being short and round, and the short beak slightly bent. The breed has a three-clump beard. This means that a gap is preferred between the throat plumage and the feathers of the muffs or whiskers. The Belgian Bearded de Watermaal Bantam has a rose comb, however not with just a single leader or spike, but with three short and rather thin ones, placed next to one another. The comb itself is short and broad. On the head, there is a little tuft, as broad as the skull and starting next to the comb, so that it in part covers this, following the line of the skull. The color of the eyes is dark brown in most variants.

Black Belgian Bearded de Watermaal Bantam cock

Black white mottled Belgian Bearded de Watermaal Bantam hen

Laceless Belgian Bearded de Watermaal Bantam hen

Belgian Bearded de Watermaal Bantam hen, cuckoo

Laceless Belgian Bearded de Watermaal Bantam cock

Belgian Bearded de Watermaal Bantam cock, cuckoo

COLORS AND MARKING PATTERNS

If you like colors, this is really a breed for you. More than thirty different variants are recognized in this breed. The most common ones are black, white, cuckoo, quail, white quail, white lemon quail, silver quail, buff columbian and golden necked black.

QUALITIES

Belgian Bearded de Watermaal Bantams fall into the category of ornamental breeds, so they are certainly not great layers. Their eggs weigh on average 35g (1¼ oz). The hens are good sitters, but should not be in the care of too many eggs: seven is the maximum. The advantage of their small size is that these bantams need little room, and can also be run free. With their slight body weight, they are good flyers, but do not make use of this feature to escape, as most of them are extremely tame. However, they sometimes tend to spread their wings out of curiosity, so do not be surprised if you find these birds on top of the henhouse or on your shed. Just give the feed tin a few shakes and they will land at your feet like pigeons. For children, they are nice pets, because they are very tame and affectionate. On the other hand, the cocks can become a bit too 'active' and then may threaten or attack their owner. Keep an eye on this, when your kids are the ones taking care of the birds. There is another disadvantage to the cocks: they crow early in the morning, keep this up for a long time and make a very shrill noise. One should insulate the roost well, so that the neighbors are not bothered by this.

PARTICULARS

- In connection with their full beard and small tuft, the animals should have a special drinker. A jar waterer (small 'water tower') is very satisfactory, as there is only a little water available at a time, the beard and tuft cannot get wet.
- The color white lemon quail is only found in this breed. This color arose more or less coincidentally in the Netherlands. Chicks that initially were white, after a while were seen to have rather yellowish feather parts. The marking corresponded with that of the color quail. The difference with the quail color is that the black is substituted by white and the golden brown by lemon yellow. The color is so light and delicate that the markings are only seen in clear daylight from close by.

Silkie Bantam

COUNTRY OF ORIGIN

The Netherlands

ORIGIN

As a large breed, the Silkie is a 'tiny tot' and is therefore not included among the large chickens in some countries, but among the bantams instead. In the second half of the twentieth century, breeders in the Netherlands wanted to create a very small bantam by

Partridge-colored Silkie Bantam hen, with beard

White Silkie Bantam hen, with beard

White Silkie Bantam hen

way of Silkies and Belgian Bearded de Watermaal Bantams. Many years passed before this goal was reached. The white color was the first to arise.

APPEARANCE

The weight of a Silkie Bantam is around 600g (21 oz). Thus, the animal weighs just under half of what its large namesakes does. At a distance, Silkie Bantams look like hairy balls. This is due to the feature from which the breed takes its name, to wit its feathers that look like hairs from a distance. These bantams have a round shape and a low stand. The tail section is short and in the cocks is covered by silk-feathered sickles. The purplish blue skin color is very typical of this breed, as is the extra fifth toe. Silkie Bantams have what is sometimes called a strawberry comb (or walnut comb). The ear-lobes are light blue. The short legs are abundantly feathered, as are the outer parts of the legs. Alongside of the regular form, there are also Bearded and Crested Silkie Bantams.

COLORS AND MARKING PATTERNS

The breed comes in various colors, including white, black, multiple penciled partridge ('triple laced'), lavender, red, buff and self blue. However, not all colors are also recognized in every country this breed is found in.

QUALITIES

Silkie Bantams are pleasant creatures: They are trusting and calm and can be easily 'trained to the hand'. If you let them run free, they will not scatter all over the neighborhood. Because of their different feather structure, they are unable to fly, so that low fences will keep these chickens on your premises. As they don't fly, you will have to place the perches close to the ground; however, many Silkies simply tend to roost on the ground. Also for those who do not have very much room, these attractive dwarfs are suitable. Small henhouses suffice and even on a balcony you can keep a few of these bantams in a 'rabbit hutch-type' coop. The hens do not lay many eggs, at most about a 100 a year, mainly in spring and summer. Still, they are very frequently – and persistently – broody. They are highly reliable sitters. That is why the hens of the Silkie Bantams are often used as foster mothers for eggs and chicks of bantams breeds that are not so expert in this field. Silkie Bantams are known for their vitality and certainly need not be pampered. Although, due to their different feather structure, you perhaps are under the impression that these birds may suffer from the cold, this is certainly not the case.

PARTICULARS

- Once a hen of this miniature breed is broody, it is very hard to get her to change her mind. Even though you leave her no eggs, she will simply keep on sitting. So, you should see to it that she eats and drinks enough, and should also take her off her nest regularly encouraging her to do so.
- The Silkie Bantam's special feather structure arises because the feather's barbicels (hamuli) are lacking, so that the feather has a disconnected structure. This feature is in-herited recessively, meaning that, in crossing silk-feathered birds with normally feathered ones, the outcome will be normally feathered.
- Not only is the Silkie Bantam's skin bluish black, also its meat and even its skeleton have this highly pigmented color. To this pigmentation, the Chinese attribute medicinal properties. However, despite the color, the meat of a Silkie Bantam is no different in taste or texture from ordinary chicken meat.

Silkie Bantam chicks

Partridge-colored Silkie Bantam, cock

White Silkie Bantam cock, with beard

White Silkie Bantam cock

Index

Addresses, Magazines and Websites

Addresses

American Poultry Association:
c/o Lorna Rhodes
APA Secretary-Treasurer
133 Millville Street
Mendon, MA 01756
USA
(508) 473-8769
www.ampltya.com

Magazines

Fancy Fowl (www.poultryclub.org/FancyFowl.htm)
TP Publications
Barn Acre Road, Saxtead Green. Suffolk, IP13 9QJ, England

Show Bird Journal (hometown.aol.com/showbird62/showbirdjournal.html)
33130 County Road 8, Killen, AL 35645-3028, USA

Poultry Press (www.poultrypress.com)
PO Box 542, Connersville, IN 47331, USA

National Poultry News (www.NationalPoultryNews.com)
PO Box 1647, Easley, SC 29641-1647, USA

Feather Fancier (www.featherfancier.on.ca)
5739 Telfer Road, Sarnia, Ontario N7T 7H2, Canada

Websites

www.feathersite.com
www.poultrypages.com
www.ansi.okstate.edu/poultry/chickens
chickscope.beckman.uiuc.edu/resources/standard_varieties

Photo Credits &

Acknowledgements

Photo credits

All photographs were taken by Esther Verhoef, with the exception of:

p. 58 all, p. 59 all, p. 61 left: these were made available by the Teurlings Company in Waalwijk; p. 11, p. 15, p. 33 below, p. 39 top, p. 40 top, p. 42 top right, p. 48 top, p. 68 top right, p. 70, p. 81, p. 89 top right, p. 97 top, p. 118 below, p. 119 below, p. 120 top, p. 140 below, p. 276 below: all taken by Aad Rijs.

The black and white photographs and drawing are from the book *Hoenderrassen in hunne vormen en kleuren*, part 1 and 2 (1909), by R. Houwink.

The color illustrations were done by Angelique van Voorst.

Acknowledgements

The following people have helped to realize the photography:

R. Van As, A.F.G.J. Bardoel, J. Beukers sr., Comb. Boerebach, Jaap Boeve, J. Bonte, R. Van De Boogaard, P. Bouw, A.A.J. Broers, E. Burgers, G. de Bruin, Christ Chabot, J.A. De Dooij, J.J. De Dooij, J. Van Dijck, C.G. Van Dijk, Willem Doesburg, H. Don, B.H. Van Drunen, Comb. De Eenselaar, R. Gatti, M. Van De Goor, I. De Graaf, Carin Van Der Griendt, J. Van Haaren, W.G.M. Haverkate, H. Van Heerde, A. Heerkens, M. Hermans, J. Van Den Heuvel, Jurgen Van Hevelingen, S. Hulleman, C. Jansen, Comb. Joco, D. De Jong, C. Joosten, Mr. & Mrs. Keijnemans, A. De Laat, C. J. Lamers, C. Maas, Mr. Mastenbroek, Comb. Van Der Mel, Mr. De Mik, Mr. & Mrs.Van Mil, B. Mimpen, Corné Monshouwer, W. Monshouwer, C.J. De Nekker, Jac. Netten, T. Nillesen, A. Van Der Nobelen, C.G. Noorloos, S. Oegema, Mr. Van Oenen, A. Van Den Oetelaar, D. Van Oord, A. Oudshoorn, C. Overeem, Mr. & Mrs. Van Der Pas, J.M. Puttenstein, L. Reedijk, Aad Rijs, Ineke Rijs, P. Roelofsen, Mr. & Mrs. Van Rooij, Willem Van Rooijen, C. Van Ruissen, W. Van Ruissen, Jan Schaareman, P. Van Schijndel, Mr. Schouwenaar, W. Schretzmeijer, Chr. Sentel, W.F. Seybel, L. Smits, D.P. Spek, Rick Spek, J. Stappenbelt, Mrs. H. Steegs, Gradus Stein, P. Stokkermans Jr., M. Straver, M.W. Struyken, G. Stuij, J. Van Suylekom, A. Tollenaar, A.G.W. Ueberbach, G. De Vaen, H. De Veer, Mark Verbaas, H. Verhees, L.A. de Vries, H. Van Weelden, H. Wezendonk, H. Wiehink, H. Witlox, Comb. Wyhorn